400335

D0719542

THE PENGUIN BOOK
OF TWENTIETH-CENTURY
Fashion Writing

Edited by
Judith Watt

VIKING

VIKING

Published by the Penguin Group
Penguin Books Ltd, 27 Wrights Lane, London w8 5tz, England
Penguin Putnam Inc., 375 Hudson Street, New York, New York 10014, USA
Penguin Books Australia Ltd, Ringwood, Victoria, Australia
Penguin Books Canada Ltd, 10 Alcorn Avenue, Toronto, Ontario, Canada m4v 3b2
Penguin Books (NZ) Ltd, Private Bag 102902, NSMC, Auckland, New Zealand

Penguin Books Ltd, Registered Offices: Harmondsworth, Middlesex, England

First published 1999
1 3 5 7 9 10 8 6 4 2

Editorial matter copyright © Judith Watt, 1999
The moral right of the editor has been asserted

The copyright permissions on pages 347–358 constitute an extension of this copyright page

Set in 12/15pt Monotype Garamond
Typeset by Rowland Phototypesetting Ltd,
Bury St Edmunds, Suffolk
Printed in England by Clays Ltd, St Ives plc

A CIP catalogue record for this book is available from the British Library

ISBN 0-670-88215-1

For my father, Thomas MacDonald Beattie Watt, 1920–1989, and grandmother, Margaret Judith May Verney, 1903–1987

Contents

Acknowledgements

With thanks to Kate Bernard, Michael Bracewell, Judith Clark, Emma Dent Coad, Basil Comely, Michael 'Goldie' Dillon, Caroline Evans, David Godwin, Margaret Halton, Philip Hoare, Robert Hodgins, Alkarim Jivani, Vanessa Nicolson, Brian Robinson, Lise Strathdee and Jane Wildgoose. Thanks to my editors at Viking/Penguin, without whom this would not be possible: Juliet Annan, Hannah Robson and Anya Waddington; to my copy editor, Anne Askwith; and especially to my agent, Joanna Weinberg, at A. P. Watt. Thanks also to the staff at the London Library and to Alison Church of the Central Saint Martin's Library. I'd also like to thank everyone who dealt with permissions and rights on this project.

Special thanks for their love and support: Mark Ellingham and Nat Janz; to Fred Burlage and my family, Ann Verney, Shona, Angus, Beattie and Ludwig Watt.

Introduction

'It is only the Shallow people who do not judge by appearances.'

Oscar Wilde, *The Picture of Dorian Gray*, 1891

Great authors are not fashion writers; their motivation is not to give accurate accounts of the modes of the past or present. It is their individual view, of clothes and fashion conditioned by experience and attitude, that adds an often fascinating perception and is a rich source for anyone interested in the history of dress. So the intention of this collection is to provide examples of some of the best writing in the English language on dress. Some fashion journalism is included, but I have limited this in preference to primary sources such as autobiography, letters and diaries, fiction, prose and poetry. The selection has been limited by copyright laws and by the fees charged by authors and representatives of estates of deceased writers; Jean Genet, J. D. Salinger and James Joyce are amongst those omitted whose contributions to the anthology were important.

In *Seeing Through Clothes* Anne Hollander argues that in literary art, depictions of clothes are most realistically rendered when connected with dramatic situations or actions. 'Descriptions of the behaviour or state of garments (leaving out how they are made or normally look) may be as universally understandable as that of states of mind ... But how garments are visually designed and how they look when ordinarily worn is the part of the image that is nearly always missing from the literary mirror when it is held directly up to nature.'[1] Literature is not there to give details of cut and construction and – although some writers do accurately describe a character's dress and the way it is worn – most authors are not fashion journalists or fashion historians. Furthermore, a writer can give an overall description of the *impression* that the clothes create and the writer's personal viewpoint can transform a green hat *pour le sport* into an emblem of an era or a black suit into an executioner's uniform. When Oscar Wilde said, 'A fashion is merely a form of ugliness so unbearable that we are compelled to alter it every six months',[2] he was referring to the body-distorting styles (bustles and corsets) created in Paris and worn, for fashion's sake, in the 'civilized' world. This perception – that fashion is inherently unnatural, disfiguring and dishonest – was shared by many twentieth-century writers: their attitude to clothes coloured the way they viewed the world and their dress coloured the way the world viewed them. Writers such as Virginia Woolf belonged to the bohemian tradition in which clothes were an *anti-fashion* statement; Wyndham Lewis in his black cape epitomized Fitzrovia; Nancy Mitford's love for the man she called 'the Colonel' led to a passion for Paris and the clothes of Christian Dior; while the gay Colin MacInnes opened a window on the gay and Black London subculture (and its clothes) of the 1950s which has not been matched. Writers have often looked into places in which dress reflects the human condition, sometimes places where most contemporary fashion commentators have feared to tread; for example, the paedophilia aroused by adolescence which is the subject of Vladimir Nabokov's *Lolita* in which Lolita's age is signified by her bobby-sox; the fetishism of Mrs Danvers expressed through clothes in Daphne du Maurier's *Rebecca*; Gore Vidal's exploration of the role of sex change and gender in *Myra Breckinridge*.

For some writers that viewpoint is concerned with the relationship of clothes to the body. Franz Kafka, whose father kept a haberdasher's shop selling frills and accessories, shows antipathy towards the excessive detail of fashionable clothes which 'dishonestly' conceal the body with unnecessary surface decoration. In his prose poem *The Clothes* he writes,

Often when I see clothes with manifold pleats, frills and appendages which fit so smoothly on to lovely bodies I think they won't keep that smoothness long, but will get creases that can't be ironed out, dust lying so thick in the embroidery that it can't be brushed away, and that no one would want to be so unhappy and so foolish as to wear the same valuable gown every day from early morning till night.[3]

The folds and creases are surely sexual imagery; and as well as a form of dishonesty – for like Eve with the apple, women deceive – Kafka perceives fashion as sexual 'dirt'. Similarly, fashion is the weapon of male downfall for Thomas Mann in *The Magic Mountain*: 'The way women dressed! They showed their necks and bosoms, they transfigured their arms by veiling them in "illusion"; they did so, the world over, to arouse our desire.'[4]

'Vain trifles as they seem, clothes have the same, more important offices than merely to keep us warm,' writes Virginia Woolf in her novel *Orlando*.[5] 'They change our view of the world and the world's view of us.' Woolf discussed what she described as 'frock conscious-ness' in literature with H. G. Wells. He probably rejected the notion as shallow, for she recorded in her diary that he'd said, 'Henry James was a formalist: he always thought of clothes. He was never intimate with anyone.'[6] In other words, 'frocks' were a veneer which concealed reality and they trivialized a work of art. What may have alienated Wells and Mann, and certainly did Kafka, who in his early years was a supporter of the *Jugendstil* dress reform movement, was the dominance of *fashion*, in which couturiers in Paris appeared to decide, apparently on whim, upon a new trend and which distorted the bodies of men and women.

'Fashion is *fantasie*,' notes Diana Vreeland, the former *Vogue* editor, in her autobiography *D. V.* 'It was always unreal to me.' Fashion was, and still is, about glamour, the magic glow that can be conferred by clothes. The transformation offered by clothes is often found in the work of writers dealing with social reality. 'Clothes are powerful things,' observes George Orwell in *Down and Out in Paris and London*. 'Dressed in a tramp's clothes, it is very difficult, at any rate for the first day, not to feel that you are genuinely degraded.' In *The Road to Wigan Pier*, he writes of the psychological importance of dress: 'You may have three-half-pence in your pocket and not a prospect in the world . . . but in your new clothes you can stand on the street corner, indulging in a private daydream of yourself as Clark Gable or Greta Garbo.' Walter Greenwood provides an invaluable document in *Love on the Dole*, written in 1933, which describes not only the social conditions of the very poor in the Depression but also the importance of fashion to 'ordinary' people, shown when Harry Hardcastle longs to achieve some kind of respectability and glamour with a new suit and his father finally purchases one from the local co-operative society. These are examples of references that are not found in fashion journalism and make valid the study of dress through literature. *Vanity Fair*'s 'Well-Dressed Man' column, for instance, which ran from its launch in 1913 through to the 1930s, dealt with the *'fantasie'* of pre-war men's style; by the late 1950s, some fashion writers were exploring the phenomenon of fashion being influenced from the street and by youth, but mainstream fashion journalists were reporting on the couture collections for women and bewailing the alien nature of the male youth. In contrast, Alan Sillitoe in *Saturday Night and Sunday Morning* gives an account of a young Teddy boy as dandy, who refuses to wear an overcoat and spends his hard earned money on creating a peerless wardrobe; Nell Dunn describes the tricks the girls of Battersea play in 'buying' a dress, wearing it for the night and returning it, unpaid for, the next day in *Up the Junction*.

Fashion dates a work. This is so with Ted Hughes's poem 'A Pink Wool Knitted Dress', which describes his and Sylvia Plath's wedding, he in demob – the clothes issued to newly demobilized troops – and she, American, side-stepping the drabness of 'Utility Britain' in a pink wedding dress. Even when a story is set in the future it is conditioned by a known, usually current, dress aesthetic. Stella Gibbons in *Cold Comfort Farm* sets her tale some time in an unspecified future, where brassières are collector's items, yet she relies on contemporary style: the sculpted white gown designed by the fictional temperamental couturier Viol evokes the work of real courturier Madeleine Vionnet. Patented in 1917, zips were just entering fashion in the early 1930s; and in *Brave New World* published in 1932, Huxley creates a bleak utopia thousands of years hence with women wearing synthetic materials with zips as futuristic fastening – 'zipp-caminicks' and 'zippyjamas'. What is also interesting is that the designer Elsa Schiaparelli made a splash with zips in her 1935 collection: 'not only did they appear for the first time in the most unexpected places, even on evening clothes. The whole collection was full of them. Astounded buyers bought and bought . . .'[7] Whereas Schiaparelli makes no reference to *Brave New World* as influence, Colette describes in *My Apprenticeships and Music Hall Highlights* how the fashion of her character Claudine in her novel of that name was adopted into mainstream fashion:

I am writing in 1935 and have this moment received a letter from a shirt and blouse maker offering me three new styles in collars, just recently named: 'Claudine à l'Ecole' for morning wear; 'Claudine à Paris' (book muslin and stitched pleats) and (we must not forget summer and the call of the wilds) 'Claudine s'en va'. So thirty years have not thrown into the rag-bag, not yet done away with the little white collar, the round, white, porcelain dish on which dark-haired Polaire's laughing, curly head was served up.[8]

Designer Andrew Groves called his spring/summer 1999 collection 'Cocaine Nites', inspired, he said, by J. G. Ballard's novel. The press, on the whole, did not 'get' this inspiration and almost unanimously condemned the event, with its runway strewn with razorblades and white powder, as decadent.

Some writers of fiction have their characters reflect attitudes towards clothes and fashion which also appear in non-fiction. In *Within a Budding Grove*, Marcel Proust describes the designer Mariano Fortuny as an artist who makes clothes and evokes the spirit of Venice in his work; Lady Diana Cooper discusses the impact of the 'Fortuni [sic]' in the first volume of her memoirs, *The Rainbow Comes and Goes*. Anthony Powell refers to the expensive glamour of the designer Christian Dior's New Look in *Books do Furnish a Room*; Nancy Mitford, one of the first British women to wear Dior, gives many descriptions of buying and wearing Dior in her letters; Dior's autobiography *Dior on Dior* gives a factual account of its launch in 1947. The *Autobiography of Malcolm X* talks of Black youth culture and identity in the USA, which can be read against Albert Camus' account of zazous in *The Outsider* and Colin MacInnes's celebration of Black style in *City of Spades*. The subculture of gay and lesbian dress is explored in Radclyffe Hall's *The Well of Loneliness*; Vita Sackville-West's description in her diary of the start of her relationship with Violet Trefusis can be read with Hall. Sylvia Plath raises questions over the role of fashion and women in *The Bell Jar*, exploring the lie that fashion gives to her own fragile reality; Germaine Greer reflects the view that fashion is a male-created reality in *The Female Eunuch*. Colin McDowell discusses the decadence of the cult of the designer label in his feature 'Depravity Bites' for the *Guardian*; Jay McInerney in *Model Behaviour* talks of the cycle of retro in fashion which is attacked by McDowell; Bret Easton Ellis uses a shorthand of 'Gucci poses' and 'Prada black' in *Glamorama*, not only describing the importance of designer labels in *fin de siècle* New York, Paris and London, but also touching on the important role played by gay designers; Julie Burchill instructs women in 'Material Boys' for the *Guardian* to remember that '[heterosexual] men love you because you have a vagina. They don't give a damn whether you've got a Versace.'

Male and female writers have different attitudes to dress. For many writers concern over appearance is perceived as feminine;

clothes might be used to describe a character but in-depth discussion belongs, in the view of some, to the second-rate 'fashionable novelist', whose work is 'dated' by the fashions they describe. Certainly women writers have historically had more contact than men with fashion; whether loving or loathing it they are more at ease with the subject, most particularly when it comes to the description of dress, the importance of a 'look' or the significance of a garment. I refer particularly to Colette, Jean Rhys, Nancy Mitford, Angela Carter, A. S. Byatt and Linda Grant. Each describes not only the immediate impact of a piece of clothing but also its texture: the touch of fur on skin, the constriction caused by a corset, the physical transformation made possible by wearing a Courrèges dress or a first pair of high heels, the liberation in wearing trousers. Male writers refer to women's fashion relatively cautiously. Tom Wolfe, while enjoying describing how the wardrobe of Sherman McCoy in *Bonfire of the Vanities* transforms him into a Master of the Universe, is almost reticent when it comes to the dress of the women characters; surely the social X-rays he describes, members of New York society, would be wearing frocks by Oscar de la Renta or Donna Karan? Wolfe's research is, however, accurate: the novel includes the puffball skirt, which Sarah Mower had a year before reported on as a sinister signifier in *The Face*; and the cloyingly feminine and uptight masculine in dress, which looking back, indicated Black Monday was in the air. A common way for male writers to describe the dress of a male character – perhaps because they are uncomfortable with the idea of fashion – is to have them study their reflection in a looking-glass; Aldous Huxley, Walter Greenwood, Stan Barstow, John Braine and J. L. Herlihy all make their men a momentary Narcissus; and the implication is that vanity is the territory of the effeminate. Will Self is an exception to the trend of reluctance by male writers to write about fashion: the short skirt worn by Ursula Bentley in *the sweet smell of psychosis* is at once a pelmet, a flange, a lappet, curtains and drapes, and its curious construction can only be by a designer's hand, rising as it does in an arch over the juncture of her thighs; lust confuses clarity but illustrates perfectly how clothes make the body sexy.

In 1930, J. C. Flugel's *The Psychology of Clothes* was published by the Woolfs' Hogarth Press. A Freudian psychoanalyst, Flugel sees fashion as a self-renewing compromise between modesty and eroticism; overt sexuality had been necessarily largely repressed in 'civilized' society, and it must therefore express itself in furtive or oblique ways, always fighting the 'reaction formation' of modesty and shame. Certain clothes signify sexual organs: the tie as a phallic symbol, fur as pubic hair. According to Freud, these are objects and textures that become fetishized as a form of sexual activity because of a fear of castration in the male. Clothes are fetishized because they are worn close to the body: they carry its smell, they are often shaped by the body beneath, and they are what we see and therefore 'know' of a person; for some, they are the essence of a person. The most obvious form of this fetishism is sexual taste; and it can be seen in the tight lacing of Jacqueline in Pauline Reage's *Story of O* and in Vladimir Nabokov's *Lolita*, in Humbert Humbert's delectation over Lolita's clothes. Linda Grant talks of the fur the narrator and her mother wore in *The Cast Iron Shore* 'They gave up their wildness and in death we civilized them, they became extensions of our humanity when we put them on . . .'; the women became more feral. But clothes are also fetishized for being imbued with the 'spirit' of the wearer or of a time that is past. Watching women wearing couturier Paul Poiret's Directoire style and men walking without top hats in *Within a Budding Grove* makes Proust's narrator recall Madame Swann and he describes his sad nostalgia as a 'fetishistic attachment to the old things which it did once animate, as if it was in them and not in ourselves that the divine spark resided . . .' In *Rebecca*, Daphne du Maurier has Mrs Danvers taunt the second Mrs de Winter with the contents of Rebecca's wardrobe, kept intact since her death: 'She looked beautiful in this velvet. Put it against your face. It's soft, isn't it? You can feel it, can't you? The scent is still fresh, isn't it? You could almost imagine she had only just taken it off.' This scene has been read as an indication of Mrs Danvers's love for Rebecca, but it may also be read as fetishizing the clothes of the dead.

Vera Brittain captures the powerful significance of clothes in death – though not in a fetishistic way – when she writes in her diary of the horror of receiving her dead fiancé's uniform back from the front in 1916. A uniform was not personal like clothing, and gave a blanket identity to all who wore it: 'one could never imagine those things the same as those in which he had lived & walked. One couldn't believe anyone alive had been in them at all. No, they were not Him . . .' Alan Jenkins's poem 'In the Hothouse' makes a play on the word, the ties given to him by his father being a rite of passage, a link to the dead, and the black tie an inadequate symbol of grief.

Black, historically the shade of death, has become *the* twentieth-century fashion colour (although black has been used too in fashion throughout European history). Perhaps this is because it is the least individual and most private of all colours: as with a uniform, it makes no personal expression; wearing black for mourning implies that no questions need to be asked. Black is anonymous in a time when 'pastels' and 'brights' denote anything from flirting to fury. Diana Vreeland devotes pages to a flow of consciousness about colour in *D.V.*, saying, 'Black is the hardest colour in the world to get right – except gray . . .' Indeed, it's become a fashion joke, with pink, grey and brown each in turn being dubbed 'the new black'. I have woven in extracts and commentary about colour throughout the anthology, as it pertains to so many different areas, from couture to identity to shopping. An opportunistic style statement is made about mourning by the couturier Lady Duff Gordon, known as 'Lucile', who recalls in her egotistical memoirs *Discretions and Indiscretions* a black frock she created called 'Consolable Sorrow', in which the wearer must have appeared the shadow of the Merry Widow: 'Every woman who lost her husband went into [it], and I must say they looked sweetly pathetic.'

Compare this with D. H. Lawrence's story of a young woman meeting her badly disfigured husband, back from the front in 'The Thimble': 'in her fashionable but inexpensive black silk dress, wearing her jewels, her string of opals, her big, ruby brooch, she went downstairs. She knew how to walk, how to hold her body according to the mode. She did it almost instinctively, so deep was her consciousness of the impression her own appearance must create.' With the millions of fatalities during the First World War, many women were forced by convention to wear black; but with Chanel's 'little black dress' of the mid-1920s, the scandal of which was that it was short in the hem and meant to be *sexy*, not sad, the emblem of mourning was turned into a chic fashion statement. Peter Jenkin, the Baudelairean-wannabe poet in Rosamund Lehmann's *Invitation to the Waltz*, set in 1920, jolts the adolescent heroine into an awareness of the glamour, the sexiness of black: 'I never let Inez wear anything but black at night. Occasionally white.'

Clothes of all colours are used in the twentieth-century novel to explore issues of identity. Proust, a homosexual, understood that clothes simultaneously conceal and reveal sexual orientation: the young Marquis de Saint-Loup-en-Bray wears a 'clinging, almost white material such as I never have believed any man would have had the audacity to wear'.[9] Franz Kafka, who was an elegantly dressed aesthete in his youth, shows his understanding of the relation of clothes and individuality in *The Trial*: in the beginning Joseph K. is required to put on clothes approved by his arrestors and at the end his execution takes place only when he has been undressed.[10] Colette's account of the disintegration of Cheri in *Cheri* and *The Last of Cheri* is marked by the character's change from smart young dandy who loves shopping to decadent recluse attired in Oriental kimono. Marguerite Duras, recalling her adolescent love affair in 1930s Saigon in *The Lover*, describes her image when she was attired in second-hand clothes – gold lamé shoes, a threadbare silk dress and a man's fedora hat: 'The crucial ambiguity of the image lies in the hat.' The second-hand clothes not only made her sexually ambiguous; while second-hand became chic in the 1970s, in the 1930s it was the mark of poverty and eccentricity, and the out-of-date clothes also meant she was not of the mode.

In the post-World-War-Two years, the attitude of the intellectual 'outsider' towards fashion was often antagonistic and youth's search to find its own identity and mark it through dress began to influence fashion itself: In 1947 Christian Dior sent a New Look dress to Juliet Greco in an attempt to gain approval from the young, black-clad existentialist.

From America came a youth style which was constructed from its own non-European culture: in Jack Kerouac's *On the Road*, for instance, Sal Paradise cherishes a wool plaid shirt, the 'shirt of Shelton, Nebraska' that marks his freedom from the convention that dogs his friend Dean Moriarty, the writer-dandy who purchases a new three-piece suit, 'blue with pencil-stripes'. The development of youth culture, with clothes defining different groups of people, saw clothes being described as a 'uniform' – the draped coats of Teds, the Italian jackets of mods, the duffle coats and jeans of the 'angries' of CND. As fashion designers picked up on the liberated sixties' style known as Youthquake on both sides of the Atlantic, fashion became closely linked with the non-fashion clothes that people wore. Malcolm Bradbury's acute satire on trendy mid-1970s' academic life, *The History Man*, describes at length the styles of the campus; the outsider is Carmody, the 'conventional' student, the only student to own a trouser press.

With punk in 1976, the late-twentieth-century pattern of fashion designers reflecting the street and street style being the wearing of fashion labels became complete. Hanif Kureishi uses the development of fashion from hippy to punk to New Wave and, finally, to the early 1980s' designer suit boom, with members of a Covent

Garden club looking like 'George Orwell lookalikes', to discuss his hero's progress in *Buddha of Suburbia*. Malcolm McLaren, who was, with Vivienne Westwood, the packager and outfitter of punk, rejects the designer cult in his article 'Hype-Allergic':

I want out of the fashion victim brigade. I no longer wish to be recognized as a grand image that sprang from someone else's brain . . .

Why pay all that money for some hallmark approved by *GQ*? How boring! Who cares? Fashion doesn't have that power any more. It reached its peak when all those designers became orators and philosophers, when they began to believe they could design their customers' lives as well as their clothes. Everybody waited for them to say something significant, but they never did.[11]

Calling for a return to the individuality that comes with a bespoke Savile Row suit, he denounces the designer decade of the 1980s. He describes shopping, identified so strongly with the label-conscious 1980s and 1990s, as alternately misery-making or elating; it is the retailer, dressmaker or tailor who holds the keys to dreams. In 1998, British designer Paul Smith set up a traditional bespoke tailoring service at his new shop in Notting Hill to cater for the demand for individual, well-crafted clothes; there is also a section in the building dedicated to selling old couture womenswear.

In the same year, William Boyd published *Armadillo*, a novel exploring clothes as disguise and signifiers of social status. He told *Harpers & Queen* magazine:

[People] are sending out sartorial signals . . . I think one of the four or five crucial things you must be as a novelist is a good observer. You have to derive satisfaction from these minutiae – so you can talk about the way handmade shirts, which are very distinctive, often tend to have an overlap of collar on the reverse of your jacket . . .[12]

Boyd's skill as a 'good observer' justifies his use of clothes in his novel and makes *Armadillo* contemporary in its reading of dress as social signal. Following on from themes such as Proust's 'fetishistic attachment' to the past, Woolf's delving into 'frock consciousness', Kafka's neurosis about fashion and appearance, Boyd has given another meaning still to fashion.

'But I must remember to write about my *clothes* next time I have an impulse to write. My love of clothes interests me profoundly: only it is not love; & what it is I must discover,' notes Virginia Woolf.[13] Julie Burchill, on the other hand, writes in 'Material Boys', 'I have met some boring people in my life, but none as boring as the fashion writer in her thirties.' I hope that this anthology and the discoveries I have made in compiling it go some way to prove that fashion writing is not always boring, and that the way clothes are used in literature and discussed in journalism is indeed of profound interest. It intends to reflect the different ways dress has been used by twentieth-century writers to entertain, enlighten, amuse or shock the reader. The extracts chosen show how social, political and cultural developments have made this century one of the most exciting periods of dress history, in which people's response to clothes has ranged from wearing or wanting the latest look to using them in an anti-fashion expression of individuality. It is the latter that has been most richly explored by authors and that has informed many of the selections which I have made to explore themes such as identity, sexuality, status, fetishism and gender.

1. 'The crucial ambiguity of the image': Clothes and Identity

People who dress up in bizarre costumes have a *savoire-faire* – not to mention the sort of personality disorder – that he admires. When he was a little boy, back in Leningrad, Tchitcherine's mother sewed by hand a costume for him to wear in a school entertainment. Tchitcherine was the wolf. The minute he put on the head, in front of the mirror by the ikon, he knew himself. He was the wolf.

Thomas Pynchon, *Gravity's Rainbow*, 1975

Fashion speaks of a tension between the crowd and the individual at every stage in the development of the nineteenth- and twentieth-century metropolis . . . Modernity creates fragmentation, dislocation. It creates the vision of 'totalitarian' societies peopled by identical zombies in uniform. The fear of depersonalization haunts our culture. 'Chic', from this perspective, is then merely the uniform of the rich, chilling, anti-human and rigid. Yet modernity has also created the individual in a new way. Modern individualism is an exaggerated yet fragile sense of self – a raw, painful condition.[1]

Clothes frame us. They express our individuality and are a means for us to interact with and belong to society. The adoption of what is fashionable at a given time or the rejection thereof may be expressed in the membership of a group or the affirmation of a personal stance. Dressing the body according to personal choice, instead of following the common herd, means that clothes can communicate, disguise or even repel. For the young Malcolm X, quoted in this chapter, dressing is part of a parade as he prepares to hustle on the streets of Harlem; for George Orwell, the adoption of a tramp's clothing in London is a revelation into the significance of dress. Fashion as an expression of individuality is too essentially an urban phenomenon: the city is where the 'getting and spending' takes place, and the city – Paris, London and New York in particular – is where the modern sense of self has evolved. One can hide on a city street in a way one can't in a rural environment; and anonymity, the freeing from background in order to evolve, makes what we wear much more personal.

In France in the nineteenth century, the poet Baudelaire, trying to analyse the dandy and his role in the modern city, observed that fashion can confer not only an individual identity but a social one; wearing *haute couture* was a mark of belonging to a 'civilized' élite. It set the *demi-mondaine* and courtesan on a par with the aristocrat: both understood that being fashionable meant not elegance but certain social status. Set against this at that time was the growing ready-to-wear industry and mass communication, which not only made 'fashion' – albeit watered down – more quickly available to women but also presented the 'ordinary' person with an ideal of dress, and the notion of people dressing in the same styles, dictated to by the fashion industry with the attendant press, was established. Opposing the dominance of a style was a growing anti-fashion movement of bohemians, dress reformers and feminists who by the 1880s had developed their own sartorial identities, which ran against the perceived 'ideal', providing rich material for novelists and reflected in the memoirs and diaries of the period and into the next century (some of which are explored in Chapter Nine).

In this way clothes as opposed to fashion were reconsidered and given value as a means of making a statement about individuality. This appeared all the more understandable in the light of Sigmund Freud's psychoanalytic work, which saw dress as an expression of the unconscious, as, for example, seen in the collaborative work of dress designer Elsa Schiaparelli and surrealist artist Salvador Dali who made fantasy clothes, such as a *trompe l'oeil* lobster dress, and a dream life which saw 'passion play and power play';[2] and he voiced the theory that fashion's change was motivated by shifting sexual interest in areas of the female body. The distaste for women's fashion that Thomas Mann voices in *The Magic Mountain* reflects an influence by Freud and raises the notion of sexuality and dress. But the connection between sexuality and fashion was not applied solely to women's dress. Men's clothing has been subject to the same theory in the history of dress; the phrase 'peacock male', for instance, fundamentally describes the way men adorn themselves as a means of attracting a mate, outdoing the latter by display. The unhappiness Kafka expresses in his diaries over the buying of a tuxedo, his anxiety over being 'badly dressed', is concerned with his place in (a potentially hostile) society and also with the image he will present to women.

Early feminists were certainly anti-fashion (although Mrs Pankhurst urged her suffragette followers not to dress in an unfeminine way and therefore challenge conventional ideas of womanhood), condemning the numerous constrictions made on the female body by fashion (such as corsetry and, later, the requirement for woman to be thin) at a time when women's dress was at its most voluptuous and statuesque – the British designer Lucile describes her models as almost six feet tall and averaging eleven stone, sometimes 'considerably more'.[3] The main problem that many feminists seem to have had – and still have – with fashion is that it is a male ideal imposed on women which subordinates them; thus women are ornamental adjuncts to men and society as a whole. The other side of this argument, however, is, as Elizabeth Wilson points out, that 'fashion has been one of the means by which women have been able to achieve self expression', and 'feminism has been as simplistic – and as moralistic – as most other theories in its denigration of fashion'.[4]

The themes of women's gender and identity run through the century, from the androgynous women of the 1920s who adopted trousers and cropped their hair to the present day. Simone de Beauvoir wrote about the 'bondage of elegance'[5] and its imposition on a female reality in *The Second Sex* in 1953, approximately four years after Christian Dior launched his New Look. 'The least sophisticated of women, once she is "dressed", does not present herself to observation; she is, like the picture or statue, or the actor on the stage, an agent through which is suggested someone not there – that is, the character she represents, but is not. It is this identification with something unreal, fixed, perfect . . . that gratifies her; she strives to identify herself with this figure and thus to seem to herself to be stabilized, justified in her splendour.'[6] In her groundbreaking work of 1970, *The Female Eunuch*, Germaine Greer talks of 'curves' and discusses the imposition of bras and corsets which shape the female body into an 'ideal' hourglass shape. 'The only way that women can opt out of such gross handling is to refuse to wear undergarments which perpetuate the fantasy of pneumatic boobs, so that men must come to terms with the varieties of the real thing.'[7] Her attack is on the nature of fetishism in fashion (discussed further in Chapter Five) and has continued to be sustained by women writers who question the imposition of the male ideal; what is different about current debate is that it also voices a disgust – and distrust – of the homosexual designer and his vision of female identity. Even though women designers become more powerful – Vivienne Westwood, Donna Karan, Katharine Hamnett – identities – sexual, social and political – continue to play an important role. Fashion utilizes the way these identities are expressed; it often exploits them to a point of unamusing irony, but they have yet to lose their meaning.

Mother had a hard time making both ends meet* and, on a day like this, wanted us to be dressed in something respectable. The day

---

*Pritchett's first volume of his memoirs recalls his Edwardian childhood.

before she put the sewing-machine on the dining-room table, took out a paper pattern and set about making me some trousers. She made many of her own dresses and a lot of our clothes; indeed, if she was making a dress for herself or my sister, I was often the model. I had to stand up while she pinned patterns all over me. She was often puzzled by the strips of pattern that were left over. If only she had her cousin Emmy or better still Cousin Louie, the dress-maker, she would say; for it was a fate with her often to cut out, say, two left sleeves, or to be short of a quarter of a yard on the length. She knitted our stockings and never learned how to turn a heel, so that a double heel often hung over the backs of our boots: jerseys for us she never finished; but for herself – for she did not want to make victims of *us* – she would knit recklessly on while I read the instructions to her, and turn out narrow tubes of wool that she would stretch, laughing till she cried, to her knees. She had to pay for the material for her dressmaking out of the house-keeping money and she would raid any free material in sight. I have described her attacks on our curtains. Her own bloomers were a byword: for in gay moments she would haul up her long skirts above her knees and show my father – who was always shocked – what could be done with a chair cover or something robust of that kind. 'You want me in the business instead of "that woman",' she'd say.

For she had a vengeful streak in her, and looking at our father, the impressive Managing Director, and counting his suits and know-ing how she couldn't get a penny out of him for our clothes, she attacked his wardrobe. She found a pair of striped trousers of the kind worn with morning dress. Just the thing for me. Out came the scissors. Slicing the enormous trousers roughly at the knees she saw that my brother and I could get into them both at once. She was upset by our laughter. She now slashed at the trousers again and narrowed them to my size. The insoluble difficulty was the fly buttons; these she pulled round to the side of one leg; cutting and then tacking her way up the middle while they were on me at the final try-on, she sewed me up totally in front.

'I won't be able to *go*, Mum,' I said.

She was flabbergasted, but in her careless way, she snipped a couple of stitches in her tacking.

These were the trousers I was wearing as I stood before Mr Timms, very pleased by Father's fashionable stripes and willing to show any boy who was interested the original touch of having Savile Row fly buttons down the side of one leg. What I feared was happening: the hole was lengthening in front. I could feel an alarming draught. I dared not look down. I hoped Mr Timms would not look down, as my mother chatted on and on about our family. Nothing happened. I went to my classroom: at playtime I dared not run, for fear the tacking would go. When I pulled the thread to tighten it I was left with a length of thread hanging down from the vulnerable part. When I went home after school the thread went altogether and I had to cover myself with my hand.

So my first day at Rosendale Road School began. Wearing my father's classy cut-downs I knew the distinction of our family and its awkward difference from the families of all the other children. No one else had a Managing Director's trousers on. No one else had (I was sure) our dark adventures. We were a race apart; abnormal but proud of our stripes, longing for the normality we saw around us.

V. S. Pritchett, *A Cab at the Door*, 1968

Presently there was a noise on the staircase. He shut up Margaret's card in the pages of Ruskin, and opened the door. A woman entered, of whom it is simplest to say that she was not respectable. Her appearance was awesome. She seemed all strings and bell-pulls – ribbons, chains, bead necklaces that clinked and caught – and a boa of azure feathers hung round her neck, with the ends uneven. Her throat was bare, wound with a double row of pearls, her arms were bare to the elbows, and might again be detected at the shoulder, through cheap lace. Her hat, which was flowery, resembled those punnets, covered with flannel, which we sowed with mustard and cress in our childhood, and which germinated here yes, and there no. She wore it on the back of her head. As for her hair, or rather hairs, they are too complicated to describe, but one system went down her back, lying in a thick pad there, while another, created for a lighter destiny, rippled around her forehead . . . Yes, Jacky was past her prime, whatever that prime may have been. She was descending quicker than most women into the colourless years, and the look in her eyes confessed it.

E. M. Forster, *Howards End*, 1910

30 December 1911

But while I thought I was distinguishing myself – I had no other motive than the desire to distinguish myself and my joy in making an impression and in the impression itself – it was only as a result of giving it insufficient thought that I endured always having to go around dressed in the wretched clothes which my parents had made for me by one customer after another, longest by a tailor in Nusle. I naturally noticed – it was obvious – that I was unusually badly dressed, and even had an eye for others who were well dressed, but for years on end my mind did not succeed in recognizing in my clothes the cause of my miserable appearance. Since even at that time, more in tendency than in fact, I was on the way to underestimating myself, I was convinced that it was only on me that clothes assumed this appearance, first looking stiff as a board, then hanging in wrinkles. I did not want new clothes at all, for if I was going to look ugly in any case, I wanted at least to be comfortable and also to avoid exhibiting the ugliness of the new clothes to the world that had grown accustomed to the old ones. These always long-drawn-out refusals on the frequent occasions when my mother (who with the eyes of an adult was still able to find differences between these new clothes and the old ones) wanted to have new clothes of this sort made for me, had this effect upon me that, with my parents concurring, I had to conclude that I was not at all concerned about my appearance.

2 January 1912

As a result I let the awful clothes affect even my posture, walked around with my back bowed, my shoulders drooping, my hands at awkward angles, was afraid of mirrors because they showed in me an ugliness which in my opinion was inevitable, which moreover could not have been an entirely truthful reflection, for had I actually looked like that, I certainly would have attracted even more attention, suffered gentle pokes in the back from my mother on Sunday walks and admonitions and prophecies which were much too abstract for me to be able to relate them to the worries I then had . . .

Once it seemed impossible to get along without a black dress suit, especially as I also had to decide whether I would join a dancing class. The tailor in Nusle was sent for and the cut of the suit discussed. I was undecided, as I always was in such cases; they made me afraid that by a definite statement I would be swept away not only into an immediate unpleasantness, but beyond that into something even worse. So at first I didn't want a dress suit, but when they shamed me before the stranger by pointing out that I had no dress suit, I put up with having a tailcoat discussed; but since I regarded a tailcoat as a fearful revolution one could for ever talk about but on which one could never decide, we agreed on a tuxedo, which, because of its similarity to the usual sack coat, seemed to me at least bearable. But when I heard that the vest of the tuxedo had to be cut low and I would therefore have to wear a stiff shirt as well, my determination almost exceeded my strength, since something like this had to be averted. I did not want such a tuxedo, rather, if I had to have one, a tuxedo lined and trimmed with silk indeed, but one that could be buttoned high. The tailor had never heard of such a tuxedo, but he remarked that no matter what I intended to do with such a jacket, it couldn't be worn for dancing. Good, then it couldn't be worn for dancing, I didn't want to dance anyhow, that hadn't been decided on yet in any case; on the contrary, I wanted the jacket made for me as I had described it. The tailor's stubborness was increased by the fact that until now I had always submitted with shamed haste to being measured for new clothes and to having tried them on, without expressing any opinions or wishes. So there was nothing else for me to do, and also since my mother insisted on it, but to go with him, painful as it was, across the Altstadter Ring to a second-hand clothing store in the window of which I had for quite some time seen displayed a simple tuxedo and recognized it as suitable for me. But unfortunately it had already been removed from the window, I could not see it inside the store even by looking my hardest, I did not dare to go into the store just to look at the tuxedo, so we returned, disagreeing as before. I felt as though the future tuxedo was already cursed by the uselessness of this errand, at least I used my annoyance with the pros and cons of the argument as an excuse to send the tailor away with some small order or other and an indefinite promise about the tuxedo while I, under the reproaches of my mother, remained wearily behind, barred for ever – everything happened to me for ever – from girls, an elegant appearance and dances. The instantaneous cheerfulness that this induced in me made me miserable, and besides, I was afraid that I had made myself ridiculous before the tailor as none of his customers ever had before.

The Diaries of Franz Kafka, 1910–1913, edited by Max Brod, 1948

The other lady put up an eyeglass and looked where Miss Blanchflower pointed; but languidly, as though it were an effort to shake herself free from preoccupying ideas. She was a woman of about thirty-five, slenderly made, with a sallow, regular face, and good though short-sighted eyes. The eyes were dark, so was the hair, the features delicate. Under the black shady hat, the hair was very closely and neatly coiled. The high collar of the white blouse, fitting tightly to the slender neck, the coat and skirt of blue serge without ornament of any kind, but well cut, emphasized the thinness, almost emaciation of the form. Her attitude, dress and expression conveyed the idea of something amazingly taut and ready – like a ship cleared for action. The body with its clothing seemed to have been simplified as much as possible, so as to become the mere instrument of the will which governed it. No superfluity whatever, whether of flesh on her small bones, or of a single unnecessary button, fold, or trimming on her dress, had Gert-rude Marvell ever allowed herself for many years. The general effect was in some way formidable; though why the neat precision of the little lady should convey any notion of this sort, it would not at first sight have been easy to say.

Mrs H. Ward, *Delia Blanchflower*, 1915

Now, this morning, her husband was coming to see her, and she was dressing to receive him. She felt heavy and inert as stone, yet inwardly trembling convulsively. The known man, he did not affect her. Heavy and inert in her soul, yet amused, she would play her part in his reception. But the unknown man, what was he? Her dark, unknown soul trembled apprehensively.

At any rate he would be different. She shuddered. The vision she had of him, of the good-looking, clean, slightly tanned, attractive man, ordinary and yet with odd streaks of understanding that made her ponder, this she must put away. They said his face was rather horribly cut up. She shivered. How she hated it, coldly hated and loathed it, the thought of disfigurement. Her fingers trembled, she rose to go downstairs. If he came he must not come into her bedroom.

So, in her fashionable but inexpensive black silk dress, wearing her jewels, her string of opals, her big, ruby brooch, she went downstairs. She knew how to walk, how to hold her body according to the mode. She did it almost instinctively, so deep was her consciousness of the impression her own appearance must create.

D. H. Lawrence, 'The Thimble',
from *The Mortal Coil and Other Stories*, 1917

Which of the two jumpers – the crimson, the fawn? The fawn today. The crimson heartened the lesser days, put a firm face on them. It suited her, as they said. But today she could suit her clothes, provide the glow, fill out the shape, warm up texture and colouring. She pulled on her brown stockinette skirt, regretting, but without irritation today, the slight bagginess at knees and bottom; fastened a broad scarlet patent-leather belt. The belt was an object that had virtue in it. She had had it for two years. It was cracked, peeling a little. Within its compass she felt a certainty of individuality, like a seal set on her, and she loved it, liked to think of it lying coiled, secret and brilliant, in the top left-hand drawer. She had another belt, a thin nigger-brown one of suede; and that was a good belt too, though less dependable.

She cast a glance at her figure in the long glass; but the image failed her, remained unequivocally familiar and utilitarian.

Nowadays a peculiar emotion accompanied the moment of looking in the mirror: fitfully, rarely a stranger might emerge: a new self.

It had happened two or three times already, beginning with a day last summer, the languid close of a burning afternoon; coming from the burdened garden into the silent, darkened house: melancholy, solitary, restless, keyed up expectantly – for what? waiting – for whom? The house was empty. She took off her creased linen frock, poured out cold water, plunged her face and arms. She must put on a new frock – her raspberry-ice-pink cotton frock with short sleeves and round neck, just back from the dressmaker. The rough crêpe stuff clung, she smelt the faint pungency of fresh unwashed cotton. She looked in the glass and saw herself . . . Well, what was it like? She knew what she looked like, had for some years thought the reflection interesting, because it was her own; though disappointing, unreliable, subject twenty times a day to blottings-out and blurrings, as if a lamp were guttering or extinguished: in any case irremediably imperfect. But this was something else. This was a mysterious face; both dark and lowing; hair tumbling down, pushed back and upwards, as if in currents of fierce energy. Was it the frock that did it? Her body seemed to assemble itself harmoniously within it, to become centralized, to expand, both static and fluid; alive. It was the portrait of a young girl in pink. All the room's reflected objects seemed to frame, to present her, whispering: Here are You.

Olivia considered serviceable dark-brown or navy-blue winters, holland and tussore summers; cream Viyella blouses, white piqué tennis skirts; all plain, neat, subdued, unbecoming. The patches of colour splashing one's wardrobe's life history were rare, now one came to think of it, as roses in December. Each one remained vivid in memory: isolated accidents, shocks of brightness: a crimson ribbon slotted through an early white party frock, exciting, evoking again the drop of blood of the fairy story piercing the cold blank, startled snow, piercing her smooth mind indelibly, as she read, with sudden stain; an orange Liberty scarf on a straw hat: a curious coat of violet frieze that winter of wearing half-mourning for Mother's father.

Now that I am grown up and can choose my own clothes, I'll wear bright colours always.

Rosamund Lehmann, *Invitation to the Waltz*, 1932

Iris walked swiftly, heroically, her eyes intent before her, impersonal, utterly unselfconscious. The glaring lights in the passage lit her swiftly moving green-and-silver shoes, or were they sandals with high heels? And so intent were the flippant silver-flashing ankles, briskly striding on, as though chiming the never-to-be-known marching song of a lady who must always meet men on their own ground.

Michael Arlen, *The Green Hat*, 1924

If skirts become much shorter
    said the flapper with a sob
There'll be two more cheeks to powder
    and one more place to bob

Eric Gill, *c.* 1925

When she went out she tripped over quite a long train which she had on her skirt and she nearly fell down. So Dorothy leaned out of the door and Dorothy called down the hall and said, 'Take a tuck in that skirt Isabel, it's 1925.'

Anita Loos, *Gentlemen Prefer Blondes:*
The Illuminating Diary of a Professional Lady, 1926

Two words have always been banned from my house – the word 'creation', which strikes me as the height of pretentiousness, and the word 'impossible'. I kept in touch with the needs of women who had confidence in me and tried to help them find their type. This I believe to be the principle secret of being well dressed.

Elsa Schiaparelli, *Shocking Life*, 1954

Hans Castorp mused, his gaze still bent on Frau Chauchat's arm. The way women dressed! They showed their necks and bosoms, they transfigured their arms by veiling them in 'illusion'; they did so, the world over, to arouse our desire. Oh God, how beautiful life was. And it was just such accepted commonplaces as this that made it beautiful – for it was a commonplace that women dressed themselves alluringly, it was so well known and recognized a fact that we never consciously realized it, but merely enjoyed it without a thought. And yet he had an inward conviction that we ought to think about it, ought to realize what a blessed, what a well-nigh miraculous arrangement it was. For of course it all had a certain end and aim; it was by a definite design that women were permitted to array themselves with irresistible allure: it was for the sake of posterity, for the perpetuation of the species. Of course. But suppose a woman were inwardly diseased, unfit for motherhood – what then? What was the sense of her wearing gauze sleeves and attracting male attention to her physical parts if these were actually unsound? Obviously there was no sense; it ought to be considered immoral, and forbidden as such. For a man to take an interest in a woman inwardly diseased had no more sense than – well, than the interest of Hans Castorp had once taken in Pribislav Hippe.

Thomas Mann, *The Magic Mountain*, 1924

Often when I see clothes with manifold pleats, frills and appendages which fit so smoothly on to lovely bodies I think they won't keep that smoothness long, but will get creases that can't be ironed out, dust lying so thick in the embroidery that it can't be brushed away, and that no one would want to be so unhappy and so foolish as to wear the same valuable gown every day from early morning till night.

Franz Kafka, *The Clothes*, 1913

30 June 1926
This is the last day of June & finds me in black despair because Clive laughed at my new hat, Vita pitied me, & I sank to the depths

of gloom. This happened at Clive's last night after going to the Sitwells' with Vita. Oh dear I was wearing the hat without thinking whether it was good or bad: & it was all very flashing & easy; & there I saw a man with braided hair, another with long red tongues in his button hole; & sat by Vita & laughed & clubbed . . . Clive suddenly said, or bawled rather, what an astonishing hat you're wearing! Then he asked where I got it. I pretended a mystery, tried to change the talk, was not allowed, & they pulled me down between them, like a hare; I never felt more humiliated. Clive said did Mary choose it? No. Todd said Vita. And the dress? Todd of course: after that I was forced to go on as if nothing terrible had happened; but it was very forced & queer & humiliating. So I talked & laughed too much. Duncan prim & acid as ever told me it was utterly impossible to do anything with a hat like that. And I joked about the Squires's party; & Leonard got silent, & I came away deeply chagrined, as unhappy as I have been these ten years; & revolved it in sleep & dreams all night; & today has been ruined.

Virginia Woolf, *Diaries: Volume III 1925–1930*,

edited by Anne Olivier Bell, 1980

Though it was nearly a year since her husband's death, Emmeline Lucas (universally known to her friends as Lucia) still wore the deepest and most uncompromising mourning. Black certainly suited her very well, but that had nothing to do with this continued use of it, whatever anybody said.

Gradually, and in increasing areas, grey and white and violet invaded the unrelieved black in which she had spent the year of her widowhood; one day she wore a white belt, another there were grey panels in her skirt, another her garden hat had a velvet riband on it. Even Georgie, who had a great eye for female attire, could not accurately follow these cumulative changes: he could not be sure whether she had worn a grey cloak before, or whether she had had white gloves in church last Sunday. Then, instead of letting her hair droop in slack and mournful braids over her ears, it resumed its old polished and corrugated appearance, and on her pale cheeks (ashen with grief) there boomed a little brown rouge, which made her look as if she had been playing golf again, and her lips certainly were ruddier. It was all intensely exciting, a series of subtle changes at the end of which, by the middle of July, her epiphany in church without anything black about her, and with the bloom of her vitality quite restored, passed almost unremarked.

E. F. Benson, *Mapp and Lucia, 1935*

The Brummell Club was some sort of betting place, he had heard; full of gamblers, and people who did and sold things on commission, he shouldn't wonder. That was the vice of the day; that and the dole. Work? No! Sell things on commission – motorcars, for choice. Brummell Club! Yes! This was the place. It had a window – he remembered. No harm, anyway, in asking if the fellow really belonged there! And entering, he enquired:

'Mr Stainford a member here!'

'Yes. Don't know if he's in. Mr Stainford been in, Bob?'

'Just come in.'

'Oh!' said Soames, rather taken aback.

'Gentleman to see him Bob.'

A rather sinking sensation occurred within Soames.

'Come with me, sir.'

Soames took a deep breath, and his legs moved. In an alcove off the entrance – somewhat shabby and constricted – he could see a man lolling in an old armchair, smoking a cigarette through a holder. He had a little red book in one hand and a small pencil in the other, and he held them as still as if he were about to jot down a conviction that he had not got. He wore a dark suit with little lines; his legs were crossed, and Soames noted that one foot in a worn brown shoe, treed and polished against age to the point of pathos, was slowly moving in a circle.

John Galsworthy, *Swan Song*, 1928

Weston [W.H. Auden] and I met again, by purest chance, seven years later. Just before Christmas, 1925, a mutual acquaintance brought him to tea. I found him very little changed. True, he had grown enormously; but his small yellow eyes were still screwed painfully together in the same short-sighted scowl and his stumpy immature fingers were still nail-bitten and stained – nicotine was now mixed with the ink. He was expensively but untidily dressed in a chocolate-brown suit which needed pressing, complete with one of the new fashionable double-breasted waistcoats. His coarse woollen socks were tumbled all anyhow, around his babyishly shapeless naked ankles. One of the laces was broken in his elegant brown shoes. While I and his introducer talked he sat silent, aggressively smoking a large pipe with a severe childish frown. Clumsy and severe, he hooked a blunt dirty finger round the tops of several of the books in my shelves, overbalancing them on to his lap and then, when his casual curiosity was satisfied, dropping them face downwards open on the floor – serenely unconscious of my outraged glances.

Six months later – this was July 1926 – Weston came down to stay with me at the seaside. I see him striding towards me, along Yarmouth pier, a tall figure with loose violent impatient movements, dressed in dirty grey flannels and a black evening bow tie. On his straw-coloured head was planted a very broad-brimmed black felt hat.

This hat I disliked from the start. It represented, I felt, something self-conscious and sham, something that Oxford had superimposed upon Weston's personality; something which he, in his turn, was trying to impose upon me. He wore it with a certain guilty defiance: he wasn't quite comfortable in it; he wanted me to accept it, with all its implications – and I wouldn't. I will never, as long as I live, accept any of Weston's hats. Since that day, he has tried me with several. There was an opera hat – belonging to the period when he decided that poets ought to dress like bank directors, in morning cut-aways and striped trousers or evening swallow tails. There was a workman's cap, with a shiny black peak, which he bought while he was living in Berlin, and which had, in the end, to be burnt, because he was sick into it one evening in a cinema. There was, and occasionally still is, a panama with a black ribbon – representing, I think, Weston's conception of himself as a lunatic clergyman; always a favourite role. Also, most insidious of all, there exists, somewhere in the background, a schoolmaster's mortarboard. He has never actually dared to show me this: but I have seen him wearing it in several photographs.

The black hat caused a considerable sensation in the village where I was staying. The village boys and girls, grouped along the inn wall by the bus stop, sniggered loudly as we got out of the bus. Weston was pleased: 'Laughter', he announced, 'is the first sign of sexual attraction.'

Christopher Isherwood, *Lions and Shadows*, 1938

I took a trip to London to buy tweeds and stormed the press with my trouser-skirts. They were made for every occasion, travelling, city suits, evening and sport. They were graceful and feminine and to my mind much more modest than skirts. After all, in all the countries where women live a retired and restricted life, they wear trousers, while men wear mostly robes.

The controversy was violent, and unexpected because it was not such a new idea. Poiret had tried it before.

People wrote angry letters to the editors, asking that it should be made a penal offence for a woman to appear in male attire.

'I have never heard such monstrous impudence,' wrote a woman to the *Daily Mail*, 'in all my life, as for a foreign woman to come here and dictate to us what we are going to wear.'

And to the *Daily Express*: 'If any woman dares to appear at Wimbledon in that divided skirt she should be soundly beaten.'

The tennis player Lily Alvarez wore this trouser-skirt at a match in Monte Carlo and was greatly admired and discussed. Later she arrived at Wimbledon for the World Championship.

'But where are your trousers?' acidly asked a rival.

'Oh,' answered Lily with a mocking smile, 'so much has been said about them that I did not dare . . .'

And she was asked away to the court ready to play, when everyone suddenly realized that she was wearing them.

Elsa Schiaparelli, *Shocking Life*, 1954

I'm wearing a dress of real silk, but it's threadbare, almost transparent. It used to belong to my mother. One day she decided the colour was too bright for her and she gave it to me. It's a sleeveless dress with a very low neck. It's the sepia colour real silk takes on with wear. It's a dress I remember. I think it suits me. I'm wearing a leather belt with it, perhaps a belt belonging to one of my brothers. I can't remember the shoes I used to wear in those days, only certain dresses. Most of the time I wore canvas sandals, no stockings. I'm speaking of the time before the high school in Saigon. Since then, of course, I've always worn shoes. This particular day I must be wearing the famous pair of gold lamé high heels. I can't see any others I could have been wearing, so I'm wearing them. Bargains, final reductions bought for me by my mother. I'm wearing these gold lamé shoes to school. Going to school in evening shoes decorated with little *diamanté* flowers. I insist on wearing them. I don't like myself in any others, and to this day I still like myself in them.

These high heels are the first in my life, they're beautiful, they've eclipsed all the shoes that went before, the flat ones, for playing and running about, made of white canvas.

It's not the shoes, though, that make the girl look so strangely, so weirdly dressed. No, it's the fact that she's wearing a man's flat-brimmed hat, a brownish-pink fedora with a broad black ribbon.

The crucial ambiguity of the image lies in the hat.

How I came by it I've forgotten. I can't think who could have given it to me. It must have been my mother who bought it for me, because I asked her. The one thing certain is that it was another mark-down, another final reduction. But why was it bought? No woman, no girl wore a man's fedora in that colony then. No native woman either. What must have happened is, I try it on just for fun, look at myself in the shopkeeper's glass, and see that there, beneath the man's hat, the thin awkward shape, the inadequacy of childhood, has turned into something else. Has ceased to be a harsh, inescapable imposition of nature. Has become, on the contrary, a provoking choice of nature, a choice of the mind. Suddenly it's deliberate. Suddenly I see myself as another, as another would be seen, outside myself, available to all, available to all eyes, in circulation for cities, journeys, desire. I take the hat, and am never parted from it. Having got it, this hat that all by itself makes me whole, I wear it all the time. With the shoes it must have been much the same, but after the hat. They contradict the hat, as the hat contradicts the puny body, so they're right for me. I wear them all the time too, go everywhere in these shoes, this hat, out of doors, in all weathers, on every occasion. And to town.

Marguerite Duras, *The Lover*, 1984

You may have three-half-pence in your pocket and not a prospect in the world . . . but in your new clothes you can stand on the street corner, indulging in a private daydream of yourself as Clark Gable or Greta Garbo.

George Orwell, *The Road to Wigan Pier*, 1937

When the *patronne* goes shopping it's her cousin who takes her place at the bar. His name is Adolphe. I began looking at him while I was sitting down and I went on because I couldn't turn my head. He is in shirtsleeves with mauve braces; he has rolled the sleeves of his shirt above his elbows. The braces can scarcely be seen against the blue shirt; they are completely obliterated, buried in the blue, but this is false modesty; in point of fact they won't allow themselves to be forgotten, they annoy me with their sheep-like stubbornness, as if, setting out to become purple, they had stopped somewhere on the way without giving up their pretentions. You feel like telling them: 'Go on, *become* purple and let's hear no more about it.'

Jean-Paul Sartre, *Nausea*, 1938

One day this summer I was riding through Letchworth when the bus stopped and two dreadful-looking old men got on to it. They were both about sixty, both very short, pink and chubby, and both hatless. One of them was obscenely bald, the other had long grey hair bobbed in the Lloyd George style. They were dressed in pistachio-coloured shirts and khaki shorts into which their huge bottoms were crammed so tightly you could study every dimple. Their appearance created a mild stir of horror on top of the bus. The man next to me, a commercial traveller I should say, glanced at me, at them, and back again at me, and murmured 'Socialists', as who should say, 'Red Indians'.

George Orwell, *The Road to Wigan Pier*, 1937

My bedroom overlooks the main street of our district. Though it was a fine afternoon the paving-blocks were black and glistening. What few people were about seemed in an absurd hurry. First of all there came a family going for their Sunday afternoon walk; two small boys in sailor suits, with short trousers hardly down to their knees, and looking rather uneasy in their Sunday best; then a little girl with a big pink bow and black patent-leather shoes. Behind them was their mother, an enormously fat woman in a brown silk dress, and their father, a dapper little man, whom I knew by sight. He had a straw hat, a walking stick, and a butterfly tie. Seeing him beside his wife, I understood why people said he came of a good family and had married beneath him.

Albert Camus, *The Outsider*, 1942

Off the train, I'd go through that Grand Central Station afternoon rush-hour crowd, and many white people simply stopped in their tracks to watch me pass. The drape and the cut of a zoot suit showed to the best advantage if you were tall – and I was over six feet. My conk was fire-red. I was really a clown, but my ignorance made me think I was 'sharp'. My knob-toed, orange-coloured 'kick-up' shoes were nothing but Florsheim's, the ghetto's Cadillac of shoes in those days. (Some shoe companies made these ridiculous styles for sale only in the black ghettoes where ignorant Negroes like me would pay the big-name price for something that we associated with being rich.) ... My conk and costume were so wild that I might have been taken as a man from Mars. I caused a minor automobile collision; one driver stopped to gape at me, and the driver behind bumped into him. My appearance staggered the older boys I had once envied; I'd stick out my hand, saying, 'Skin me, daddy-o!'

Malcolm X and Alex Haley, *The Autobiography of Malcom X*, 1965

At this distance of time I cannot remember precisely what sort of an overcoat Widmerpool was said to have worn in the first instance. Stories about it had grown into legend: so much so that even five or six years later you might still occasionally hear an obtrusive or inappropriate garment referred to as 'a Widmerpool'; and Templer, for example, would sometimes say, 'I'm afraid I'm wearing rather Widmerpool socks today,' or, 'I've bought a wonderfully Widmerpool tie to go home in.' My impression is that the overcoat's initial deviation from normal was slight, depending on the existence or absence of a belt at the back, the fact that the cut was single or double-breasted, or, again, irregularity may have had something to do with the collar; perhaps the cloth, even, was of the wrong colour or texture.

As a matter of fact the overcoat was only remarkable in itself as a vehicle for the comment it aroused, insomuch that an element in Widmerpool himself had proved indigestible to the community. An overcoat (which never achieved the smallest notoriety) belonging to a boy called Offord whose parents lived in Madeira, where they had possibly purchased the garment was indeed once pointed out to me as 'very like Widmerpool's'. There was on no occasion the slightest question of Widmerpool being bullied, or even seriously ragged about the matter. On the contrary, his deviation seems scarcely to have been mentioned to him, except by cruder spirits; the coat becoming recognized almost immediately as a traditionally ludicrous aspect of everyday life. Years later, if you questioned his contemporaries on the subject, they were vague in their answers, and would only laugh and say that he wore the coat for a couple of terms; and then, by the time winter came round again, he was found to possess an overcoat of a more conventional sort.

This overcoat gave Widmerpool a lasting notoriety which his otherwise unscintillating career at school could never wholly dispel.

Anthony Powell, *A Question of Upbringing,* 1951

A PINK WOOL KNITTED DRESS

In your pink wool knitted dress
Before anything had smudged anything
You stood at the altar. Bloomsday.

Rain – so that a just-bought umbrella
Was the only furnishing about me
Newer than three years inured.
My tie – sole, drab, veteran RAF black –
Was the used-up symbol of a tie.
My cord jacket – thrice-dyed black,
    exhausted,
Just hanging on to itself.

I was a post-war, Utility son-in-law!
Not quite the Frog-Prince. Maybe the Swineherd
Stealing this daughter's pedigree dreams
From under her watchtowered search lit future.

No ceremony could conscript me
Out of my uniform. I wore my whole wardrobe –
Except for the odd, spare, identical item
My wedding, like Nature, wanted to hide.
However – if we were going to be married
It had better be Westminster Abbey. Why not?
The Dean told us why not. That is how
I learned that I had a Parish Church.
St George of the Chimney Sweeps
So we squeezed into marriage finally.
Your mother, brave even in this
US Foreign Affairs gamble,
Acted all bridesmaids and all guests,

Even – magnanimity – represented
My family
Who had heard nothing about it.
I had invited only their ancestors.
I had not even confided my theft of you
To a closest friend. For Best Man – my squire
To hold the meanwhile rings –
We requisitioned the sexton. Twist of the outrage:
He was packing children into a bus,
Taking them to the Zoo in that downpour!
All the prison animals had to be patient
While we married.
                    You were transfigured.
So slender and new and naked,
A nodding spray of wet lilac
You shook, you sobbed with joy, you were ocean
    depth
Brimming with God.
You said you saw the heavens open
And show riches, ready to drop upon us.
Levitated beside you, I stood subjected
To a strange tense: the spellbound future.
In that echo-gaunt weekday chancel.
I see you.
Wrestling to contain your flames
In your pink wool knitted dress
And in your eye-pupils –
Great cut jewels
Jostling their tearflames, truly like big jewels
Shaken in a dice-cup and held up to me.

Ted Hughes, from *The Birthday Letters*, 1998

Because, of course, we were all disaffected and most of us were students and, for a variety of reasons, had adopted a style of dress which was a more or less conscious form of social affront or visual insult. Caught in a limbo of fashionable anti-style (that is, unofficial or 'underground' style) between the demise of the beatnik and the ascent of hippy, we had adopted the only style there was around, the CND or generalized 'protesters' style, army-surplus sweaters and jeans usually manufactured by Levi-Strauss and Company. There was a lot of status about a pair of genuine Levis at this time.

We young chicks all wore Levis, of course, and we chose the men's styles because they offered a trimmer fit around the thigh. Though we did not know it, these trousers were a quite unambiguous sign saying, in effect, we could not or did not need to work. That is, we were either workshy or else were students – the old excuse for not getting your hands mucky.

Angela Carter, 'Trouser Protest', *New Society*, 1975

A fantastically beautiful girl called Gloria Gordon holds court at one table, wearing a silver lamé evening gown, cut to the navel, while rock-and-roll singers do an impromptu number in the center of the room, to the delight of the western stars in their boots and chaps: a pleasure not shared by the motorcyclists in their black leather, bedecked with swastikas and chains, radiating hostility, so unlike the Easterners who are solemnly catatonic in their Brooks Brothers suits and button-down collars, each clutching an empty attaché case. The students regard the Easterners respectfully as the farthest-out of all for they are, reputedly, the drugtakers.

Gore Vidal, *Myra Breckinridge*, 1968

In college, my coterie and I were mods and beats rather than hippies. Feld cut a striking figure on campus in his green-vinyl car coat, a badge of British dandyism purchased on Carnaby Street and 'coveted' by Jarratt. It was an exact copy, Feld boasts, of the one worn by Julie Christie in Paris in *Darling*, a favorite film of ours. I affected men's ties, paisley Tom Jones shirts, Edwardian pin-striped bell-bottoms, naval pea coats, and antique jodhpur boots. My favorite piece of everyday clothing, however, was Feld's khaki jean jacket, which I appropriated like a family hand-me-down and wore for several years. Hard as it may be to understand now, since the style has become universal, it was a radical gesture for a woman then. Hippie girls did don their boyfriends' jean jackets, but only with reinforced feminine iconography – long, flowing hair, peasant blouses, dirndl skirts. I aggressively wore Feld's jacket with cropped hair and trousers (as can be seen in a period photo reproduced in my *Vanity Fair* profile of September 1992). The hippie clique who ruled the student-center scene didn't like it one bit, as I certainly heard while traversing the snack bar on the way to class.

Camille Paglia, 'Memoirs and Adventures', from
Vamps and Tramps, 1994

The only way that women can opt out of such gross handling is to refuse to wear undergarments which perpetuate the fantasy of pneumatic boobs, so that men must come to terms with the varieties of the real thing. Recent emphasis on the nipple, which was absent from the breast of popular pornography, is in women's favour, for the nipple is expressive and responsive. The vegetable creep of women's liberation has freed some breasts from the domination of foam and wire. One way to continue progress in the same direction might be to remind men that they have sensitive nipples too.

Germaine Greer, *The Female Eunuch*, 1970

She had a ruby-colored satin dressing gown, a gorgeous garment, fruitily molding, when she sat down, the bulges of her stomach and thighs. She wore it Sunday mornings, when she sat in our dining room smoking, drinking tea, until it was time to get ready for church. It parted at the knees to show some place clinging rayon – a night-gown. Nightgowns were garments I could not bear, because of the way they twisted around and worked up on you while you slept and also because they left you uncovered between the legs. Naomi and I when we were younger used to draw pictures of men and women with startling gross genitals, the women's fat, bristling with needly hair, like a porcupine's back. Wearing a nightgown one could not help being aware of this vile bundle, which pajamas could decently shroud and contain. My mother at the same Sunday breakfast table wore large striped pajamas, a faded rust-colored kimono with a tasseled tie, the sort of slippers that are wooly socks, with a sole sewn in.

Alice Munro, *Lives of Girls and Women*, 1971

They look the way new people do look, this autumn. Howard, small, dark and compact, has long hair, though not quite so long as it was last year, and a Zapata moustache; he wears neat white sweatshirts, with rousing symbols on the front, like clenched fists, and hairy loose waistcoats, and pyjama-style blue jeans. Barbara, who is big and has frizzled yellow hair, wears green eyeshadow, and clown-white make-up, and long caftan dresses, and no bra, so that her stubby nipples show through the light cotton.

For in the new parade of styles, which undergoes subtle shifts year by year, like the campus itself, bits of military uniform, bedraggled scraps of garments, fur hats and forage caps and kepis, tank tops and denims and coats which have lost their buttons have become the norm; the crowds troop along raggedly, avoiding the paths which have been laid out for them, hairy human bundles fresh from some

sinister experience ... There are people in old suits that look
new and new jeans that look old. There are students and youths in
Afghan yak, loon-pants, combat-wear, wet-look plastic; bearded
Jesuses, long-haired androgynes, girls with pouting plum-coloured
mouths.

Malcolm Bradbury, *The History Man*, 1975

On the subway, the D train, heading for the Bronx, Kramer stood
in the aisle holding on to a stainless-steel pole while the car bucked
and lurched and screamed. On the plastic bench across from him
sat a bony old man who seemed to be growing like a fungus out of
a backdrop of graffiti. He was reading a newspaper. The headline
on the newspaper said 'HARLEM MOB CHASES MAYOR'.
The words were so big, they took up the entire page. Up above, in
smaller letters, it said 'Go Back Down to Hymietown!' The old man
was wearing a pair of purple-and-white-striped running sneakers.
They looked weird on such an old man, but there was nothing really
odd about them, not on the D train. Kramer scanned the floor. Half
the people in the car were wearing sneakers with splashy designs on
them and molded soles that looked like gravy boats. Young people
were wearing them, old men were wearing them, mothers with
children on their laps were wearing them, and for that matter, the
children were wearing them. This was not for reasons of Young Fit
and Firm Chic, the way it was downtown, where you saw a lot of
well-dressed young white people going off to work in the morning
wearing these sneakers. No, on the D train the reason was, they
were cheap. On the D train these sneakers were like a sign around
the neck reading 'SLUM' or 'EL BARRIO'.

Tom Wolfe, *The Bonfire of the Vanities*, 1988

Two of the boys wore glasses, curiously enough the same kind: tiny, old-fashioned, with round steel rims. The larger of the two – and he was quite large, well over six feet – was dark-haired, with a square jaw and coarse, pale skin. He might have been handsome had his features been less set, or his eyes, behind the glasses, less expressionless and blank. He wore dark English suits and carried an umbrella (a bizarre sight in Hampden) and he walked stiffly through the throngs of hippies and beatniks and preppies and punks with the self-conscious formality of an old ballerina, surprising in one so large as he. 'Henry Winter', said my friends when I pointed him out, at a distance, making a wide circle to avoid a group of bongo players on the lawn.

The smaller of the two – but not by much – was a sloppy blond boy, rosy-cheeked and gum-chewing, with a relentlessly cheery demeanor and his fists thrust deep in the pockets of his knee-sprung trousers. He wore the same jacket every day, a shapeless brown tweed that was frayed at the elbows and short in the sleeves, and his sandy hair was parted on the left, so a long forelock fell over one bespectacled eye. Bunny Corcoran was his name. Bunny being somehow short for Edmund. His voice was loud and honking, and carried in the dining halls. The third boy was the most exotic of the set. Angular and elegant, he was precariously thin, with nervous hands and a shrewd albino face and a short, fiery mop of the reddest hair I had ever seen. I thought (erroneously) that he dressed like Alfred Douglas, or the Comte de Montesquieu; beautiful starchy shirts with French cuffs; magnificent neckties; a black greatcoat that billowed behind him as he walked and made him look like a cross between a student prince and Jack the Ripper. Once, to my delight, I even saw him wearing pince-nez. (Later, I discovered that they weren't real pince-nez, but only had glass in them, and that his eyes were a good deal sharper than my own.) Francis Abernathy was his name. Further inquiries elicited suspicion from male acquaintances, who wondered at my interest in such a person.

And then there were a pair, boy and girl. I saw them together a great deal, and at first I thought they were boyfriend and girlfriend, until one day I saw them up close and realized they had to be siblings. Later I heard they were twins. They looked very much alike, with heavy dark-blond hair and epicene faces as clear, as cheerful and grave, as a couple of Flemish angels. And perhaps most unusual in the context of Hampden – where pseudo-intellects and teenage decadents abounded, and where black clothing was *de rigueur* – they liked to wear pale clothes, particularly white. In this swarm of cigarettes and dark sophistication they appeared here and there like figures from an allegory, or long-dead celebrants from some forgotten garden party. It was easy to find out who they were, as they shared the distinction of being the only twins on campus. Their names were Charles and Camilla Macaulay.

Donna Tartt, *The Secret History*, 1992

Courtney Love, lead singer of the pop group Hole, is a woman with problems. Earlier this year she had the role of rock widow thrust upon her overnight, securing her a place in that élite but unenviable club whose most famous member is Yoko Ono. Unlike Ono, Love was not actually present at the death of her husband. Nor was his suicide entirely unexpected. Kurt Cobain, tormented singer and guitarist with the Seattle-based band Nirvana, had made at least one unsuccessful attempt on his life a few weeks before.

Together Love and Cobain personified grunge, as publicly self-destructive as their predecessors in this sad rock pantheon, punk icons Sid Vicious and Nancy Spungen.

Yet their dress signals were misread in much the same way: as a spunky, two-fingered rejection of convention when their real target was much more dangerously accessible, which is to say themselves.

Vicious murdered Spungen and overdosed on heroin; Cobain blew his brains out; Love is the sole survivor among these starry and star-crossed lovers. But at what cost?

In a recent issue, *Elle* magazine ran a picture of her alongside an article on trends of the 1990s. Above the caption 'Courtney Love, Hole role model', the grunge widow was shown wearing white, in one of her trade-mark little-girl dresses, all frills and bows and pink ribbon sash with a baby-blue knitted toy hanging from her waist. Her mouth, by contrast, was lipstick red, and a word had been scrawled in the same bright colour on each pale forearm: 'witch' on the right, 'slut' on the left.

Love's sartorial style, bizarre as it may seem, has been widely copied. Teenagers have begun to wear accessories made out of Barbie dolls and turn up at clubs wearing dummies or cot toys strapped to their waists. Style gurus defend the fashion as ironic appropriation of designer baby clothes but the *Elle* article which singled out Love was unusually perceptive in characterizing her appeal as the 'glamour of self-destruction'.

Her clothes are not merely a fashion statement but a reflection of emotional disorder, a painful exposure of vulnerability, self-hatred and confusion. She is at once a little girl, a baby doll without responsibility for the paedophiliac response courted by her appearance and – in a curious piece of self-objectification – the site on which the sexual disgust accompanying that response can be inscribed. Rarely has the sinister nexus between sex, faux-innocence and death which motivates the recurring craze for dressing adult women as schoolgirls or baby dolls been so frankly exposed.

That is not, of course, how designers and their acolytes on the fashion pages express it. The American designer Anna Sui has built her entire business on baby doll dresses and is never seen out of one. A feature in *The Times*'s Saturday magazine earlier this month consisted of four colour pages in which the same girlish model posed in a series of skimpy skirts and shrunken jumpers which exposed her midriff. Under the unambiguous headline 'Sugar Baby Love', the feature nervously hedged its bets, announcing 'the return of the sweater girl. Pretty pastel knits lose some of their sweetness with the ultra-modern sexy tight fits. Complete the colourful, clean look with A-line miniskirts and high heels.'

It is hard to imagine a more confusing description of a look, evoking a type – the old-fashioned sweater girl with the big breasts – which is the antithesis of the flat-chested girl-woman it seeks to extol. Pastel colours, baby pinks and blues, suddenly become sexy, yet the look as a whole manages to remain 'clean'. The feature is followed by an advert for Gianni Versace which, with his trade-mark vulgarity, makes the true appeal of 'Sugar Baby Love' absolutely clear.

Clothes have traditionally prompted moral panics. When Dior launched his New Look in 1947, it seems unlikely that he gave much thought to how it would be received by the British Labour Party. But the full skirt and wasp waist of the New Look outraged Socialist politicians including the rising Labour star Harold Wilson, who denounced it as 'damn silly'. Bessie Braddock thought it was 'the ridiculous whim of idle people'. Sir Stafford Cripps wanted to ban it, although it is not obvious who would take on the role of clothes police or how they would persuade women to co-operate.

In its defence, the fashion industry has easy arguments to deploy. Designers can stigmatize their critics as humourless, joyless, envious, and suggest that fashion is not a serious business; that it shouldn't be subjected to the same degree of rigorous deconstructive scrutiny as other aspects of high and low culture. This is disingenuous, for there are few more eloquent indicators of current thinking about femininity, female roles and the status of women than the clothes they are encouraged to wear at any given moment.

When Naomi Campbell walked out of a London nightclub wearing a crochet minidress over French knickers, suspenders and combat boots, she embodied the contemporary, upmarket version of Kinderwhore.

It is not an accident that dressing up as baby dolls has come back into fashion at a time of sexual confusion, anxiety about Aids and fast-changing gender roles – a familiar *fin-de-siècle* sexual panic, in other words.

After decades in which women have sought to define their own sexuality and overcome taboos about seeking sexual pleasure, the spectacle of Naomi or Courtney stepping out in their frilly dresses defuses male fears, pretending that adult women are little girls at heart. At the same time, the Kinderwhore look replays the tiredest trick in the paedophile book, that of absolving the partner of responsibility either for his desire or its satisfaction.

Vladimir Nabokov's *Lolita* is a key text for understanding the intellectual games which paedophiles play, a novel of startling ambiguity in which Humbert Humbert's self-flagellation for his uncontrollable desires is also a form of self-exculpation. Humbert drugs his teenage stepdaughter, intending to have sex with her while she is unconscious, but the pill fails to work, leaving him to lie awake all night, trying to think up a new plan of seduction. He fretfully concludes that he will have to wait months or even years to gain Lolita's confidence, 'but by six she was wide awake, and by six fifteen we were technically lovers. I am going to tell you something very strange: it was she who seduced me.'

It soon transpires that Humbert is not even the thirteen-year-old's first lover. Lolita creeps into his arms 'like the cheapest of cheap cuties. For that is what nymphets imitate – while we moan and die.' *Lolita* – and its fashion counterpart Kinderwhore – involves a special kind of dishonesty which allows men to indulge a fantasy not just of defloration but of defilement.

It is a species of doublethink in which the pervert's celebration of his victim's innocence is always an illusion, but one of which he is in complete control. It is up to him to choose the point at which it has served its purpose and he names the girl 'slut' or 'whore'.

Courtney Love, grunge icon and nineties's role model, anticipates that dismal metamorphosis by painting crude insults on her own arms. Her intention may be ironic but, with her recently dead husband and history of drug problems, she gives the impression of someone just managing to cling on to life. A peroxide blonde in a torn baby-doll dress, her clothes and arms smeared with lipstick, bears an uncomfortable resemblance to a murder victim: anyone who chooses to dress like this, to abuse and mock herself as jailbait and a whore, is surely teetering on the brink. Appearances are not always deceptive: sometimes, what you see is frighteningly close to what you get.

Joan Smith, 'Kinderwhoring', *Guardian*, 1994

When I walk into the sitting room, I can see immediately that I'm doomed to die a long, slow, suffocating death. There's a man wearing a sort of brick-red jacket and another man in a carefully rumpled linen suit and Charlie in her cocktail dress and another woman wearing fluorescent leggings and a dazzling white silk blouse and another woman wearing those trousers that look like a dress but aren't. Whatever. And the moment I see them I want to cry, not only through terror, but through sheer *envy: Why isn't my life like this?*

Nick Hornby, *High Fidelity*, 1995

Q. Did Proust have any relevant thoughts on dating? What should one talk about on a first date? And is it good to wear black?

A. Advice is scant. A more fundamental doubt is whether one should accept dinner in the first place.

There is no doubt that a person's charms are less frequently a cause of love than a remark such as: 'No, this evening I shan't be free.'

If this response proves bewitching, it is because of the connection made in Noah's case between appreciation and absence. Though a person may be filled with attributes, an incentive is nevertheless required to ensure that a seducer will focus wholeheartedly on these, an incentive which finds perfect form in a dinner rebuff, the dating equivalent of forty days at sea.

Proust demonstrates the benefits of delay in his thoughts on the appreciation of clothes. Both Albertine and the Duchesse de Guermantes are interested in fashion. However, Albertine has very little money and the Duchesse owns half of France. The Duchesse's wardrobes are therefore overflowing; as soon as she sees something she wants she can send for the dressmaker and her desire is fulfilled as rapidly as hands can sew. Albertine on the other hand can hardly buy anything, and has to think at length before she does so. She spends hours studying clothes, dreaming of a particular coat or hat or dressing gown.

The result is that, though Albertine has far fewer clothes than the Duchesse, her understanding, appreciation and love of them is far greater: 'Like every obstacle in the way of possessing something . . . poverty, more generous than opulence, gives women far more than the clothes they cannot afford to buy: the desire for those clothes, which creates a genuine, detailed, thorough knowledge of them.'

Proust compares Albertine to a student who visits Dresden after cultivating a desire to see a particular painting, whereas the Duchesse is like a wealthy tourist who travels without any desire or knowledge, and experiences nothing but bewilderment, boredom and exhaustion when she arrives.

It emphasizes the extent to which physical possession is only one component of appreciation. If the rich are fortunate in being able to travel to Dresden as soon as the desire to do so arises, or buy a dress just after they have seen it in a catalogue, they are cursed because of the speed with which their wealth fulfils their desires. No sooner have they thought of Dresden than they can be on a train there, no sooner have they seen a dress than it can be in their wardrobe. They therefore have no opportunity to suffer the interval between desire and gratification which the less privileged endure, and which, for all its apparent unpleasantness, has the incalculable benefit of allowing people to know and fall deeply in love with paintings in Dresden, hats, dressing gowns and someone who isn't free this evening.

Alain de Botton, *How Proust Can Change Your Life*, 1997

Sarah sat at the bar of the Sealink Club being propositioned by men. Some men propositioned her with their eyes, some with their mouths, some with their heads, some with their hair. Some men propositioned her with nuance, exquisite subtlety, others propositioned her with chutzpah, their suit as obvious as a schlong slammed down on the zinc counter. Some men's propositioning was so slight as to be peripheral, a seductive play of the minor parts, an invitation to touch cuticles, rub corns, hang nails. Other men's propositioning was a Bayreuth production, complete with mechanical effects; great flats descending, garishly depicting their Taste, their Intellect, their Status. The men were like apes – she thought – attempting to impress her by waving and kicking things about in a display of mock potency.

She sat, a small blonde eye to this storm of impersonality. A young woman who believed, when it suited her, in defying expectation. This evening she was dressed in a little black suit, little black toque, little black veil, black heels, black tights, cream silk blouse with long pointed collar. She shifted a little and sensed silken surfaces move around her, accommodating her in a sheeny embrasure. She felt very much present on the barstool. Beamed down to, the molecules of her still fizzing, delighted to play a part in assuming her form.

Perhaps, Sarah thought, it's this that really whistles up the men, this call of the urbane.

Will Self, *Great Apes*, 1998

In Nike's huge department store called Niketown the trainer has its own cathedral. But this is an anachronism because the trainer itself is our contemporary cathedral. It's not that trainer sweat is a secular incense, though trainers do indeed smell like teen spirit. It's just that trainers aren't simply shoes. The trainer is our new template of architecture. Trainer design has invaded everything, and chunkiness is everywhere. While the cathedral was a monument to the glory of God, the trainer has become a post-monumental symbol to the values of freedom and equality.

In *Sneakers: Size Isn't Everything,* a book about trainers and their culture, Richard Wharton, who runs Office Shoes and Offspring, which is a major retailer of trainers, says, 'In ten years' time they won't be talking about pine dressers on the *Antiques Roadshow.* A kid will be on there with a 1969 Adidas tracksuit. People have to understand that the first-ever performance outerwear has a place in our culture. A Reebok Instapump will cost you £440 now. In four years' time £4,000.' . . .

In the 1990s the trainer has transcended all previous conventions and rules of fashion and footwear. As an object it has the status of a modern archetype because simply by definition the archetype is something that resolves contradictions. The trainer is both fashion and anti-fashion, shoe and anti-shoe. It denotes both uniformity and the expression of non-conformity, the casual and the active. It is hard to conceive of a more synthetic object in the history of footwear, yet it is sold by laying claim to some instinctive, natural energy – just do it.

John O'Reilly, 'All That is Solid Melts into Air Jordans', *Guardian*, 1998

2. 'On the brink of fashion': Clothes and Sexuality

'In every human being a vacillation from one sex to the other takes place, and often it is only the clothes that keep the male or female likeness, while underneath the sex is the very opposite of what it is above.'

Virginia Woolf, *Orlando*, 1928

'Have you taken up transvestism? I'd no idea our marriage teetered on the brink of fashion.'

Joe Orton, *What the Butler Saw*, 1969

'Just about everyone dresses a little gay these days,' wrote the Metropolitan Museum of Art's Curator of Costume, Richard Martin, in 1993, citing the appearance at Manhattan dinner parties of Thierry Mugler's gay bondage-inspired dresses. The theme of sexual identity in fashion and dress has run throughout the history of twentieth-century culture and is comprehensively illustrated in literature, but such acceptance of the gay element – his comments were published in an article in (American) *Esquire* – has been a long time in arriving.

The fashion industry at its highest level was – and is – largely run by gay men and by women, with changing ideas of gender and the growing awareness of sexual orientation influencing both image and product. Chanel, who promoted the androgynous dandyism of the 1920s, may have railed against '*ces messieurs*' working in fashion, and there may be a continuing debate about the role of homosexual designers in female identity but the creative influence of the gay –

and to a lesser, but significant extent, lesbian – personae in all areas
has been enormous.

A century ago, the situation could not have been more different
from the openness celebrated by Richard Martin. Proust's portrayal
of fellow homosexual Comte Robert de Montesquieu as M. de
Charlus gives some indication of the *double entendres*, the sartorial
codes revealed and concealed by the gay man after the trial of Oscar
Wilde in 1895 made secrecy advisable. Montesquieu became more
sober in attire as he grew older, unlike Charlus, who 'would now
utter unconsciously almost the same little cries . . . as are uttered
unconsciously by the inverts who refer to one another as "she" . . .
As a matter of fact – and this is what this purely unconscious
"camping" revealed – the difference between the stern Charlus,
dressed all in black . . . whom I had known, and the painted young
men, loaded with rings, was no more than [a] purely imaginary
difference.'[1]

The 'painted young men, loaded with rings' bear more than a
passing resemblance to the 'Knights of the Bracelet', the artists who
worked for Lucian Vogel's fashion magazine *Gazette du Bon Ton*, first
published in 1912, whose adoption of jewellery was an indication of
sexual ambiguity. Dress historian James Laver identified the gender
confusion of the androgyny that became fashionable for men and
women after the First World War on both sides of the Channel, and
the passion for jazz, dancing and partying, as natural consequences
of the trauma of war; not only had several millions died in the war
itself, but the septic flu epidemic that followed killed 200,000 more
in 1919 in Britain alone.[2] After the Terror of 1793–4, Revolutionary
Paris had also seen a blurring of the masculine and feminine, dancing
in the streets and rapid developments in fashion.

The British designer Lucile was more prosaic, attributing the look
to the decision made by couturiers and manufacturers to respond
to the shortage of fabric by introducing shorter hemlines and less
use of fabric: 'The Rue de la Paix is nothing if not resourceful. It

brought in the ideal of the "boyish woman". Here was the perfect solution to the problem. Slight figures covered with three yards of material, skirt ending just below the knees, tiny cloche hat trimmed with a band of ribbon.'[3] But this 'decision' could never have been carried off unless the mood was right. The war had seen women in shorter skirts and trousers, clothes in which they could move, and they did not want to return to the restriction of pre-war fashion.

Aldous Huxley describes the new shape in *Antic Hay* (published in 1923) as 'fairly tall but seemed taller than she actually was, by reason of her remarkable slenderness. Not that she looked disagreeably thin, far from it. It was a rounded slenderness. The Complete Man decided to consider her as tubular – flexible and tubular, like a section of a boa constrictor . . . dressed in clothes that emphasized this serpentine slimness . . .'[4] The modern girl shocked the older generation with her make-up, smoking and short hair; but the acceptance of a fashion diktat by women that promoted the boy in them probably made the publication of Radclyffe Hall's *The Well of Loneliness* and Virginia Woolf's *Orlando* in 1928 easier. However, interest in lesbians became both hostile and prurient. Dress historian Doris Langley Moore tried to bring a sense of balance, arguing that, while the boyish look of the 1920s could be identified as lesbian, in fact, it was simply manifesting a desire by women to enjoy the freedom of men.[5]

Hall blended in with the androgynous Eton-cropped young women of fashion, but her interest – and Woolf's – was not in fashion but in the language of clothes and the identity of which they spoke. And they could speak of a homosexual identity, too. Noël Coward's *The Vortex* (1924) spoke of homosexuality and as a result the roll-neck sweaters he wore had been taken up by numerous gay chorus boys. Oxford bags, as worn by Sir Harold Acton and Beverly Nichols, were regarded as a sign of effeminacy. By 1930, published investigations into the lives of 'effeminate men' described exotic creatures in bright coloured, tightly fitting jackets. Terence Greenidge suggests the reader 'go down the High or Cornmarket . . . you will observe several of them with their locks shining through the sun and with their faces subtly adorned by the art which seeks to improve upon nature . . . they will be wearing rather brightly coloured coats [jackets], cut short and very tight in the waist, their grey flannel trousers will be a conspicuously silver hue and flow loosely, their feet will be shod with gay suede shoes . . .'[6]

Taylor Croft is even more lurid: 'The real invert . . . is proud of his near approach to the feminine . . . He will dress with the most elaborate care . . . is fond of colour as his shirts and ties testify, while any new fashion will appeal to him.'[7] The Hon. Stephen Tennant, who dressed with 'elaborate care', was, to a certain extent, protected from homophobia by his class; even so, Cecil Beaton recalls the not altogether positive comments he caused wherever he went. Quentin Crisp was not protected by anything except his own bravado; his account in *The Naked Civil Servant* of hostility and violence illustrates the reality of being 'out' in the city in the 1920s.

Images of masculinity were changing by the late 1960s, following the publication of the Wolfenden Report in December 1966, which brought about the legalization of homosexuality in the following year. When Cecil Beaton learned of the report's publication, he called it 'one of the most important milestones in English law', writing in his diary: 'Of recent years the tolerance towards the subject has made a nonsense of many of the prejudices from which I myself suffered acutely as a young man.'[8] Whereas descriptions of men looking at themselves in a mirror as they dress in the 1950s show no self-doubt on the part of the character, in *Myra Breckinridge*, Gore Vidal satirizes the male ego which was soon to crumble in the face of the rising power of women and the homosexual. Andy Warhol talks of how the drag queen Candy Darling longed to play the part of the sex-change diva Myra in the movie (it was played by Raquel Welch)[9] and describes the way in which drag queens were moving into the fashion arena. The Stonewall riots of 28 June 1969 saw drag queens chanting, 'We are the Stonewall girls – we wear our hair in curls; we wear no underwear; we show our pubic hair,' as they attacked the police with their stilettos.[10] Stonewall is widely regarded as a watershed, as if gay men were in-the-closet before and out of it afterwards. While dress for homosexuals had always been an important part of proclaiming their identity, after Stonewall gay style became more assertive, more expressive. While the pop group Village People brought to public attention the masculine stereotypes – the Leather Man, Construction Worker, Cowboy, Indian, Cop and Soldier – that gay men had satirized in the United States,[11] Calvin Klein marketed the white T-shirt and jeans – another stereotype – to the gay and straight market. By the mid-1990s, drag had become an acceptable part of fashion imagery with New York drag queen RuPaul as the MAC cosmetics girl and television drag artist Lily Savage promoting a brand of tights. Doris Langley Moore's assertion that the classic manifestation of lesbianism – women dressing in trousers – would not happen has been proved wrong. The achievement of gay and lesbian questioning of the role of gender in fashion is the open adoption of gay and lesbian iconography by the consumer and mainstream industry at the end of the century.

One afternoon of scorching heat I was in the dining room of the hotel, plunged in semi-darkness so as to shield it from the sun, which gilded the drawn curtains through the gaps between which twinkled the blue of the sea, when along the central gangway leading from the beach to the road I saw approaching, tall, slim, bare-necked, his head held proudly erect, a young man with searching eyes whose skin was as fair and his hair as golden as if they had absorbed all the rays of the sun. Dressed in a suit of soft, whitish material such as I could never have believed that any man would have the audacity to wear, the thinness of which suggested no less vividly than the coolness of the dining room the heat and brightness of the glorious day outside, he was walking fast. His penetrating eyes, from one of which a monocle kept dropping, were the colour of the sea. Everyone looked at him with interest as he passed, knowing that this young Marquis de Saint-Loup-en-Bray was famed for his elegance. All the newspapers had described the suit in which he had recently acted as second to the young Duc d'Uzes in a duel. One felt that the distinctive quality of his hair, his eyes, his skin, his bearing, which would have marked him out in a crowd like a precious vein of opal, azure-shot and luminous, embedded in a mass of coarser substance, must correspond to a life different from that led by other men.

> Marcel Proust, *Remembrance of Things Past: Within a Budding Grove*,
> translated by C. K. Scott Moncrieff and Terence Kilmartin, 1919

It was impossible to make even half of our pre-war profits, for so few people had the money to spend large sums on dress. The old standard of extravagant dressing had gone for ever; it passed away with the day of the great courtesans, whose whims and follies had so delighted the Parisians of 1912. Even the women who were noted as the best dressed in Europe had cut down their dressmaker's bills to half the previous amounts. There was consternation in the Rue de la Paix. World-famous houses were faced with the prospect of closing down.

Something had to be done about it; there was need for drastic measures. The great couturières, the leaders of fashion, took counsel among themselves.

There was only one remedy, they must cut down the cost of production to the lowest possible limit. There must be no more 'picture dresses' with trailing yards of lovely satins and brocades, no more filmy chiffon dresses veiling heavy silk underslips, no more waste of material even on linings. Lace must be taboo, so must expensive embroideries; hats must be plain and practically untrimmed. Every yard of material saved must be looked upon as a yard to the good. It was, they said, the only plan to work on.

But the new measures must be inaugurated with tact. No couturière could possibly say in effect to his clients, 'I am going to dress you as cheaply as possible,' such a thing would be an outrage to feminine vanity. No, there must be a flourish of trumpets, women must be made to feel that the revolutionary styles were the last word in chic.

The Rue de la Paix is nothing if not resourceful. It brought in the ideal of the 'boyish woman'. Here was the perfect solution to the problem. Slight figures covered with three yards of material, skirt ending just below the knees, tiny cloche hat trimmed with a band of ribbon.

No woman, at least no woman in civilization, could cost less to clothe! And best of all the women were delighted with the new presentation of themselves. They improved on the idea, shingled their hair, adopted boyish mannerisms and slang and flew to the cocktail bar (long, silk-stockinged legs looked so well dangling from a high stool). Critics wrote learnedly of the 'modern girl's emancipation' and the older generation were harsh in their condemnation. But neither the 'modern' nor her critics knew that she was a creation of the dressmakers, just as much as the clothes she wore, and all because some solution had to be found to the problems of the Rue de la Paix!

You see, all dressmakers know that women are in many ways an expression of their clothes. Put a woman into a certain type of dress and she will instinctively find a pose to wear it.

'Lucile', Lady Duff Gordon, *Discretions and Indiscretions*, 1932

Chanel's personality, like her designs, was something of a paradox, a mingling of the masculine and the intensely feminine. Actually the concept she had of women was entirely feminine: she wanted them to be charming and simple and natural, bemoaning the fact that the young were not sufficiently romantic. She detested affectation and believed that women should let their hair grow white if it was inclined to do so. This last opinion had such effect that many younger women went so far as to simulate, by using powder in their hair, a premature streak of white. The professions of men bored her. When Cocteau told her that she had a masculine mind, she became furious and, as a gesture of defiance, put a small girl's hair ribbon round her head, knotting it in a bow on the top: a fad was created.

Cecil Beaton, *The Glass of Fashion*, 1954

Her modesty as to her writing, her vanity as to her person, her fears for safety, all seem to hint that what was said a short time ago about there being no change in Orlando the man and Orlando the woman, was ceasing to be altogether true. She was becoming a little more modest, as women are, of her brains, and a little more vain, as women are, of her person. Certain susceptibilities were asserting themselves, and others were diminishing. The change of clothes had, some philosophers will say, much to do with it. Vain trifles as they seem, clothes have the same, more important offices than merely to keep us warm. They change our view of the world and the world's view of us.

Virginia Woolf, *Orlando*, 1928

'It was the 18 April [1918]. An absurd circumstance gave rise to the whole thing; I [Vita Sackville-West] had just got clothes like the women-on-the-land were wearing, and in the unaccustomed freedom of breeches and gaiters I went into wild spirits; I ran, I shouted, I jumped, I climbed, vaulted over gates, I felt like a schoolboy let out on a holiday; and Violet [Trefusis] followed me across the fields and woods with a new meekness, saying very little, but never taking her eyes off me, and in the midst of my exuberance I knew that all the old undercurrent had come back stronger than ever, and that my old domination of her had never been diminished. I remember that wild irresponsible day. It was one of the most vibrant days of my life . . .

'[At dinner that evening, Violet wore] a dress of red velvet, that was exactly the colour of a red rose, and that made her, with her white skin and tawny hair, the most seductive being. She pulled me down until I kissed her.'

Nigel Nicolson, *Portrait of a Marriage*, 1973

'It was really outrageous because John and I – of course Radclyffe Hall was always called John – always wore dinner jackets and skirts with striped braid down the side, not trousers,' Evelyn [Irons] recalls. 'And I had a shirt and black bow tie and she always wore jabots and ruffles which I thought was rather effeminate. Then we had Spanish cloaks, a very dramatic sort with scarlet linings which you flung around you. Una [Lady Troubridge] and John both wore monocles, and at one point I had a monocle too but I didn't need one, so it was plain glass. I didn't wear it all the time because I did think it was a bit silly.'

Alkarim Jivani, *It's Not Unusual:*
A History of Lesbian and Gay Britain in the Twentieth Century, 1997

Staring at her own reflection in the glass, Stephen would feel just a little uneasy: 'Am I queer looking or not?' she would wonder; 'Suppose I wore my hair more like Mother's?' and then she would undo her splendid, thick hair, and would part it in the middle and draw it back loosely.

The result was always far from becoming, so that Stephen would hastily plait it again. She now wore the plait screwed up very tightly in the nape of her neck with a bow of black ribbon. Anna hated this fashion and constantly said so, but Stephen was stubborn: 'I've tried your way, Mother, and I look like a scarecrow; you're beautiful, darling, but your young daughter isn't, which is jolly hard on you.'

'She makes no effort to improve her appearance,' Anna would reproach, very gravely.

These days there was constant warfare between them on the subject of clothes; quite a seemly warfare, for Stephen was learning to control her hot temper, and Anna was seldom anything but gentle. Nevertheless it was open warfare, the inevitable clash of two opposing natures who sought to express themselves in apparel, since clothes, after all, are a form of self-expression. The victory would be now on this side, now on that; sometimes Stephen would appear in a thick woollen jersey, or a suit of rough tweeds surreptitiously ordered from the excellent tailor in Malvern. Sometimes Anna would triumph, having journeyed to London to procure soft and very expensive dresses, which her daughter must wear in order to please her, because she would come home quite tired by such journeys. On the whole, Anna got her own way at this time, for Stephen would suddenly give up the contest, reduced to submission by Anna's disappointment, always more efficacious than mere disapproval.

'Here, give it to me!' she would say gruffly, grabbing the delicate dress from her mother.

Then off she would rush and put it on all wrong, so that Anna would sigh in a kind of desperation, and would pat, readjust, unfasten and fasten, striving to make peace between wearer and model, whose inimical feelings were evidently mutual.

She became much more anxious about her appearance; for five mornings she studied her face in the glass as she dressed – after all she was not so bad-looking. Her hair spoilt her a little, it was too thick and long, but she noticed with pleasure that at least it was wavy – then she suddenly admired the colour of her hair. Opening cupboard after cupboard she went through her clothes. They were old, for the most part distinctly shabby. She would go into Malvern that very afternoon and order a new flannel suit at her tailor's. The suit should be grey with a little white pin stripe, and the jacket, she decided, must have a breast pocket. She would wear a black tie – no, better a grey one to match the new suit with the little white pin stripe. She ordered not one new suit but three, and she also ordered a pair of brown shoes; indeed she spent most of the afternoon in ordering things for her personal adornment. She heard herself being ridiculously fussy about details, disputing with her tailor over buttons; disputing with her bootmaker over the shoes, their thickness of sole, their amount of broguing; disputing regarding the match of her ties with the young man who sold her handkerchiefs and neckties – for such trifles had assumed an enormous importance; she had, in fact, grown quite long-winded about them.

That evening she showed her smart neckties to Puddle, whose manner was most unsatisfactory – she grunted.

And now someone seemed to be always near Stephen, someone for whom these things were accomplished – the purchase of three new suits, the brown shoes, the six carefully chosen, expensive neckties.

Radclyffe Hall, *The Well of Loneliness*, 1928

Rory Freemantle did not allow evening to interfere with her masculine style. She came down to dinner at the Augusto in a good imitation of a dinner jacket, though without the stiff-fronted shirt which she would have liked to affect every night, but which owing to the inconsiderate femininity of her bust caused her so much discomfort that she could only affect it on the grandest occasions. Rosalba on the other hand in her dress after sunset was always frankly feminine. As for poor Giulia Monforte she might have been anything after sunset. Nobody cared.

This first evening Rosalba wore a frock of dead white crêpe de Chine with round her waist a galloon of silver and round her left forearm a silver bracelet so heavy as almost to seem like a fetter.

Her shoes were vivid scarlet, and it was upon these shoes that the eyes of the dull people scattered sparsely about the dining room were fixed in disapproval. The old maids peered round the half-consumed bottles of white wine left over from other meals at these shoes as if they were scarlet tanagers escaped from an aviary, and when they were hidden under the table they stared censoriously at Rosalba's face.

Compton Mackenzie, Extraordinary Women, 1928

I remember, when I was a young child before the war, a popular fancy-dress costume representing 'the Woman of 1920' (it was then about 1913). It included a garment of which one half was a trouser-leg, and the other a remnant of femininity – a portion of a chequered cloth skirt. A man's morning coat, monocle and top hat completed the mockery. I am sure the modes which inspired these far-fetched caricatures were not due to any homosexual movement. Women have nearly always been supposed to be on the verge of taking to definitely male attire, but they have never done so yet, and it is quite unlikely that they ever will.

Doris Langley Moore, Pandora's Letter Box, 1929

A barber came regularly to the house in Mulberry Walk to crop Joe's hair. Her suits and jackets were flawlessly cut by the best tailors, and kept immaculately clean. She wore stiffly starched Peter Pan collars, navy-blue berets, reefer jackets. But she did not consider herself butch: boyishness lent her lightness and elegance. 'I did look like a boy,' Joe said later. 'I really did. But I was not a stomper.'

Joe would walk into a room, head straight for the mirror and strike a pose, three fingers inside her jacket pocket, the thumb and little finger outside. 'Marvellous,' she exclaimed.

Joe was one of the few people able to shock Marlene Dietrich. One evening Joe, Dietrich and the American soprano Grace Moore were invited to a formal dinner on the Riviera. When Joe met the other two women in the hotel for cocktails they were horrified to see that she was dressed in men's black tie, and insisted she change into a dress. Shortly afterwards, Joe reappeared in an elegant gown and Dietrich and Moore saw, to their even greater consternation, that her arms were bare and covered with tattoos; she was sent to put back on the tuxedo. Even in this milieu, Joe was outlandish.

Kate Summerscale, *The Queen of Whale Cay: The Eccentric Story of 'Joe' Carstairs, Fastest Woman on Water,* 1997

The whole set of stylizations that are known as 'camp' (a word that I was hearing for the first time) was, in 1926, self-explanatory. Women moved and gesticulated in this way. Homosexuals wished for obvious reasons to copy them. The strange thing about 'camp' is that it has become fossilized. The mannerisms have never changed. If I were to now see a woman sitting with her knees clamped together, one hand on her hip and the other lightly touching her back hair, I should think, 'Either she scored her last social triumph in 1926 or it is a man in drag.' Perhaps 'camp' is set in the twenties because after that differences between the sexes – especially visible differences – began to fade. This, of course, has never mattered to women in the least. They know they are women. To homosexuals, who must, with every breath they draw, with every step they take, demonstrate that they are feminine, it is frustrating. They look back in sorrow to that more formal era and try to re-live it.

The whole structure of society was at that time much more rigid than it has ever been since, and in two main ways. The first of these was sexual. The short skirts, bobbed hair and flat chests that were in fashion were in fact symbols of immaturity. No one ever drew attention to this, presumably out of politeness. The word 'boyish' was used to describe the girls of that era. This epithet they accepted graciously. They knew that they looked nothing like boys. They also realized that it was meant to be a compliment. Manliness was all the rage. The men of the twenties searched themselves for vestiges of effeminacy as though for lice. They did not worry about their characters but about their hair and their clothes. Their predicament was that they must never be caught worrying about either. I once heard a slightly dandified friend of my brother say, 'People are always accusing me of taking care of my appearance.'

Quentin Crisp, *The Naked Civil Servant*, 1968

Contrary to the general impression, perverts, male or female, do not always carry an unmistakable stamp upon their person and bearing. Neither has the fashion had much effect upon dress. The average man is still too undesirous of being suspected of corruption to adopt the style of clothing which appeals – or might appeal – to the homosexual. To exemplify, the garments called polo jerseys were abandoned by normal men shortly after they had been introduced, simply because they were seen on many who were known to be unmanly.

Doris Langley Moore, *Pandora's Letter Box*, 1929

It was a group of children gathered around a little wicker table, under the protection of a teacher or governess: three young girls, apparently fifteen to seventeen, and a long-haired boy about fourteen years old. With astonishment Aschenbach noted that the boy was absolutely beautiful. His face, pale and reserved, framed with honey-coloured hair, the straight sloping nose, the lovely mouth, the expression of sweet and godlike seriousness, recalled Greek sculpture of the noblest period; and the complete purity of the forms was accompanied by such a rare personal charm that, as he watched, he felt that he had never met with anything equally felicitous in nature or the plastic arts. He was further struck by the obviously intentional contrast with the principles of upbringing which showed in the sisters' attire and bearing. The three girls, the eldest of whom could be considered grown up, were dressed with a chasteness and severity bordering on disfigurement. Uniformly cloister-like costumes, of medium length, slate-coloured, sober, and deliberately unbecoming in cut, with white turned-down collars as the only relief, suppressed every possible appeal of shapeliness. Their hair, brushed down flat and tight against the head, gave their faces a nun-like emptiness and lack of character. Surely this was a mother's influence, and it had not even occurred to her to apply the pedagogical strictness to the boy which she seemed to find necessary for her girls. It was clear that in his existence the first factors were gentleness and tenderness. The shears had been resolutely kept from his beautiful hair; like a Prince Charming's, it fell in curls over his forehead, his ears, and still deeper, across his neck. The English sailor suit, with its braids, stitchings and embroideries, its puffy sleeves narrowing at the ends and fitting snugly about the fine wrists of his still childish but slender hands, gave the delicate figure something rich and luxurious. He was sitting, half-profile to the observer, one foot in its black patent-leather shoe placed before the other, an elbow resting on the arm of his wicker chair, a cheek pressed against his fist, in a position of negligent good manners, entirely free of the almost subservient stiffness to which his sisters seemed accustomed.

Thomas Mann, *Death in Venice* (1912),
translated by Kenneth Burke, 1925

I invited one of Poiret's models to accompany us [to see the dress rehearsal for Bataille's *La Phalene* at the Théâtre de Vaudeville]. His models were allowed to borrow dresses from his collection if they were going to a party which was a particularly smart affair. The girl

I invited managed to get hold of the most extravagant dress in the whole collection together with a fantastic ermine and red velvet coat, which I believe was called 'Eminence'. I wore the dress and coat, with a red velvet turban (no wig), long red gloves and huge earrings. My four friends were in tails with red camellias in their buttonholes.

As soon as we entered our box, the whole audience turned to stare at us. Next morning one of the biggest newspapers published a report on the event:

In that brilliant audience all eyes were fixed on one of the boxes where two of Paul Poiret's models were sitting, accompanied by four gentlemen in impeccable evening dress. One model was an attractive blonde, but the other, with her scarlet turban, was irresistible, wearing her remarkable ensemble with an air and a sense of style that few models are lucky enough to possess.

Poiret read the article and, after checking some further details, summoned me to his office. Expecting the worst, I was extremely surprised when, instead, he made me an offer to design a variety of dresses especially for me, which I would then model at his next collection. I found the idea vastly entertaining, but begged off with the excuse that I felt I was born to be an artist and designer, not a model!

Erté, *Things I Remember*, 1975

July 1930
The event of today was a Hermaphrodite Party given by Eddy Sackville-West and Nancy Morris. It didn't begin until eleven, so that the first part of a sweltering evening had to be got through first. Ralph wore a red wig and Spanish shawl over trousers, but failed to look in any way feminine. I put on my yellow silk Empire dress, a bowler hat and a tiny moustache. Most of the young men had loaded themselves with pearls, powder and paint; the atmosphere was

stifling and the noise so deafening that even the music from a vast gramophone horn was inaudible. There is a vogue now for such parties as this: all the creative energy of the participants goes on their dress, and there are none of the elaborate performances of earlier parties. Personally I think this is a sad come-down, a sign of decadence. Eddie Gathorne-Hardy was genial and very tipsy, though near to tears because he had been twice rebuffed by a young German who refused to dance with him.

'I've been simply *mis*erable about my costume, my dear. I've had a *good* cry about it.' And then, edging me towards the German he said almost in the young man's ears: 'Now do, my dear, just take him by the hand and *throw* him into my arms.' I did my best, but most unfortunately the German took a fancy to me instead.

Frances Partridge, *Memories*, 1981

Adam and Miss Runcible and Miles and Archie Schwert went up to the motor races in Archie Schwert's car. It was a long and cold drive. Miss Runcible wore trousers and Miles touched up his eyelashes in the dining room of the hotel where they stopped for luncheon. So they were asked to leave.

Evelyn Waugh, *Vile Bodies*, 1930

[Daffodil] had nothing of the modern girl about him; he was as delicately feminine as a keepsake of fifty years ago. He was indeed a real womanly man, with his wide forget-me-not-blue eyes, his silky yellow hair and exquisite rose-leaf complexion, of which he took the greatest care, never going out without a parasol and always wearing a mask when he was bathing.

Compton Mackenzie, *Extraordinary Women: Theme and Variations*, 1928

5 April 1930

I arranged to do a drawing of Noël Coward and went to his cabin:

'We've been absolutely beastly to you,' he admitted. 'But you've shown spirit and let's hope you've learnt a lesson. It is important not to let the public have a loophole to lampoon you.' That, he explained, was why he studied his own 'facade'. Now take his voice: it was definite, harsh, rugged. He moved firmly and solidly, dressed quietly.

'I see.'

'You should appraise yourself,' he went on. 'Your sleeves are too tight, your voice is too high and too precise. You mustn't do it. It closes so many doors. It limits you unnecessarily, and young men with half your intelligence will laugh at you.' He shook his head, wrinkled his forehead and added disarmingly, 'It's hard, I know. One would like to indulge one's own taste. I myself dearly love a good match, yet I know it is overdoing it to wear tie, socks and handkerchief of the same colour. I take ruthless stock of myself in the mirror before going out. A polo jumper or unfortunate tie exposes one to danger.' He cocked an eye at me in mockery.

Cecil Beaton, *The Wandering Years*, 1961

The door opened silently, and I was looking at a tall blond man in a white flannel suit with a violet satin scarf around his neck.

There was a cornflower in the lapel of his white coat and his pale blue eyes looked faded out by comparison. The violet scarf was loose enough to show that he wore no tie and that he had a thick, soft brown neck, like the neck of a strong woman.

Raymond Chandler, *Farewell My Lovely*, 1940

There, by candlelight, beneath a photograph of Jean Cocteau, they tried on some of the couturier's latest creations. [Charles] James, the designer of Stephen's Sicilian wardrobe (though he did not generally design for men and often modelled dresses for intimate clients), was a notoriously effeminate young man of Oriental appearance, the same age as Stephen but considerably more *outré*. The idea of these two in *haute couture* trailing round his all-white studio, with its dyed pampas grass in huge vases, must rate high in images of between-the-wars camp.

Philip Hoare, *Serious Pleasures: The Life of Stephen Tennant*, 1990

During the Christmas season, a great costume ball was held in one of the dance halls of the In Den Zelten; a ball for men. Many of them wore female clothes. There was a famous character who had inherited a whole wardrobe of beautiful family ball gowns, seventy or eighty years old. These he was wearing out at the rate of one a year. At each ball, he encouraged his friends to rip his gown off his body in handfuls until he had nothing but a few rags to return home in.

Christopher went to the ball with Francis. He had dressed himself in some clothes lent him by a boy from the Cosy Corner – a big sweater with a collar and a pair of sailor's bell-bottomed trousers. It gave him an erotic thrill to masquerade thus as his own sex partner. A little make-up applied by Francis took the necessary five years off his age; the effect was so convincing that a friend of Karl Giese, who didn't know Christopher, later protested to Karl that Francis had really gone too far – bringing a common street hustler into this respectable social gathering.

The respectability of the ball was open to doubt. But it did have one dazzling guest; Conrad Veidt. The great film star sat apart at his own table, impeccable in evening tails. He watched the dancing benevolently through his monocle as he sipped champagne and smoked a cigarette in a long holder. He seemed a supernatural figure, the guardian god of these festivities, who was graciously manifesting himself to his devotees. A few favoured ones approached and talked to him but without presuming to sit down.

Christopher Isherwood, Christopher and His Kind, 1977

She wore a steel-grey business suit and under the jacket a dark blue shirt and a man's tie of lighter shade. The edges of the folded handkerchief in the breast pocket looked sharp enough to slice bread. She wore a linked bracelet and no other jewellery. Her light hair was parted and fell in loose but not unstudied waves. She had a smooth ivory skin and rather severe eyebrows and large dark eyes that looked as if they might warm up at the right time and in the right place.

Raymond Chandler, The Lady in the Lake, 1944

Even before this, my position in society had undergone a change for reasons over which I had no control. The women of London had gone butch. At all ages and on every social level, they had taken to uniforms – or near-uniforms. They wore jackets, trousers and sensible shoes. I could now buy easily the footwear that I had always favoured – black lace-up shoes with firm, medium heels. I became indistinguishable from a woman . . .

Once, as I stood at a bus stop, a policeman accused me of this. After looking me up and down for nearly a minute he asked me what I was doing.

Me: I'm waiting for a bus.

Policeman: You're dressed as a woman.

Me (amazed): I'm wearing trousers.

Policeman: Women wear trousers.

Me: Are you blaming me because everybody else is so eccentric?

Policeman (louder): You're dressed as a woman and you'd better catch a bus quick or there will be trouble. People don't like that sort of thing (pointing at my flyless trousers and my high-heeled shoes).

Quentin Crisp, *The Naked Civil Servant*, 1968

Abruptly, without apparent premeditation (though he closed his eyes fast as if to shut the subject away out of sight for ever), Scobie lay back on the bed, hands behind his head, and said:

'Before you go, there's a small confession I'd like to make to you, old man. Right?'

I sat down on the uncomfortable chair and nodded. 'Right,' he said emphatically and drew a breath. 'Well then: sometimes at the full moon, *I'm Took*. I come under *An Influence*.'

This was on the face of it a somewhat puzzling departure from accepted form, for the old man looked quite disturbed by his own revelation. He gobbled for a moment and then went on in a humbled voice devoid of his customary swagger. 'I don't know what comes over me.' I did not quite understand all this. 'Do you mean you walk in your sleep, or what?' He shook his head and gulped again. 'Do you turn into a werewolf, Scobie?' Once more he shook his head like a child on the point of tears. 'I slip on female duds and my Dolly Varden,' he said, and opened his eyes fully to stare pathetically at me.

'You *what?*' I said.

To my intense surprise he rose now and walked stiffly to a cupboard which he unlocked. Inside, hanging up, moth-eaten and unbrushed, was a suit of female clothes of ancient cut, and on a nail beside it a greasy old cloche hat which I took to be the so-called 'Dolly Varden'. A pair of antediluvian court shoes with very high heels and long pointed toes completed this staggering outfit. He did not know how quite to respond to the laugh which I was now compelled to utter. He gave a weak giggle. 'It's silly, isn't it?' he said, still hovering somewhere on the edge of tears despite his smiling face, and still by his tone inviting sympathy in misfortune. 'I don't know what comes over me. And yet, you know, it's always the old thrill.'

A sudden and characteristic change of mood came over him at the words: his disharmony, his discomfiture gave place to a new jauntiness. His look became arch now, not wishful, and crossing to the mirror before my astonished eyes, he placed the hat upon his bald head. In a second he replaced his own image with that of a little old tart, button-eyed and razor-nosed – a tart of the Waterloo Bridge epoch, a veritable Tuppenny Upright. Laughter and astonishment packed themselves into a huge parcel inside me, neither finding expression. 'For God's sake!' I said at last. 'You don't go around like that, do you, Scobie?'

'Only,' said Scobie, sitting helplessly down on the bed again and relapsing into a gloom which gave his funny little face an even more comical expression (he still wore the Dolly Varden), 'only when the Influence comes over me. When I'm not fully Answerable, old man.'

He sat there looking crushed. I gave a low whistle of surprise which the parrot immediately copied. This was indeed serious. I understood now why the deliberations which had consumed him all morning had been so full of heart-searching. Obviously if one went around in a rig like that in the Arab quarter . . . He must have been following my train of thought, for he said, 'It's only sometime when the Fleet's in.' Then he went on with a touch of self-righteousness: 'Of course, if there was ever any trouble, I'd say I was in disguise. I am a policeman when you come to think of it. After all, even Lawrence of Arabia wore a nightshirt, didn't he?' I nodded. 'But not a Dolly Varden,' I said. 'You must admit, Scobie, it's most original . . .' And here the laughter overtook me.

Lawrence Durrell, *Balthazar*, 1958

The two young Americans made a royal progress down the streets that lay between the Candy Bowl and the Marchioness Theatre, catching the eyes of the pedestrians as much by the extravagance of their luminous sweaters and skin-tight slacks as by the eloquence of their bodily gyrations, shrill voices and vivid gesticulations; and did anyone fail to look at them, his conquest was affected by their bending down suddenly in front of him or her to adjust an enamelled shoe, so that the recalcitrant bowler-hatted or tweed-skirted natives found themselves obstructed by an exotic, questioning behind.

Colin MacInnes, *City of Spades*, 1957

Piers had gone over into a corner where a small dark young man wearing black jeans and a blue tartan shirt, whom I had not noticed before, was peering into some biscuit tins.

'Wilmet, this is Keith – I don't think you've met before,' said Piers in a rather jolly tone which did not seem quite natural to him.

Keith gave a stiff little bow and looked at me warily. He was about twenty-five years old, with a neat-featured rather appealing face and sombre brown eyes. His hair was cropped very short in the fashionable style of the moment. I noticed that it glistened like the wet fur of an animal.

In bed I turned the pages of the knitting book, looking for Keith. I soon found him, on the opposite page to a rugged looking pipe-smoking man who was wearing a cable-stitch sweater which took thirty ounces of double knitting wool. Keith was leaning against a tree, one hand absently playing with a low-hanging branch. He wore a kind of lumber jacket with a shawl collar, knitted crossways in an intricate and rather pleasing stitch. 'For Leisure Hours', the pattern said, 'to fit a 36–38-inch chest. Commence at right cuff by casting on 64 sts. on No. 11 needles . . .'. I went on looking at the patterns, comparing the expressions, and finding that though most were smiling and jolly, the sort of men one could imagine pottering about in the garden at the weekend or playing a round of golf, some were a little shamefaced, as if they hoped nobody they knew would come upon them posing for knitting patterns. None seemed to me to have Keith's air of romantic detachment. Was he thinking of French verbs, dreaming of the day when he could read Baudelaire with ease, I wondered? Or was his mind a blank, in the way that minds of beautiful people are sometimes said to be?

Barbara Pym, *A Glass of Blessings*, 1958

The door at the back of the room opened. A woman in a black masculine-cut suit with a high coffee-coloured lace jabot stood in the doorway. She walked slowly, unselfconsciously down the room and stood behind the empty chair. Goldfinger had got to his feet. She examined him carefully and then ran her eyes round the table. She said a collective, bored 'Hi' and sat down. Mr Strap said, 'Hi Pussy,' and the others, except Mr Stringer who merely bowed, made careful sounds of welcome. Goldfinger said, 'Good afternoon, Miss Galore.' . . . Bond liked the look of her. He felt the sexual challenge all beautiful lesbians have for men.

Ian Fleming, *Goldfinger*, 1959

Accidents will happen; wine is spilled on her dress, a cigarette burns it; this marks the disappearance of the luxurious and festive creature who bore herself with smiling pride into the ballroom, for she now assumes the serious and severe look of the housekeeper; it becomes all at once evident that her toilette was not a set piece like fireworks, a transient burst of splendour, intended for the lavish illumination of a moment. It is rather a rich possession, capital goods, an investment; it has meant sacrifice; its loss is a real disaster. Spots, tears, botched dressmaking, bad hairdos are catastrophes still more serious than a burnt-roast or a broken vase, for not only does the woman of fashion project herself into things, she has chosen to make herself a thing.

Simone de Beauvoir, *The Second Sex*, 1953

One could see that Holly had a laundry problem; the room was strewn, like a girl's gymnasium.

'– and you know, she's quite a successful model: isn't that *fan*tastic? But a good thing,' she said, hobbling out of the bathroom as she adjusted a garter. 'It ought to keep her out of my hair most of the day. And there shouldn't be too much trouble on the man front. She's engaged. Nice guy, too. Though there's a tiny difference in height: I'd say a foot, her favour. Where the hell–' She was on her knees poking under the bed. After she'd found what she was looking for, a pair of lizard shoes, she had to search for a blouse, a belt, and it was a subject to ponder, how, from such wreckage, she evolved the eventual effect: pampered, calmly immaculate, as though she'd been attended by Cleopatra's maids. She said, 'Listen,' and cupped her hand under my chin, 'I'm glad about the story. Really I am.'

Truman Capote, *Breakfast at Tiffany's*, 1958

I was having a wash down, at the bathroom sink, when up came the Hoplite, nervously patting his hair which was done in a new style of hairdo like as if a large animal had licked the Hoplite's locks down flat, then licked the tip of them over his forehead vertical up, like a cockatoo with its crest on back-to-front. He was wearing a pair of skintight, rubber-glove thin, almost transparent cotton slacks, white nylon-stretch and black wafer-sole casuals, and a sort of maternity jacket, I can only call it, coloured blue. He looked over my shoulder into the mirror, patting his head and saying nothing, till when I said nothing too, he asked me, 'Well?'

'Smashing, Hoplite,' I said. 'It gives you a rugged, shaggy, Burt Lancaster appearance.'

'I'm not so sure,' the Hoplite said, 'it's me.'

'It's you, all right, boy. Of course, anything is, Fabulous. You're the one who can wear anything, even a swimsuit or a tuxedo, and look nice in it.'

'I know you're one of my fans,' the Hoplite said, smiling sadly at me in the mirror, 'but don't mock.'

'No mockery, man. You've got dress sense.'

The Hoplite sat down on the lavatory seat, and sighed. 'It's not dress sense I need,' he said, 'but horse sense.'

Colin MacInnes, Absolute Beginners, 1959

He was resplendent in a light blue Italian silk suit and a pink hand-painted tie. Larry, rather surprisingly, was a woolman; he'd come to live in Warley some ten years ago and now had become part of the place. He was a gossip and a scandalmonger and the sort of man who was never described in conversation simply as being a bachelor but always as being a bachelor of course, with heavy emphasis on the amplification. But everyone liked him; without having any special party accomplishments he was always the life and soul of the party. Even Mrs Brown liked him; I expect that she felt that having so exotic a creature in her house was proof she was a woman of the world, a role which occasionally she enjoyed as a relief from the star part of Lady of the Manor.

John Braine, Life at the Top, 1962

25 February 1967

Went down to the Criterion. Not a full house. I took heart from the fact that outside the Globe, where usually the 'HOUSE FULL' sign is up for *A Girl in My Soup*, was no sign at all of the sign. I wore a leather jacket (which I'd found at the bottom of a suitcase, put away from 1964 when leather jackets went out of date) and my cap from Hamburg. As uniforms are now 'in' it looked very way out. 'Oh,' Sheila Ballantine said, 'how trendy.' Stayed until the rise of the curtain and then left. In Piccadilly a rather slant-eyed and pissed (or drugged) poove sidled past me and said in a low, hot tone, 'I say, how camp.' But, as Kenneth Halliwell said, it's rather pointless making to pick up when the object of your desires is clearly with someone else.

Joe Orton, *The Orton Diaries*, edited by John Lahr, 1986

1966

Gerard had on his leather bikini, and he looked confident that it would turn somebody on, but everybody up there seemed more into the Boston-Irish look.

1967

This was the summer I met Candy Darling.

As late as '67 drag queens still weren't accepted in the mainstream freak circles. They were still hanging around where they'd always hung around – on the fringes, around the big cities, usually in crummy little hotels, sticking to their own circles – outcasts with bad teeth and body odor and cheap make-up and creepy clothes. But then, just like drugs had come into the average person's life, sexual blurs did too, and people began identifying a little more with drag queens, seeing them more as 'sexual radicals' than as depressing losers.

One hot August afternoon during that Love Summer of '67, Fred and I were out walking around the West Village on our way to pick up some pants I was having made up at the Leather Man. There were lots of flower children tripping and lots of tourists watching them trip. 8th Street was a total carnival. Every store had purple trip books and psychedelic posters and plastic flowers and beads and incense and candles, and there were Spin-Art places where you squeezed paint on to a spinning wheel and made your own Pop Art painting (which the kids loved to do on acid), and pizza parlors and ice-cream stands – just like an amusement park.

Walking just ahead of us was a boy about nineteen or twenty with wispy Beatle bangs, and next to him was a tall, sensational blonde drag queen in very high heels and a sundress that she made sure had one strap falling on to her upper arm. The two of them were laughing, and as we turned on to Greenwich Avenue, where the hustlers leaned against the wall, we saw the blonde throw her head back and say loud, for all the cruising fags to hear, 'Oh, just look at all these Green Witches.' Then the boy happened to turn round. He recognized me and asked for my autograph on the paper bag he had from the English clothes boutique Countdown. I asked him what was in the bag.

'Satin shorts for the tap-dancing in my new play, *Glamour, Glory and Gold*. It opens in September; I'll send you an invitation. My name's Jackie Curtis.'

I was taking a closer look at the blonde. She was much more attractive from a distance – up close, I could see that she had real problems with her teeth, but she was still the most striking queen around. Jackie introduced the blonde as 'Hope Slattery', which was the name Candy was using in those days – her real name was Jimmy Slattery and she was from Massapequa, Long Island.

At some point much later on, after I'd gotten to know both of them very well, Jackie told me how he and Candy had gotten together:

'I met her in practically the same spot that we met you – right by Sutter's ice-cream parlor – and I told her, "There's something, uh, different about you." And she said, "I draw attention because I'm like women on the screen." And I looked at her and thought, "Now, *please*. Just *who* is this one like on the screen? . . ." Because, Andy, she was a mess. Before she started taking care of herself a little, she looked like the maid in *Dinner at Eight.*'

Andy Warhol and Pat Hackett, *POPism: The Warhol '60s*, 1981

After class, Rusty came to my office and sat on the straight chair beside the desk, listing to one side, legs wide apart. He was not in the least nervous. In fact, he was downright defiant, even contemptuous of me, so secure did he think himself in his masculine superiority.

As usual, he wore a sport shirt with two missing buttons. Today, however, a T-shirt hid the chest from view. Faded blue jeans and desert boots completed the costume, and – as I have already noted – it is costumes that the young men now wear as they act out their simple-minded roles, hopefully constructing a fantasy world in order to avoid confronting the fact that to be a man in a society of machines is to be an expendable, soft auxiliary to what is useful and hard. Today there is nothing left for the old-fashioned male to do, no ritual testing of his manhood through initiation or personal contest, no physical struggle to survive or mate. Nothing is left him but to put on clothes reminiscent of a different time; only in travesty can he act out the classic hero who was a law unto himself, moving at ease through a landscape filled with admiring women. Mercifully that age is finished . . . Young men compensate by playing at being men, wearing cowboy clothes, boots, black leather, attempting through clothes (what an age for the fetishist!) to impersonate the kind of man our society claims to admire but swiftly puts down should he attempt to be anything more than an illusionist, playing a part.

Gore Vidal, *Myra Breckinridge*, 1968

The Liberace Fan Club had booked the Rainbow Room for their banquet to coincide with the maestro's visit to London to launch his book . . .

The door slid open and the lovely fresh-faced, sparkling Liberace sailed into the Rainbow Room. He looked magnificent in his white mink double-breasted coat fastened by rows of real diamond buttons. What puzzled me was that right behind me were Andrew Logan and Zandra Rhodes wearing a Sheherezade turban. I wandered over to Andrew and asked them how on earth they'd got invitations. They replied that they hadn't. They were just gatecrashing, but with such panache. They were both armed with instamatic cameras and Andrew was clutching a bread roll. Before the evening was out he had got Liberace's autograph on his tie *and* on the roll.

Perhaps our *pièce de résistance* was the New Year's Eve party of 1973. Andrew Logan had just started his Alternative Miss World Competition. I had met him a few years before, when Biba was part of the Cecil Beaton Exhibition at the Victoria & Albert Museum, and he had become a friend. The central part of the evening was to be a fancy-dress competition organized and judged by Andrew and his friends. Mynah Bird, a well-known lady about town, was to leap out of a huge cake carried by four professional strong men. Aina had taped Big Ben at midnight and was responsible for playing it at the right time. There was a net full of balloons to be released and the Rainbow Room was packed out. Our personal guests were a good cross-section of our friends: Molly Parkin and her then husband Patrick Hughes . . . and Michael Roberts of the *Sunday Times*, who was dressed as Diana Ross.

The evening was a riot. Fitz was introduced by Del to the strong men that she had hired to lift the cake. Four enormous and polite men, immaculately dressed in dark suits, shook him gravely by the hand and asked if it was all right to bring in their wives and girlfriends. Fitz thought they looked familiar. When he saw them stripped for action in the leopard loincloths we had had made for them, he realized that Del had unknowingly hired the cream of professional wrestlers, headed by the great Tibor Sackas.

'Christ!' said Fitz. 'Thank heavens I was nice to them.'

We had built a catwalk several feet off the ground, which ran for twenty yards up the middle of the room. By the time the contest started, at about ten, many of the predominantly male entrants, dressed in the most exotic evening clothes, had become remarkably drunk. The catwalk was a challenge that several failed to beat. I will never forget one sedate couple who had secured a prize seat beside the catwalk, gazing in stunned disbelief at a hairy male bottom emerging from a white dress whose owner had collapsed, stomach first, across their table.

Barbara Hulanicki, From A to Biba, 1983

GLENDDA: Well, you know, what I like about drag is we have these extremes. You can be ultra-butch, and then you can be ultra-feminine. And I think sometimes feminism tries to push everyone into the middle and say, 'No, we have to whitewash everyone,' and everyone has to be, like, kind of unsexy and androgynous.

PAGLIA: Yeah.

GLENDDA: Androgyny *can* be sexy. But I think they want a kind of unsexy state of androgyny.

PAGLIA: This is exactly right. Right now in the Ivy League, OK, there's a lot of talk that the prominence of the drag queens right now is due to the new interest in androgyny, the dissolution of sex roles. Now I think that's *wrong*. The drag queen flourishes in periods when sex roles are actually very *firm*. Like the fifties, OK?

GLENDDA. Right.

PAGLIA: That was a great period of drag, drag went underground. It fell apart in the seventies and eighties. So I'm saying that the dominance of the drag queen now in the nineties is due to us looking again for what it is to be a man, what it is to be a woman. And we're looking historically again. We no longer like the kind of Mao suit, unisex look. That's *tired*! That's *stale*! Androgyny is *dead*! Drag queen-ism is in!

> Camille Paglia, 'Glendda and Camille Go Downtown',
> from *Vamps and Tramps*, 1994

Gay men, by dint of their attraction to their own gender, have refined and defined the symbols of masculine style. The history of men's fashion has always had this underlying, sometimes invisible, current. And it has never been more pronounced than it is now.

For one thing, gay men play a central role in the fashion business – from the design rooms where clothes are created to photography sessions for magazines and advertising – which to a large degree determines the seasonal progress of fashion. For another, the influence of gay style on the street has become pervasive . . .

'Fashion is the homo sport,' declared *The Advocate*, the gay and lesbian magazine, last year. 'Elsa Klench is our Howard Cosell; the collections, our Super Bowl.' But if the homosexual lifestyle is likely to promote interest in personal appearance and style before (or instead of) investment in family and children, what cultural group is not subject to these same interests in recent years? Heterosexuals are not necessarily pairing off at twenty-four and seeking 1.8 children, either.

Is there some special gene or scene that causes gay men to want to drape fabric? Gay power is indisputable in the industry, but that doesn't mean that there is a cartel of mincing gay men dictating style from on high. Rather, the creative forces behind both men's and women's fashion have looked increasingly to vernacular street styles for inspiration in recent years. With discriminating connoisseurship, designers like Vivienne Westwood, Karl Lagerfeld, Claude Montana and others have watched gay styles on the streets and the downtown clubs.

A tough, edgy, leather-bar look turned up in the Paris women's ready-to-wear collections of the eighties and still permeates fashion. The so-called bondage collection Gianni Versace showed in Milan last year, with its criss-crossed leather bodices, seemed to take the downtown sex-bar idea to another level altogether. Now it is not the least bit shocking to see wealthy socialites at a black-tie dinner wearing bondage dresses that have their origins in the meat-packing district of New York's lower West Side. Just about everyone dresses a little gay these days.

Richard Martin, 'The Gay Factor in Fashion', *Esquire Gentleman*, 1993

Later I was talking to Matt. Matt was lean and pale, with slicked-back hair, and a cynical smile that never quite extended to the left side of his mouth. There was an affected calm to him; he looked at you with a glancing stare as if you had already come to an agreement. When I'd seen him here before he had been over-smart, and showed a spivvish self-consciousness about his cuffs and the creases in his flannels. I understood that he was something to do with computers, he was in the money, which explained his groomed composure among the transient youngsters of the bar and added to the static of sex and faithlessness he knew he gave off. Tonight he was in a clean new denim and a Tom of Finland T-shirt; a bulging biker armlocked another across the shallow dip of his chest.

Alan Hollinghurst, *The Folding Star*, 1994

There's nothing wrong with homosexuality – I gave it a shot myself a couple of years ago, and thoroughly enjoyed it. My best male friend, Marcus, is a trolley dolly who looks like Gianni from *Eastenders*, and he is the sweetest-natured person I have ever met. He is young and beautiful, though, and this matters more than anything on the gay male scene. When gay men begin to lose their looks, or never had looks, or when they start to age, as we all do, they can become bitter.

If all fashion designers looked like Marcus, they'd want nothing more than to create the most glorious frocks with which to gild the female lily. But they don't. Instead, they're sending out the most beautiful women of their generation to parade in front of the world's media dressed as schoolgirls and sluts, space cadets and beekeepers, with their arms shackled to their legs and wearing trousers as jackets. A recent craze was patches of gauze and silk that cover the mouth: you don't have to be Emma Freud to get the subconscious wish behind this.

Jobs for the boys rule the roost in fashion as nowhere else, except possibly, the police force: the hot new names in womenswear this year are Scott Henshall, Sean McGowan, Anthony Symonds, Robert Cary-Williams and Simon Thorogood, joining golden boys Antonio Berardi, Alexander McQueen and Matthew Williamson. Female designers – Amanda Wakely, Caroline Charles, Nicole Farhi, for example – who create clothes that anyone outside a circus would want to wear, are often dismissed by their male peers as 'dressmakers'.

How many girls want to be designers? How many graduate each year from the big colleges? And why do so few get the glamour jobs, and are instead shunted into sensible shoes and chain stores? Maybe it says something for female graduates that they do not possess the silliness and vanity that the boys do, but it speaks volumes about high fashion, too.

No, if a girl wants to get to the top in fashion, she had better become a model. If you have the look, you will be paid handsomely by designers to parade their monstrosities down the catwalk. And because newspaper photographers and editors are so robustly heterosexual, you will end up on the front page. Soon, though, the designer will become aware that people are looking at you, not his clothes, and he will start to hate you, loudly and in public. The recent spectacle of the raddled old designer queens, living like princes and as right wing as kings, coming on like some Marxist scourge about how disgustingly overpaid the supermodels are, was truly disgusting to behold – these are girls who earn a literal pittance when compared with the designers themselves. Their attempt to portray the new wave of undermodels as some sort of feminist triumph over the supers is amazing in its audacity, too. The new girls are, on average, fifteen years old, thin as rakes, and with skin like unborn lambs; they make the supers look lovably human. At least they were women.

If Claudia Schiffer is a joke, finished, what does Karl Lagerfeld think he is? If supermodels are so stupid, how come it's Christy Turlington and not Jean-Paul Gaultier who has gone back to college? No, the supermodels' crime was not greed and temper – which are lauded in male designers – but being women who dared open their mouths and express opinions and ambitions beyond acting as clothes horses. Designers like the new girls because they don't talk back and they're cheap, but there never has been and never will be any integrity in preferring children over women as either sex objects or employees.

Models, though treated like simpletons, are not sad; they do their best with what they've got, and make a tidy pile, and know enough *never* to wear stupid clothes without getting paid for it. It is the people who follow fashion past the age of thirty who are truly sad. I have met some boring people in my life, but none as boring as the fashion writer in her thirties. Hanging around with gay men to the exclusion of heterosexual ones has dulled what charm and spirit she might have once had. And make no mistake: no one despises a fag hag as much as that fag.

When a civilian dares to play the little boy swinging from the lamp-post and ask why the Emperor's new clothes are unwearable, and exactly what fashion is for, we are told that it is to brighten up our little lives. But, frankly, only someone with a very dull life indeed could find fashion interesting. *It's just material!* The Technicolor wonderlands are in our heads, not on our backs. It seems to me that women have never spent more time and effort on making themselves beautiful; and never before have women moaned so much about not being able to Get a Man. The answer to this may well be that, by buying the gay male agenda – that looks are the only important thing to offer a prospective sex partner – they have made themselves into horrible copies of these men, total narcissists, and therefore no red-blooded boy wants to go out with them. When all you care about is your hair and your make-up, you're not much fun. And everybody wants to have fun.

The much discussed emptiness that Bridget McBeal feels is often thought to be the result of too much feminism, but I would say that, on the contrary, it comes from too much girlyism: so much effort goes into the outer self that the inner self is a barren husk. Men don't give a damn what you wear, as long as you take it off a lot.

The fashion and beauty industries have done a great job selling insecure women the idea that men have to be *made* to want them, and that only by spending half their salary on clothes, scent and make-up will this miracle come about. But men wanted women a long time before pore-strips and eyelash-curlers were ever invented. One of the lessons modern woman has not yet got her head around is that men love you because you have a vagina. They don't give a damn whether you've got a Versace.

Julie Burchill, 'Material Boys', Guardian, 1998

3. 'Fashion is fantasie':
Couture and the Designer

Fashion is at once both caterpillar and butterfly. Be a caterpillar by day and a butterfly by night. Nothing could be more comfortable than a caterpillar and nothing more made for love than a butterfly. There must be dresses that crawl and dresses that fly. The butterfly does not go to the market, and the caterpillar does not go to a ball.

Coco Chanel, from Edmonde Charles-Roux,
Chanel and Her World, 1979

'Well, do you like your dress?' she asked Elfine, as they sat at lunch in the New River Club.

'It's heavenly,' said Elfine, solemnly. She, like M. Solide, was pale with exhaustion. 'It's better than poetry, Flora.'

Stella Gibbons, *Cold Comfort Farm*, 1932

The story of twentieth-century fashion is the story of the designer: the establishment of the couturier at its start and the power of *haute couture* and the designer label at its end. It was an Englishman, Charles Frederick Worth, who was the first couturier who dictated to the client in nineteenth-century Paris; it is an Englishman, John Galliano, who has re-established the role of *haute couture* in international fashion at Christian Dior in the late 1990s. Between Worth and Galliano, Paris has seen enormously powerful women designers holding sway over their male counterparts in the so-called 'golden age' of couture between the wars. This chapter looks at these women, in particular Coco Chanel and Elsa Schiaparelli, and at Paul Poiret, Christian

Dior and Christabal Balenciaga, and the ways in which they have been written about by journalists and novelists, such as Nancy Mitford and Angela Carter.

At the start of the century, Doucet, the Callot Soeurs, Paquin and Worth were the most powerful couture houses in Paris, although garments produced by these houses were often still a collaboration between client and designer. Paul Poiret trained under Jacques Doucet and understood the importance of personality and publicity for the couturier; artists were becoming stars – why not couturiers? In 1908 Poiret launched his Directoire line (in which the constricting S-bend corset that transformed the body through tight lacing was abandoned) and had his work illustrated in a *de luxe* album of drawings by Paul Iribe. *Les Robes de Paul Poiret* presented the work of the couturier at its most desirable, moving on from the tradition of fashion illustration which concentrated on factual detail and communicating instead the modern spirit of dress.[1] The twentieth-century notion of couturier as dictator of style and artist was born, and the soft pastel colours, the lace and chiffon that characterized Belle Epoque style of the early years of the century were replaced with bold colour and embroidery as Poiret played potentate reflecting contemporary Orientalism inspired by Diaghilev's Ballet Russes. However, style is a social phenomenon and reflects changing social ideologies. Poiret became fixed in his personal taste for grand gesture and ornamentation and the appeal of his work failed to survive the transition of contemporary tastes to modernism and simplicity in design.

His successor Gabrielle 'Coco' Chanel could not have been more different. Her cult of the personality of the couturier was similar, but she understood the changing aesthetic of fashion and she understood modern women. Her work personified modernism, the rejection of ornamentation called for by architect and theorist Adolf Loos in 1908: 'cultural evolution is equivalent to the removal of ornament from articles of everyday use.'[2]

Chanel opened a sportswear boutique in Biarritz in 1916 and, designed the first 'modern' clothes for women in beige lock-knit and grey flannel: sweaters, jersey dresses[3] and suits in the male tradition of the dandy, whose 'uniform' of black clothes and white linen had challenged the notion of fashion as ostentatious display. Her power as a couturière – she charged 7,000 francs for a radically simple dress[4] – is demonstrated by the success of her 'little black dress', which *Vogue* dubbed 'A Fashion Ford' in 1926. Others designed black dresses;[5] but it was Chanel who made the black dress fashionable.

Chanel was antagonistic towards her rivals. Calling Elsa Schiaparelli 'that Italian artist who makes clothes'; she was contemptuous of '*ces messieurs*' Dior, Jacques Fath and Balenciaga and held forth at length on the iniquities visited on society by the homosexual. But for her women rivals especially she was a catalyst; and the opening of her couture house in Paris in 1919 was a symbol of the beginning of the 'golden age of the couturière'[6] – Chanel, Elsa Schiaparelli, Alix (Madame Gres), Sonia Delaunay, Madeleine Vionnet and Jeanne Lanvin were women designing *for* women, and the last two finally established the couturier as artist, cutting and fitting dresses with their own hands. In the 1930s, Schiaparelli's collaboration with artists, which produced her lobster dresses and hats inspired by newspaper print, brought surrealism to fashion, the motifs questioning fashion itself.[7] Vionnet's bias cut and Alix's draping brought a sculptural form to fashion and celebrated the body. The mass market adopted the styles and brought the couturier's collections to the street. By the 1930s, style had become more romantic, and when Christian Dior launched his New Look in February 1947 he was continuing from where Paris, and particularly the work of Mainbocher, had left off before the start of the Second World War. Dior, Fath, Balmain and Balenciaga re-instituted the male role in *haute couture*; Dior's boned bodices and long skirts were questioned by Chanel, Schiaparelli and Vionnet, who saw his work as dress in the hands of men, controlling the movement, and ultimately the lives, of women.

During the 1950s the dominance of Paris and couture itself was challenged by the ready-to-wear industry. This was largely brought about by Chanel, who re-launched in 1953 with a collection of chic separates, telling *Vogue*, 'I am no longer interested in dressing a few hundred women; private clients; I shall dress thousands of women . . .'[8] The Chanel suit was reproduced everywhere, especially in the United States,[9] where it was ideal for the 'working girl', a blend of the new and classic style. In the 1960s, the designers of New York – Tiger Morse – and of London – Mary Quant and Barbara Hulanicki – catered for the youth market, who simply did not want to dress as their mothers did. Pierre Cardin and André Courreges both picked up the gauntlet, producing couture lines that reflected the youth spirit which called for the new. Yves Saint Laurent turned the mods' parka and jacket and the working-class pea-coat into couture; in 1966, opening his Rive Gauche ready-to-wear boutique, he anticipated the demand for designer ready-to-wear and looked to the needs of the modern woman, creating women's daywear that was essentially masculine – jacket, trousers and shirt – and evening wear that was romantically feminine. Like Cardin, Saint Laurent and his business partner Pierre Bergé saw licensing agreements as market-making and other designers followed suit; the branding of scent, make-up and toiletries has resulted in a label-awareness which is global and menswear (discussed in Chapter Six) was also part of the designer vision. Fashion at this level during the late sixties through to the mid-eighties was not about the couture collections but about the ready-to-wear catwalk shows; Italy's Nino Cerruti, Giorgio Armani, Valentino Caravani and Gianni Versace, and America's Ralph Lauren, Calvin Klein and Donna Karan all fed a first world consumer market for whom the wearing of a designer label was a mark of personal success. However, the Japanese conceptual designer Rei Kawakubo of Comme des Garçons, who designed clothes to feel comfortable on the body, and Issey Miyake, who created clothes which explored form through fabric, were and are basing their work on a non-western tradition and moved fashion back into the 'dress as art' arena.

Couture received a much vaunted re-vamp with Christian Lacroix for the House of Patou (the fashion label founded by Jean Patou in the 1920s) in 1981, when the theatricality and fantasy of his work placed him at the forefront of couture.[10] The 1990s have seen a renaissance in the art, with British designers John Galliano at Christian Dior, Alexander McQueen at Givenchy and Stella McCartney at Chloe; this is balanced with the success of 1990s' aspirational ready-to-wear designer labels, particularly Gucci by Tom Ford and Prada.

Overshadowing the end of the fashion century is the death of Versace in July 1997, which marked the designer as international celebrity, a position that Poiret, who died in poverty, did not achieve. Now that his legacy, the role of couturier as artist, has, as I have already said, been revived in the person of John Galliano, the question is: how relevant is the art of couture to *fin de siècle* consumers and what does the term 'fashion' mean to them?

At the end of the Avenue Gabriel, the magnificent roadway bordering the open gardens of the Champs-Élysées, a beautiful girl, beautifully dressed in a formal evening dress of blue satin brocade, is leaning back with arms uplifted against the trunk of a chestnut tree. Three yards away from her, a photographer standing with one eye glued to his Leica grimaces as he calls out his instructions: 'Lean back a bit more, can you?' The beautiful girl obeys. Her dress, with its short train, makes her look like a professional vamp. Her pose is exaggerated, completely out of harmony with her surroundings, the early morning hour, the hurrying preoccupied air of the passers-by. As she stares unseeing into the chestnut foliage, just starting to redden under its coating of dust, her eyes are filled with a sense of importance due to something more than her own beauty. She is smiling with a touch of disdain that has nothing to do with her attitude towards the world around her. She is not trying to copy the hauteur of a sophisticated woman nor the outraged expression of some heroine of melodrama surprised by an intruder. Her manner is simply calculated to give value to the dress she is wearing.

How did I start to haunt the fashion houses? I am no longer very clear about it. I feel rather as though I found my way into this milieu as one finds oneself beginning to fall in love. Afterwards one's memories are disjointed, and one can no longer remember what life was like before this love existed. But once inside the charmed circle it was curiosity that kept me there. For weeks and months on end – months that seemed shorter than some days had seemed in the past – I would set off first thing in the morning. Leaving the room where as a rule I stayed shut up for hours together at my typewriter. I no longer made any engagements before the evening. I was 'in *couture*' – submerged and buried in it. I had to see everything, and try to understand everything I saw.

I remember one encounter – not my first, but undoubtedly the most spectacular to date – with this world I was bent on exploring.

Late one morning I found myself, a little breathless but not at all disconcerted, in the boutique of one of our couturiers, the most famous of them all: Christian Dior. There was a canopy over the entrance, some green plants under the vaulted roof of the staircase, and a cloakroom installed at the back of the hall. The commissionaires and the woman in charge of the crowded cloakroom kept on coming into the deserted shop, where two *vendeuses*, to while away the time, were trying on necklaces in front of a looking-glass. Two young brunettes dressed in black, both beautiful; and the necklace they were passing back and forth between them was made of many rows of little glass pearls, the colour of red currants.

'With matching earrings, it would be too dark,' said one of them.

'I adore necklaces,' said the other, taking off her triple rows of pearls. 'Necklaces, earrings and bracelets, but I don't like wearing rings. This red is divine.' She fastened the clasp, also red, and pulled down the neck of her sweater to study the effect of the pearls against her skin.

'I'm mad about rubies,' the other one said. 'If I had a really generous lover who'd give me whatever I wanted . . .'

'What curious taste! Now I, on the other hand, would gladly make up to the most awful little fat old man for the sake of pearls and emeralds.'

Both of them laughed. The one who had just tried on the red-currant necklace laid it down, and put on her three rows of baroque pearls once more.

'These will be just as good with my printed satin dress,' she said. 'I haven't the slightest desire to go to this dinner anyway. I'm all in.'

She is a *vendeuse*, and she goes out almost every evening; not simply for pleasure, but in order to keep in touch with her clientele, composed very largely of her relatives. She has two little girls, a great name. Her colleagues appreciate her courage and good humour, the gaiety which enables her to adopt these midinette airs as though to the manner born, and to keep her conversation as racy as that of a daughter of the people, full of freshness and verve. Everything she says sounds natural. She is never the sophisticated woman playing at having come down in the world. She is quite simply herself, a woman who has at once too much imagination and too much honesty to accept the conventional existence to which she was born.

Haute couture is a form of teamwork. By talking to several of our couturiers, I have learnt how much they rely on the work of their fitters and workgirls. There is a constant, indispensable collaboration between the studio, where the designs are worked out, and the workrooms. The more I realized how widely the styles of the individual couturiers vary, how different are the ways in which they conceive their aim and even their ideas of fashion itself, the more I saw that it must be very difficult for a workhand to go from one house to another, or even from one designer to another. This means that, if they are to carry out their task with the maximum of taste and efficiency, the workhands must become very much attached to their chief. If he goes elsewhere, or if the firm closes down, they often prefer to leave rather than to go on working in the same place under a different management.

At the first showing of a collection by Jacques Griffe, I noticed a striking woman in the front row of chairs in the big salon. Small, white-haired and dressed in black, with a fresh complexion and sparkling eyes behind her round spectacles, she was wearing a kind of top hat with a fine black veil. Her coat was thrown over her knees like a rug.

She was busy inspecting and peering at the models. Nothing escaped those observant eyes, those hands outstretched towards the dress as it went by, to feel the material, lift a wide skirt, confirm the placing of a seam.

I had seen her before in one of the couturier boutiques, attentive and absorbed. Someone had whispered her name to me, and it brought back strange memories. When I escaped from Paris at the time of the German occupation, I found, in a village in the Jura mountains, peasant families who, like her, bore the name of Vionnet; and now this familiar name brought back a memory of the nostalgia I had felt in those days for my city and all the life of Paris that I had lost . . .

'My head is a real workbox,' she says. 'It has always held scissors, needles and thread. Even when I'm walking down the street I can't stop myself looking to see how the clothes of passers-by are made, even men's clothes! I say to myself: "Supposing one were to put a tuck there, to give more breadth to the shoulder . . ."' And as she talks she suits the action to the words, pulling up the shoulder seam of her own jacket. She has all the finesse of people who have remained in close contact with a manual craft.

But she has more to give than stories, and she knows, with an agreeable precision, the role she has played in couture. She isn't conceited. She only wants people to recognize, and give her credit for, the revolutions she brought about.

'It was I who got rid of corsets,' she says. 'At Doucet's, in 1907, I presented mannequins for the first time with bare feet and sandals, and in their own skins.'

Celia Bertin, *Paris à la Mode*, 1956

Lady Katherine and Mrs Mackintosh came into my room on the way up to bed. She – Lady Katherine – wanted to show Mary how beautifully they had done it up; it used to be hers before she was married. They looked all round at the dead-daffodil-coloured cretonne and things, and at last I could see their eyes often straying to my night-gown and dressing gown, laid out on a chair beside the fire.

'Oh, Lady Katherine, I am afraid you are wondering at my having pink silk,' I said, apologetically, 'as I am in mourning, but I have not had time to get a white dressing gown yet.'

'It is not that, dear,' said Lady Katherine, in a grave duty voice. 'I – I – do not think such a nightgown is suitable for a girl.'

'Oh! but I am very strong,' I said. 'I never catch cold.'

Mary Mackintosh held it up, with a face of stern disapproval. Of course it has short sleeves ruffled with Valenciennes, and is fine linen cambric nicely embroidered. Mrs Carruthers was always very particular about them, and chose them herself at Doucet's. She said one never could know when places might catch on fire.

'Evangeline, dear, you are very young, so you probably cannot understand,' Mary said, 'but I consider this garment not in any way fit for a girl – or for any good woman for that matter. Mother, I hope my sisters have not seen it!!'

I looked so puzzled.

She examined the stuff. One could see the chair through it, beyond.

'What would Alexander say if I were to wear such a thing!'

This thought seemed almost to suffocate them both, they looked genuinely pained and shocked.

'Of course it would be too tight for you,' I said, humbly, 'but it is otherwise a very good pattern, and does not tear when one puts up one's arms. Mrs Carruthers made a fuss at Doucet's because my last set tore so soon, and they altered these.'

At the mention of my late adopted mother, both of them pulled themselves up.

'Mrs Carruthers we know had very odd notions,' Lady Katherine said stiffly, 'but I hope, Evangeline, you have sufficient sense to understand now for yourself that such a – a – garment is not at all seemly.'

'Oh! Why not, dear Lady Katherine?' I said. 'You don't know how becoming it is.'

'Becoming!' almost screamed Mary Mackintosh. 'But no nice-minded woman wants things to look becoming in bed!'

The whole matter appeared so painful to them I covered up the offending 'nighty' with my dressing gown, and coughed. It made a break, and they went away, saying goodnight frigidly.

And now I am alone. But I do wonder why it is wrong to look pretty in bed – considering nobody sees one, too!

Elinor Glyn, *The Vicissitudes of Evangeline*, 1905

'She is extremely pretty,' added Lady Stoat. 'Those American girls so very often are; but they are all like the *poupées de modiste*. The very best of them are only very perfect likenesses of the young ladies that try the confections on for us at Pingat's or Worth's, and the dress has always a sort of look of being the first toilette they ever had. I don't know why, for I hear they dress extremely well over there, and should be used to it, but it has that look, and they never get rid of it. No, my dear, no; you are right. Those new people are not gentlewomen any more than men's modern manners are like the Broad Stone of Honour.'

Ouida, *Moths*, 1919

It was still the age of the corset. I waged war upon it. The last representative of this abominated apparatus was called the Gache Sarraute. It divided its wearer into two distinct masses: on the one side there was the bust and the bosom, on the other, the whole behindward aspect, so that the lady looked as if she were hauling a trailer. It was almost a return to the bustle. Like all great revolutions, that one had been made in the name of Liberty – to give free play to the abdomen: it was equally in the name of Liberty that I proclaimed the fall of the corset and the adoption of the brassiere which, since then, has won the day.

Yes, I freed the bust but I shackled the legs. You will remember the tears, the cries, the gnashings of teeth caused by this ukase of fashion. Women complained of being no longer able to walk, nor get into a carriage. All their jeremiads pleaded in favour of my innovation. Are their protestations still heard? Did they not utter the same groans when they returned to fullness? Have their complaints or grumblings ever arrested the movement of fashion, or have they not rather, on the contrary, helped it by advertising it?

Everyone wore the tight skirt.

People have been good enough to say that I have exercised a powerful influence over my age, and that I have inspired the whole of my generation. I dare not make the pretension that this is true, and I feel, indeed, extremely diffident about it, but yet, if I summon up my memories, I am truly obliged to admit that, when I began to do what I wanted to do in dress-designing, there were absolutely no tints left on the palette of the colourists. The taste for the refinements of the eighteenth century had led all the women into a sort of deliquescence, and on the pretext that it was 'distinguished', all vitality had been suppressed. Nuances of nymph's thigh, lilacs, swooning mauves, tender blue hortensias, niles, maizes, straws, all that was soft, washed out, and insipid, was held in honour. I threw into this sheepcote a few rough wolves; reds, greens, violets, royal blues, that made all the rest sing aloud. I had to wake up the good people of Lyons, whose stomach is a bit heavy, and put a little gaiety, a little new freshness, into their colour schemes. There were orange and lemon crêpe de Chines which they would have not dared to imagine. On the other hand, the morbid mauves were hunted out of existence: there appeared a new dawn – the gamut of pastel shades. I carried with me the colourists when I took each tone at its most vivid, and I restored to health all the exhausted nuances. I am truly forced to accord myself the merit of all this, and to recognize also that since I have ceased to stimulate the colours, they have fallen once more into neurasthenic anaemia.

Paul Poiret, *My First Fifty Years*,
translated by Stephen Haden Guest, 1931

Paul Poiret was the Leonardo of fashion.

Elsa Schiaparelli, *Shocking Life*, 1954

This first parade of mine [*c.* 1912], in addition to the mannequins, originated another custom which has been in use ever since – the naming of different models. Before that they were generally referred to as 'the pink silk' or 'the black velvet', or even by numbers. It offended my sense of the dramatic that some creation of mine, the expression of a mood, should be spoken of only as 'number nine', or whatever it might be. So I gave them all names and personalities of their own. How they made my audience smile as they were called out one by one. 'The Captain with Whiskers', 'When Passion's Thrall is O'er', 'Give me Your Heart', 'Do you Love Me?' 'Gowns of Emotion' I called them and they caught the fancy of all those women who sat and watched the girls from Balham and Bermondsey showing them how they ought to walk. I shall never forget the long-drawn breath of admiration that rippled round the room as the curtains parted slowly and the first of my glorious girls stepped out on to the stage, pausing to show herself a moment before floating gracefully down the room to a burst of applause.

'Lucile', Lady Duff Gordon, *Discretions and Indiscretions*, 1932

Looking up to apologize she found that the little body's eyes were set derisively on her coat, which was a very lovely fantasy in checks by Molyneux. She was not hurt by that, for often before she had noticed that good clothes, like any other form of fine art, were always greeted with ridicule when they were brought out into the open among ordinary people; and she knew that there is nothing base about this ridicule, since it springs, like the giggling of children who are taken to see a tragedy, not from a lack of sensibility but from its excess. Children are as far as possible from all knowledge of tragedy, ordinary people have few chances of encountering the rarer sorts of decoration, so these contacts are to them news of an unfamiliar variation in life. They are dismayed that it should exist at all, for it intimates that life covers a range far wider than the octave of their daily routine and that the demands which it may make upon them are endless and incalculable. They are dismayed, too, at its quality: for the beauty of tragedy and the beauty of good clothes, which is one and the same beauty, asks from those who use it a sympathetic nobility and an unembittered but firm discontent with the emotion that is not right, with the colour, the line that is not right. It sends them off on that search for harmony which is as delicious as love for a woman who is perfect and loving, as agonizing as love for a woman about whom one knows nothing, not even that she has been born. This is a hard thing to lay on children, on simple people. They will not have it, they pretend that what they have seen is of no significance, and merely a ludicrous accident of folly which calls for nothing from the same but laughter. Essington had made her see all that when she had told him how the people in Cricklewood Broadway had giggled at her when her car had broken down on the way to the Fairshams' at Harrow, and she had to step out into the street in a Nicole Groult picture gown and cloak.

Rebecca West, *Sunflower*, 1986

Black is the hardest color in the world to get right – except for gray . . .

Diana Vreeland, *D. V.*, 1984

'You've got possibilities. But you don't give yourself a chance. Why don't you make up? If there's one thing in the world I find distressing it's these schoolgirl complexions. You ought to take a lesson from my friend Inez. God! she's got style! I choose her clothes for her. You ought to meet her.'

She was silent, thinking how much she would prefer not to meet Inez.

'That dress of yours, now,' he said. 'It won't do, will it? Honestly . . . ?'

She attempted a smile; but she felt strangled.

'I'm afraid it doesn't fit very well.'

He went on:

'Besides, the colour. So *crude*. I never let Inez wear anything but black at night. Occasionally white.'

'I don't like black,' she said in a weak, high, defiant, voice. He disregarded this and continued unmoved:

'I dare say it's not your fault. You've never been taught. It takes a man to teach a woman how to dress. The majority of them don't develop a clothes-sense till they've had a lover. Or a face either, for that matter. No woman under twenty-five's worth looking at.'

Rosamund Lehmann, *Invitation to the Waltz*, 1932

Flora first took Elfine to Maison Viol, of Brass Street, in Lambeth, to have her hair cut. Short hair was just coming back into fashion, yet it was still new enough to be distinguished. M. Viol himself cut Elfine's hair, and dressed it in a careless, simple, fiendishly expensive way that showed the tips of her ears.

Flora then took Elfine to Maison Solide. M. Solide had dressed Flora for the last two years and did not despise her as much as he despised most of the women whom he dressed. His eyes widened when he saw Elfine. He looked at her broad shoulders and slim waist and long legs. His fingers made the gestures of a pair of scissors, and he groped blindly towards a roll of snow-coloured satin which a well-trained assistant put into his arms.

'White?' ventured Flora.

'But what else?' screamed M. Solide, ripping the scissors across the satin. 'It is to wear white that God, once in a hundred years, makes such a young girl.'

Flora sat and watched for an hour while M. Solide worried the satin like a terrier, tore it into breadths, swathed and caped and draped it. Flora was pleased to see that Elfine did not seem nervous or bored. She seemed to take naturally to the atmosphere of a world-famous dress-maker's establishment. She bathed delightedly in white satin, like a swan in foam. She twisted her neck this way and that, and peered down the length of her body, as though down a snow slope, to watch the assistants like busy black ants pinning and rearranging the hem a thousand feet below.

Flora opened a new romance, and became absorbed in it, until Julia arrived at one o'clock to take them to lunch.

M. Solide, pale and cross after his orgy, assured Flora that the dress would be ready by tomorrow morning. Flora said that they would call for it. No, he must not send it, it was too rare. Would he post a picture by Gauguin to Australia? A thousand evils might befall it on the way. But, secretly, she wished to protect the dress from Urk. She was sure that he would destroy it if he got a glimmer of a chance.

'Well, do you like your dress?' she asked Elfine, as they sat at lunch in the New River Club.

'It's heavenly,' said Elfine, solemnly. She, like M. Solide, was pale with exhaustion. 'It's better than poetry, Flora.'

'It's not at all the sort of thing St Francis of Assisi wore,' pointed out Julia, who considered that Flora was doing a lot for Elfine and should be appreciated.

Elfine blushed, and bent her head over her cutlet. Flora looked at her benignly. The dress had cost fifty guineas, but Flora did not grudge the sum. She felt at this moment that any sum would have been sacrificed by her to score off the Starkadders.

Stella Gibbons, *Cold Comfort Farm*, 1932

At least I could think her dress was quite horrid. I could pity her for that. A short white chemise, straight as a pinafore, not even a sequin to liven things up, it was high to the collar bone, where a six-inch diamond bar held up one minimal orchid. At the back it was open to a long U of brown flesh – an unfortunate garment for a girl as big (if in different places) as myself.

Molly Keane, *Good Behaviour*, 1981

Marlene Dietrich trying on hats, her famous legs crossed, smoking a perennial cigarette as if she was posing for the movies, and like nobody else does. Claudette Colbert, mischievous and twinkling . . . Norma Shearer . . . Merle Oberon perfumed like the Queen of Sheba . . . Lauren Bogart with her aristocratic face and Brooklyn vocabulary saying a deep, long *bonjour* that sounded like a high note . . . Gary Cooper, shy, following with his navy-blue eyes his latest conquest . . . Michele Morgan straight out of her mamma's *concierge* lodge . . . Annabella playing the grown-up in a René Clair film and looking like a little boy . . . Simone Simon tearing her dress to pieces in the face of the fitter because she did not want to wear it in spite of Sacha Guitry's wish . . . and Constance Bennett turned into a fox, so many fox furs encircled her person . . . Gloria Swanson and Cecile Sorel.

Elsa Schiaparelli, *Shocking Life*, 1954

The third was the blonde. She was dressed to go out, in a pale greenish blue. I didn't pay much attention to her clothes. They were what the guy designed for her and she would go to the right man. The effect was to make her look very young and to make her lapis lazuli eyes look very blue. Her hair was of the gold of oil paintings and had been fussed with just enough but not too much. She had a full set of curves which nobody had been able to improve on. The dress was rather plain, except for a clasp of diamonds at the throat.

Raymond Chandler, *Farewell My Lovely*, 1940

The only physical disparity between Nicole at present and the Nicole of five years before was simply that she was no longer a young girl. But she was enough ridden by the current youth worship, the moving pictures with their myriad faces of girl-children, blandly represented as carrying on the work and wisdom of the world, to feel a jealousy of youth.

She put on the first ankle-length day dress that she had owned
for many years and crossed herself reverently with Chanel Sixteen.
When Tommy drove up at one o'clock she had made her person
into the trimmest of gardens.

F. Scott Fitzgerald, *Tender is the Night*, 1934

I loved the clothes I had in the thirties. I can remember a dress I
had of Schiaparelli's that had fake ba-zooms – these funny little
things that stuck out here. When you sat down, they sort of went
. . . all I can say is that it was terribly chic. Don't ask me why, but it
was. Another of my Schiaparellis that sticks in my mind was a black
sheath with a long train in the form of a padded fishtail – I gave it
to Gypsy Rose Lee, and she performed in it at the World's Fair –
stalking the runway six times a day.

I loved my clothes from Chanel. Everyone thinks of suits when
they think of Chanel. That came later. If you could have seen my
clothes from Chanel in the thirties – the *dégagés* gypsy skirts, the
divine brocades, the little boleros, the roses in the hair, the pailletted
nose *veils* – day and evening! And the ribbons were so pretty.

I remember my great friend Leo d'Erlanger saying to me in Paris,
'Diana, I want to give you a present. I know that what you love
more than anything in the world is clothes, and I know that you
love Chanel's clothes more than anyone else's. So I want you to go
to Chanel and buy anything you want.' . . .

This was the dress I ordered: the huge skirt was of silver lamé,
quilted in pearls, which gave it a marvellous weight; then the bolero
was lace entirely encrusted with pearls and diamanté; then, underneath the bolero was the most beautiful shirt of linen lace. I think
it was the most beautiful dress I've ever owned.

Diana Vreeland, *D. V.*, 1984

I remember that my mother, during one of her rare visits to England, brought me a little jacket in scarlet cloth from Schiaparelli. It seemed to me quite plain and uninteresting except for the label in its lining, and I longed to put this on the outside so that people would know where it came from. I was wearing it, instead of a cardigan, in my house when Cedric happened to call, and the first thing he said was,

'Aha! So now we dress at Schiaparelli, I see! Whatever next?'

'Cedric! How can you tell?'

'My dear, one can always tell. Things have a signature, if you use your eyes, and mine seem to be trained over a greater range of objects than yours, Schiaparelli – Reboux – Fabergé – Viollet-le-Duc – I can tell at a glance, literally a glance.'

Nancy Mitford, *Love in a Cold Climate*, 1949

First came a very ugly woman dressed (as I thought then) with hideous severity. She wore a tight black suit, black hat and high white blouse, and clanked with gold jewellery as she moved. She was nearly six feet tall and emaciatedly thin, with short dark hair and protruding teeth. She struck me as repulsive.

'That was Mrs van Elder, the Merchandise Editor,' said Rose. 'She's the chicest woman here. She's always divinely dressed. And such wonderful bones.' I felt an ass.

Anne Scott-James, *In the Mink*, 1952

There we are, see? On the front page of the *New York Post*, in our best suits – Schiaparelli, I kid you not – charcoal wool, fox wrap collar and cuffs, buttons, typical Schiap touch, in the shape of crotchets and quavers, soft little high-crowned hats pulled down over our left eyes. Look hot, stay cool, we'd instructed one another; we'd got the stance to match the suits off pat, you stuck your hipbone forward, let your shoulders droop, put all your weight on one leg.

Angela Carter, *Wise Children*, 1991

One day, for reasons which I have forgotten, I found myself in Norman Hartnell's pleasantly regal establishment in Bruton Street. Norman was busy but he said that I could wander round. I did so, and opening a great many doors which should not have been opened, I found myself in a large deserted workroom filled with busts. On each bust was a label: 'the Countess of X', 'Madame de P', 'the Hon. Mrs Q'.

I realized that I was in the most rarified atmosphere of *la haute couture*. Here, in a sort of waxless, headless Madame Tussauds, were the corporeal likenesses of the great ladies of the town. The Countess of X, Madame de P, and the Hon. Mrs Q were all far, far too busy to come and be fitted in person; they were all roaring off to Ascot, or – much smarter – standing in a queue outside the Café de Paris to see the latest pantry-boy banging a biscuit tin at £100 a night. So these ladies had their busts copied, and kept at Norman's, and when they wanted a new frock they just rang up and the bust got all the boredom and pinpricks. There may be minor errors in this piece of rapportage but that is the rough idea, and if I were very rich I should have a permanent model of my hips, preferably in marble, in the basement of Messrs Kilgour and French.

Now for the climax of our tale. My eyes wandered round the room and lit upon a bust standing all by itself in the corner. Or rather, on the vague outlines of a bust, for it was reverently wrapped up in a lot of brown paper. Even so, there was something about this truncated material that seemed vaguely familiar. It looked the sort of bust that would stand no nonsense. It had an aura – yes – an aura of majesty.

Then Norman came into the room. And suddenly I realized who the bust was.

I turned to him. 'That bust in the parcel,' I began. 'Is it Queen Ma . . .'

But the second syllable froze on my lips. It was, of course. But Norman never discusses his royal clients. Which is one of the reasons why they gave him the CMG.

Beverly Nichols, The Sweet and Twenties, 1958

Women today imagine they can distinguish themselves and recognize themselves in the gamut of beiges and greys. On the contrary, they are confounded in a nebulous fog, which will be the symbol of our epoch. Fashion today needs a new master. It has need of a tyrant to castigate it, and liberate it from its scruples. He who shall render it this service will be loved, and he will become rich. He will have to do what I did then, and not look behind him, and consider nothing save women and what becomes them.

Paul Poiret, My First Fifty Years,
translated by Stephen Haden Guest, 1931

In December 1946, as a result of the war and uniforms, women still looked and dressed like Amazons. But I designed clothes for flower-like women, with rounded shoulders, full feminine busts, and hand-span waists above enormous spreading skirts. An ethereal appearance is only achieved by elaborate workmanship: in order to satisfy my love of architecture, and clear-cut design, I wanted to employ quite a different technique in fashioning my clothes, from the methods then in use – I wanted them to be constructed like buildings. Thus I moulded my dresses to the curves of the female body, so that they called attention to its shape. I emphasized the width of the hips, and gave the bust its true prominence; and in order to give my models more 'presence' I lined nearly all of them with cambric or taffeta, thus reverting to an old tradition.

My return to long-forgotten techniques aroused a host of difficulties, for of course none of my staff had any experience of them. As soon as I had exhibited my designs, they applied themselves to the problem, with Mme Marguerite at their head. The work was carried out under conditions of unbelievable difficulty. The lack of space in my studio – formerly a boudoir – forced us to make use of every inch of free space in order to have enough elbow room. Eventually I fled from the growing invasion of materials on to the landing, and even found myself working on the steps of the staircase. The whole building was in a fever. One of our key *premières* collapsed with a nervous breakdown, a victim of the mad regime; we had to replace her in the midst of the battle by a particularly talented underling, Monique, who luckily was more than equal to the task. With Christiane, she deserves every credit for the success of the collection. They even had to make the suits, because the expert whom I engaged for the purpose proved incapable of doing it.

My own thoughts and energies were concentrated on the most perfect reproductions of the ninety models I had designed. All around me, at the orders of Mme Marguerite, the *premières* and their subordinates were rediscovering or inventing the appropriate technique to execute the designs which had been entrusted to them. They were mostly complete strangers to one another, but within a few weeks, they were working together as proper teams.

Worn out by the triple task of organizing the business, recruiting the staff and creating the dresses, I sometimes let myself flop down exhausted on to the heaps of material. By now there was practically nowhere else to sit.

We all felt the strain. There were only six mannequins and the thousands of different fittings imposed such a nervous and physical strain upon them that on one occasion an extremely pretty blonde

English girl turned faint and collapsed into my arms. I thought I was clutching her securely, but she continued to slide to the floor – and I found myself holding . . . her bust! I had completely forgotten that in my desire to give prominence to this most feminine attribute, I had asked those whom nature had neglected to equip themselves with 'falsies'.

The materials themselves were another source of worry. In those days there was nothing like the high standard of quality we have today. I wanted silk fabrics where the yarn itself and not the woven material had been dyed – but anything which had any body to it was extremely hard to find. For years, crêpe romain, georgette, muslin and clinging jersey had supplanted taffeta, duchesse satin and wool taffeta.

Inexorably, the date at which I would have to show my collection* crept forward. I intentionally had not worried about publicity but trusted to a few loyal friends to get the new house talked about in Paris. The intellectual and social standing of Comte Etienne de Beaumont and Mme Lariviere, and the fervour which Marie-Louise Bousquet, Christian Berard and several friends of mine who were journalists, including Michel de Brunhoff, Paul Caldagues and James de Coquet, managed to communicate to others, aroused a fever of popular curiosity, from which, all at once, I recoiled in alarm. I felt that too many hopes were being pinned on me, and that I was incapable of fulfilling them.

It was only with the greatest possible reluctance that I was finally persuaded to show my dresses to my friends one evening just before their formal presentation to the public. Berard cried out that I had achieved a miracle, and Marie-Louise Bousquet chimed in with other flattering exclamations. Being superstitious by nature, I immediately looked round for a piece of wood to touch: it all seemed a little too good to be true, and therefore ominous.

*This was the collection that was to become known as the 'New Look'.

But my most fortunate piece of publicity was quite unplanned: *Life* magazine asked me to pose with a smile and the supposed 'natural' or 'inspired' expression, which I have had to try and assume so often since. At the time I had no idea of the importance of an article in *Life* in launching anything. Like Fortune, the goddess of Publicity often seems to smile most favourably on those who court her least.

Up till now I had only held hasty rehearsals, in a *salon* cluttered up with mannequins, seamstresses and *premières*: but it was essential to have some sort of a dress rehearsal. Nevertheless I knew it would give absolutely no idea of the collection as it would ultimately appear to the public: until the opening, the true significance of the dresses would be lost on anyone except those who had actually created and sewn them. So I decided not even to show the models to the *vendeuses*. For them, as for the press and my future *clientele*, the curtain would rise on the collection for the first time on the appointed day. I have stuck to this decision ever since, in spite of the pleas which have been made to me to yield. I suppose I am subconsciously trying to halt the invasions of the commercial spirit into the milieu which I love.

At last the finishing touches were put to the dresses. Now that there was no further opportunity to alter them, I suddenly felt a strange calm come over me. I had only one thing to say about my collection – though it 'would do', that is to say, I thought it would please and satisfy the *clientele* at which it was aimed.

Fortunately the anxiety of receiving my guests correctly took my mind off my actual collection. By a miracle the decor was finished, as in spite of my constant nagging the decorators had lagged behind their schedule. As Mme Delahaye had predicted, the last bang of the last hammer was actually heard as the first visitor entered.

I myself arrived very early on the great day and fidgeted about on the carpet which was still being tacked down. By dawn, the whole house was in a state of uproar which made it seem more like late afternoon. Carmen Colle had spent the last hours of darkness transforming the cubbyhole, which was supposed to be our *boutique*, into a proper little miniature shop. In the *salon*, Lachaume was arranging the last vases of flowers, and I thought the curtains and hangings of grey satin made it look very elegant. In the dressing room, the mannequins were ready for the fray, and by a miracle all the models seemed to be there too, having arrived safely from the workrooms.

At ten thirty, with the *salons* full to bursting, the first mannequin showed the first dress. Marie-Thérèse, half dead with fright, stumbled at her first appearance, collapsed in tears, and was henceforth incapable of showing a dress. Very soon, the entry of each model was accompanied by gusts of applause. I stuffed my ears, terrified of feeling confident too soon; but a series of short bulletins from the field of battle confirmed to me that my troops – led, flags flying, by my star mannequin, the inimitable Tania – had triumphed.

Now the last dress had been shown, amid a tumult of enthusiasm, and Mme Marguerite, Mme Bricard and I stood gazing at each other in the dressing room. We were none of us able to speak. Then Raymonde came to look for us, crying with joy, in order to propel us into the big *salon*, where we were greeted by a salvo of applause. As long as I live, whatever triumphs I win, nothing will ever exceed my feelings at that supreme moment.

Christian Dior, *Dior on Dior*, translated by Antonia Fraser, 1954

Was he mad, this man? Was he making fun of women? How, dressed in 'that thing', could they come and go, live or anything?

Coco Chanel, from Edmonde Charles-Roux,
Chanel and Her World, 1979

This brings me to 1947, the tolling of the bell, when the New Look, cleverly planned and magnificently financed, achieved the greatest din of publicity ever known, the shortest life of any fashion in history.

Elsa Schiaparelli, *Shocking Life*, 1954

To Lady Redesdale   7 rue Monsieur, VII
                                          20 October 1950

I've got a beautiful Dior dress, which is worn over a crinoline, I feel like a Victorian lady for the purposes of loo – very inconvenient! It's so plain however that I can wear it in the street & I see by the looks I get that, like *The Hut*, it is a smash hit. *'Tu ne te prives de rien'* [You certainly spoil yourself], a French friend remarked.

Nancy Mitford, *Love From Nancy: The Letters of Nancy Mitford*,
edited by Charlotte Mosley, 1993

Jean, rather superb in what was called the 'New Look' (another recent phrase), was dressed in a manner to which hardly any woman in this country, unless she possessed unusually powerful tentacles, could at that time aspire. She greeted us at the door. That she had become so fashionable had to be attributed, one supposed, to her husband. In the old days much of her charm – so it had seemed – had been to look like a well-turned-out schoolgirl, rather than an enchantress on the cover of a fashion magazine. The slight, inexpressibly slight, foreign intonation she had now acquired, or affected, went well with the splendours of *haute couture*.

Anthony Powell, *Books Do Furnish a Room*, 1971

Oh, but violets. You should have seen Balenciaga's violets. He was the greatest dressmaker who ever lived. Those were the days when people dressed for dinner, and I mean dressed – not just changed their clothes. If a woman came in in a Balenciaga dress, no other woman in the room existed.

He wasn't interested in youth. He didn't care a bit about bones or anything to do with what we admire today. Oh, those collections! They were the most thrilling things! We'd stand in the corner of the salon if we couldn't get a chair to see his collections. You've never seen such colors – you've never seen such violets! My God, pink violets, blue violets! Suddenly you were in a nunnery, you were in a monastery.

Nobody else compared to him.

His voice was very low, and often you had to concentrate to hear it. His first name was Cristobal. His inspiration came from the bullrings, the flamenco dancers, the loose blouses the fishermen wear, the cool of the cloisters . . . and he took these moods and colors and, adapting them to his own tastes, literally dressed those who cared about such things for *thirty* years. He loved the coquetry of lace and ribbon, and yet he believed totally in the dignity of women. Balenciaga often said that women did not have to be perfect or beautiful to wear his clothes. When they wore his clothes, they became beautiful.

One never knew what one was going to see at a Balenciaga opening. One fainted. It was possible to blow up and die. I remember at one show in the early sixties – one put on for clients rather than for commercial buyers – Audrey Hepburn turned to me and asked why I wasn't frothing at the mouth at what I was seeing. I told her I was trying to act calm and detached because, after all, I was a member of the press. Across the way Gloria Guinness was sliding out of her chair on to the floor. Everyone was going up in foam and thunder. We didn't know what we were *doing*, it was so glorious. Well, what was going on was that Balenciaga was introducing the maillot for the first time. A maillot is like a body stocking, closed at the neck, ankle, and wrist. At this show it was a nude color, half-gold and pink, and over it was a tent of chiffon surrounding the model, the girl. It was *incredibly* beautiful. And don't forget, Balenciaga didn't use long-legged models – he used rather short-limbed, plump models, because he liked Spanish women. It was the most exciting garment I've ever seen. It was a dream. And do you know, I tried to get it for my Balenciaga show at the Met and no one could even remember it – how like a dream it had passed!

And then one day Balenciaga just closed his doors. He never even told Bunny Mellon, who of course was his greatest client . . . I suppose she had the greatest collection of Balenciagas in the world.

I was staying with Mona Bismark in Capri when the news came. I was downstairs, dressed for dinner, having a drink. Consuelo Crespi telephoned me from Rome, saying it had just come over the radio that Balenciaga had closed his doors for ever that afternoon, and that he'd never open them again. Mona didn't come out of her room for three days. I mean, she went into a complete . . . I mean, it was the end of a certain part of her *life*!

Diana Vreeland, *D. V.*, 1984

Frederica comes back wearing the dress. In its honour she has put on black tights and carefully dressed her hair in a chignon. She is beautiful. Frederica is never beautiful, though often alive with attractive energy, but just for the moment, in the Courrèges dress, she is wholly beautiful, it is the word. The dress fits almost too perfectly: her small high breasts sit neat and elegant inside its beautiful seams; her thin wrists, her narrow waist, her long thin hips, are beautiful where the silk-lined cloth skims past them, making them look like necessary forms in relation to each other. It is a strange style, formal, tailored, severe, ending so far above the knee that the brevity of the skirt should be childish, a gym-slip, a dolly-dress, but it is not. Frederica's long thin legs are set off by it; another inch on her thighs would spoil its up and down simple complexity.

A. S. Byatt, *Babel Tower*, 1996

1965

Edie [Sedgewick] was wearing a pink Rudi Gernreich floor-length T-shirt dress made out of stretchy Lurex-type material. It had elastic sleeves that were supposed to stay rolled up but she unrolled one of them about twelve feet past her arm – perfect for this set-up, because she could have a drink in one hand and be draping and dipping and dangling her sleeve over the heads of the crowd below.

1966

Tiger [Morse] designed that famous dress that said 'Love' on the front and 'Hate' on the back. And she did dresses that lit up on the dance floor, only there would always be some problem with the technology – the lights wouldn't work or the batteries would be dead, etc. Women used to have old-fashioned problems like slips hanging and bra straps showing, but now there was this whole new slew of problems. I've heard people say, 'Tiger Morse was a fraud.' Well, of course she was, but she was a real fraud. She'd make up more stories about herself for the newspapers than I did. Nobody knew where she came from, really, but who cared. She was an original, and she showed a lot of people how to have fun.

Andy Warhol and Pat Hackett, *POPism: The Warhol '60s*, 1981

Paris, 28 July 1983: Tired, tired. A heat wave. Chanel show later on in the Beaux Arts School. James talked to his stuffed dog for an hour this morning. Mlle Marie, from Kids Service (an extravagantly expensive babysitting service), says he's advanced for his age.

M. Alexandre stops his teaching and drops his comb, scurrying off to usher Jerry Hall to someone else's comfortable seat. She has arrived as colorfully made up as a full crayon box, accompanied by her baby daughter and the nurse. The more the merrier. The master begins, he's been saving himself, assisted by three apprentices, a quarter of the blondy locks each. The four of them back up about a yard, brushing the golden wheatfield to its horizontal length. The only space left in the room is underneath Jerry's hair.

I remember when she started and watching her rise, inventing compliments for everyone along her path paved with men and dresses, including me. Once we ended up next to each other during a Valentino show bis, bowing, crouching, taking porcelain figure positions on full-skirted ball gowns straight out of *War and Peace*. She lifted up her skirt and fluffed it out on both sides, thus crushing and covering mine. My blood rose. I was hurt. She'd told me I looked like Vanessa Redgrave. I fluffed my skirt over hers. And she fluffed her skirt over mine. And I fluffed my skirt over hers. She finally backed down. I would have gone on for ever. She started it.

First time out I'm taken aback by the spectacle of two thousand white invitation cards silently fanning their holders beneath a high vaulted ceiling covered in priceless frescoes. A crowded tropical fish bowl. I swim shyly down the podium.

All those multi-colored sequined embroidered jackets, hundreds of hours of work each, the price of a big house, wrenched off with less ceremony than a boxer peeling off his T-shirt after training, soaked with sweat, then stampeded, by my feet or someone's running past, undressing, re-dressing, like a speeded up film ran backwards, forward, backwards, forward . . .

I was often applauded, especially in the pink high-tea-with-the-Queen number. Painless, even gratifying, for my first *haute couture* show in over a year.

Ines had said to me, sauntering in just in time to put on her first dress (she enters and exits on the right side of the podium; plebeians on the left):

'You see? I told you you would do Chanel.' She had told me nothing. We hadn't spoken in months.

'Maybe it's because of you?' I queried.

'No darling, it's because of *you*!'

'Thanks, darling.' I'd wondered why Karl Lagerfeld had suddenly decided to exhume my remains after years of hasty greetings at parties. Soon-to-be-Queen Coco had used the old influence, in yet another act of exemplary behavior, thus saving her over-the-hill friend's pride with a magnanimous reassurance of her ever constant and eternal worth.

Susan Moncur, *They Still Shoot Models My Age*, 1991

Male designers rarely create clothes that give priority to the feeling of wearing them, rather than to their visual impact; they prefer to dress a woman in a striking way, no matter how uncomfortable or inappropriate she may feel. Female designers, by contrast, tend to construct clothes on their own bodies, and are consequently alert to the sensuality and freedom of movement achieved by their craft. In some cases the sensation of wearing the garment overrides the aesthetic impact. The Japanese conceptual designer Rei Kawakubo of Comme des Garçons, for example, is so insistent that customers feel comfortable in her clothes that at first she refused to hang mirrors in her shops; this uncommercial but altruistic experiment failed. The British designer Jean Muir was dedicated to the manner in which clothes enhanced a woman's sense of self-confidence; physical freedom was never subordinated to visual effect. Vivienne took this sensual preoccupation of women designers and inverted it. Her abiding design signature became the physical restriction of a woman's body. This, she calculated, would arouse the wearer's sense of sexuality and theatricality.

Jane Mulvagh, *Vivienne Westwood: An Unfashionable Life*, 1998

The vintage Kawakubo years were 1982 and '83. Conventions were overthrown or remodelled with irony. In Paris, models stormed the catwalks wrapped and twisted in layers of fabric, silhouettes exaggerated almost to the point of caricature. Ripped and torn, pallid and vaguely bruised, they looked like the last stragglers from the Foreign Legion. The sinister overtones were magnified when flashes of lightning illuminated the catwalk. There were sweaters that were all sleeve, bound Medusa-like about the body. Others that looked like the aftermath of a moths' Last Supper were in fact realized by industrial sabotage typical of Kawakubo's irreverent approach. 'The machines that are making fabrics are more and more making uniform, flawless textures. I like it when something is off – not perfect. Hand weaving is the best way to achieve this. Since that isn't always possible we loosen a screw of the machines here and there so they can't do exactly what they're supposed to do.'

It was relentless and aggressive. It didn't particularly function as clothing. The 'confrontational' dressing of Vivienne Westwood was raised to the level of the exquisite. The glossy idealization of high fashion had its magnetic poles in a twist.

'What I do is not influenced by what has happened in fashion or culture. I work from obscure abstract images to create a fresh concept of beauty' [says Kawakubo].

Comme des Garçons seemed to lock into a certain consumer level. It was designer but it went beyond the label syndrome. It retained a subversive undercurrent, it demanded independence – a certain discipline. When, just a few seasons back, Kawakubo fused the monochrome aggression with a sweetly cloying collection, more body-conscious and in cocktail pastels, the devotees erupted in howls of betrayal.

Kawakubo denies any political message in her work. When she hears such howls, she is liable to retreat into a shell. 'I am not an artist. I make clothes.'

The fashion market in Japan throws the different readings of her clothes between East and West into perspective. Outside Japan Comme sold a minimal $5 million last year, a sum that can hardly keep afloat the substantial chain of boutiques established to promote the image abroad . . . In Japan, meanwhile, Comme's turnover was $39m last year. As in Teenage Britain, so in Japan, style is a prime language, but there the parallel ends. The kind of affluence Japanese youth enjoy today vanished in the UK with the sixties.

Jane Withers, 'Black the Zero Option: Rei Kawakubo', *The Face*, 1987

Chanel clothes are designed by the German Karl Lagerfeld, a man of protean talents who holds a dominant position in international fashion. As the models skip down the runway in revealing chiffon skirts, little-girl straw hats and a plethora of extraneous jewels and accessories, I think of how Coco Chanel would have despised this tasteless display. It is ironic that, forced to flee into exile after the Second World War because she had openly been the mistress of a high-ranking German officer, Chanel should now have her memory torn apart by another German who, like a modern storm-trooper, has jack-booted his way through her philosophy of how women should appear in the twentieth century. As the show piles excess on excess, it is hard to recall that this is the house founded on a belief that clothes should never degenerate into fancy dress.

'Clothes must be logical,' the ghost of Coco Chanel moans in despair above the raucous music and loud cheers from an audience which is looking for bread and circuses, not fashion.

Colin McDowell, *Dressed to Kill: Sex, Power and Clothes*, 1992

Rudolf Nureyev and Jack Lang, the Minister for Culture, were there; so were Danielle Mitterand, Ines de la Fressange, Paloma Picasso, one or two Rothschilds and some of the most enduring style icons of our times. Altogether, 2,800 guests were invited to L'Opéra-Bastille in Paris this month to celebrate the thirtieth anniversary in business of Yves Saint Laurent, the divine light of French fashion.

The designer himself arrived with the president of YSL, his old friend Pierre Bergé, and clutched the hand of his guest of honour, Catherine Deneuve, dressed – of course – in Saint Laurent. As banks of flashbulbs detonated around them, he looked happy and well. And as he settled back to watch an army of models, looking like toy soldiers, march along the cavernous stage in vintage Saint Laurent outfits, there was a collective sigh of relief . . .

To imagine what life without Saint Laurent means, consider the extent to which France reveres its cultural monuments. At forty-eight, Deneuve remains its biggest film star; Johnny Halliday, who would have been tossed on the scrapheap of pop aberrations years ago in Britain, and his ex-wife Sylvie Vartan, also retain immensely loyal followings.

And Saint Laurent is special. He dressed women in trapeze shapes in the fifties, blazers and men's smoking jackets in the sixties, and took risks by turning working-class uniforms such as the parka and the pea-coat into couture. A decade later he dreamt up ethnic prints and put shoulder padding back into jackets. He always did it first, and he always did it elegantly.

By the seventies, there was no other designer. Manolo Blahnik, the shoe designer, remembers visiting the headquarters. 'It was a hothouse, with *the* most glamorous women dashing in and out. And the shows were like religious experiences. It was really a case of see Saint Laurent and die!' Bianca Jagger, high priestess of seventies' chic, wore white Saint Laurent when she married Mick in 1971; Lauren Bacall announced that 'when it's pants, it's YSL'; and every middle-class girl in France, Britain and America wanted a bottle of YSL Rive Gauche.

The French smothered him with admiration almost from the start. The former *Harper's & Queen* writer Meredith Etherington-Smith believes it was 'partly because he began his career at that other great French institution, the house of Christian Dior. He commands their affections in a way Karl Lagerfeld, as a German and also as one of fashion's great mercenaries, never could. Saint Laurent is quite simply their national treasure.'

The French press has been kind in its reactions to his most recent collections, which most observers privately agree have been lacklustre. Fashion is worth £11.5 billion annually in France, and as Janie Samet, fashion editor of *Le Figaro*, says: 'In France it is not our job to criticize. These houses employ hundreds of people – thousands indirectly.' Bergé is fond of declaiming: 'There is no successor to Yves. When he goes we will close down the house.' YSL staff have refused to countenance the possibility that they might one day have to produce an heir to Saint Laurent . . .

A devotee of Proust, Saint Laurent often escapes into reams of self-penned prose exposing his misery, his past addictions to cocaine and alcohol, and his neuroses about losing his position as the Sun King of fashion. Back from his mental abyss of two years ago, when for the first time he was forced to miss one of his own shows because of 'overwhelming nervous exhaustion', he recently told *Elle*: 'Once I was suffering so much that I considered attaching the heaviest bronze from my collection around my neck and throwing myself into the Seine.' . . .

The man who counted Andy Warhol and Françoise Sagan among his friends, who partied through the seventies and once posed naked in an advertisement for his first men's perfume, never goes out to restaurants or the cinema these days. 'He lives in a world of Matisses and Picassos,' says [Andre Leon] Talley. 'He depends a great deal on his muses – Catherine [Deneuve], Loulou [de la Falaise] and Betty Tatroux, and Loulou's niece, Lucie. He's rarely shown the negative press.'

That may be, but last month Saint Laurent told *Le Monde* that he considered Chanel, 'Where they drape chains and leather thongs over everything, to be the depths of bad taste.' [John] Fairchild [publisher and editor of *Women's Wear Daily*] thinks Saint Laurent isn't quite the innocent others believe. 'He knows he doesn't influence in the way he used to ... Heaven knows, he berates all the other designers enough. But his attitude is that fashion has gone the wrong way and he won't change.'

Funnily enough, the winds of fashion are starting to blow his way again: mannish trouser suits are back, and so are the forties-inspired looks that Saint Laurent did to perfection two decades ago. But whether he can become truly influential again is questionable.

Bergé for one seems resigned to contemplating life without Yves. A few weeks ago he launched a YSL skin-care range which is marketed on Deneuve's cachet as much, if not more, than Saint Laurent's (he was not present at the launch, but she was). And Bergé finally has a new protégé, Robert Merlioz, whom he tried out on the fur collection and is now promoting to a new line. John Fairchild notes: 'When he says he'll close down the house, that's just Bergé using words. We are talking a multi-million-dollar business. There are shareholders to consider. It's Bergé's responsibility to ensure the name continues. But it won't be easy.'

The skill of Saint Laurent and Bergé has been to build a huge empire while retaining its mystique. Without Saint Laurent the empire will still grow, but the mystique may evaporate. No wonder the thirtieth anniversary celebrations sometimes look less like a semi-colon and more like a full stop, and the arias sometimes sound like dirges.

Lisa Armstrong, 'All About Yves', Independent, 1992

A look of inexpressible weariness crosses the fine features of Comte Hubert de Givenchy when he hears the words 'fashion today'. 'I think,' he says, with a sad little laugh, 'that it is a total disaster. It's neither elegant nor new; it means nothing. It is not wearable.'

If the grand old Paris dressmaker and confidante to Audrey Hepburn, Jackie Kennedy and other young lovelies of yesteryear speaks with feeling, he has good reason. His is not simply the nostalgia of a supplanted generation, but the sadness of a seventy-year-old man who has lived to see the traditional skills he cherished slashed into shreds on the workroom floor where once he ruled supreme.

Since Givenchy bowed out of his stucco premises on the Avenue George V in 1995, kissing his sixty seamstresses farewell with tears in his eyes, the barbarians – he calls them simply 'these young people' – have stormed the gates.

'These young people, with their weird ideas, they think they know everything. They think they are geniuses,' he murmurs, more in sorrow than in anger. 'Well, it's great to think you are a genius. But before being a genius, you must be a real couturier; you have to work a lot, you have to see what other people have done and reach an understanding of what couture is. Some of the young designers straight out of England, they just don't have enough experience.'

Givenchy strives gallantly to keep his comments general, but two individuals slip out past his guard: 'Galliano, OK, he's not especially young, but McQueen is.'

It is no coincidence that John Galliano and Alexander McQueen are his first and second successors at the helm of Givenchy – but the distinction Givenchy makes between them is important. Galliano has a reputation for designing inspired yet wearable clothes, whereas McQueen . . . Givenchy's eyes roll at the name alone.

Gone is the cult of the perfect pleat or underarm seam, to be replaced by the *fin-de-siècle* shock-art of torn black leather and bottom-skimming skirts. Gone, too, are the grand customers: Princess Grace, the Countess von Bismarck, the Empress of Iran, the Duchess of Windsor . . .

What, I ask Givenchy, has changed between his day and McQueen's? 'The whole epoch is different. I have old clients who tell me they still wear the suits I made them decades ago. They are very troubled now, though it is true they can go to Yves Saint Laurent or to other places, where they try to make women feel well dressed, elegant.

'These days, what I see is neither elegant nor even new. It's just disconcerting. Shows where the models are half naked? Well, making a spectacle of nudity is always amusing, though not necessarily in such a huge quantity. But you are dealing here with an industry that's not just there to crack gags, amuse, stage spectacular shows that are utterly mad and meaningless.'

Mental images dance before me of Beatrice Dalle – McQueen's centrepiece model for last year's collection – leaning sulkily on a lamp-post in microscopic leather and spike heels, like a Pigalle tart. Anything further from Hepburn in *Breakfast at Tiffany's*, immaculate in pearls and Givenchy black, would be hard to imagine.

'Couture dresses have to be expensive, because it is necessary for each garment to be absolutely impeccable,' Givenchy continues, turning his hands as if examining some invisible seam. 'The hidden bits inside have to be every bit as perfect as the externals. To sell a dress at that kind of price and make it badly – well, that's dishonest. It's dishonest to sell something which you can wear only once or in a very limited way. And making dresses which are unsellable, or at least unwearable, what good is that? It is the road to destruction. To want to make things which are simply fantasy is disastrous, because it is not a representative image of good taste in France.' . . .

Givenchy's real gripe, though, is that his successors lack reverence for the art and detailed architecture of creation – and for women. 'The modern couturier immediately thinks he's a great *monsieur* and that he can do whatever he likes. He doesn't think how a woman is going to dress and live with what he makes.'

In Givenchy's heyday, when the Duchess of Windsor called him in tears begging him to dash off a black ensemble for her husband's funeral, or when Princess Grace needed a pretty frock for her infant daughter, Caroline, the customer was queen. The idea pleases him, not simply for snobbish reasons, but because he continues to cherish the complicity between creator and creation. And, in a way, his clients were his creations, relying on his taste to guide them past the traps that lurk in the world of enormous wealth . . .

'I would have liked to die with my scissors in my hand in my own studio. It is the dream of every artist. I would have liked to go on making dresses – I love making dresses. But not . . .' he gives that sad little laugh again, 'not in those conditions. Not in this epoch.'

Susannah Herbert, When I See Fashion Now,

I Suffer, *Daily Telegraph*, 1998

The show's at Bryant's Park even though it was supposed to be in an abandoned synagogue on Norfolk Street but Todd freaked when he heard it was haunted by the ghosts of two feuding rabbis and a giant floating knish and as I roll up to the back entrance – 42nd Street jammed with TV vans and satellite dishes and limousines and black sedans – photographers have already lined up, calling out my name as I flash my pass at the security guards. Behind barricades groups of teenagers shout out for Madonna even though she's not expected to show because she's too busy facing down her latest stalker in court but Guy from Maverick Records promised to appear and Elsa Klensch and a CNN camera crew are interviewing FIT students about their favorite designers and just an hour ago the runway was shortened because of the supposed overflow of five hundred and there was a desperate need to add room for the three hundred standees. Video monitors have been set up outside for the overflow's overflow. The show cost $350,000 to put on so everyone needs to see it.

Backstage pre-show is a blur of clothes racks and taped instruction sheets and Polaroids of outfits and tables of wigs along with a lot of fierce airkissing and hundreds of cigarettes being lit and naked girls running around and basically no one really paying attention. A huge poster overlooking the scene screams 'WORK IT' in giant black letters, the sound track from *Kids* plays at an excruciating decibel level. Rumors abound that two models are missing, either running late from another show or being abused by their scummy new boyfriends in a limo stalled in traffic somewhere on Lexington but no one really knows.

'The buzzword today is *tardy*, no?' Paull, the director of the show, bitches direly at me. 'I don't think so.'

'As if,' I Alicia-Silverstone-in-Clueless back at him.

'OK – five minutes to first looks,' calls out Kevin, the producer from Hastings, Minnesota.

Todd runs around frantically, managing to somehow calm shaking, frightened, wiped-out models with just a kiss. I'm kissing a heavily eye-shadowed Chloe, who is surrounded by clothes hanging from racks and looking exactly like someone should look who has been shooting a Japanese soda-pop commercial for most of the day, but I tell her she looks like a 'total doll' and she does. She complains about blisters and the brown-paper pedicure sandals on her feet while Kevyn Aucoin, wearing a clear-plastic tool belt and an orange ruffled Gaultier body shirt, powders her cleavage and glosses her lips. Orlando Pita has done the girls' hair and we're all definitely opting for semi-understatement here and pearly cream-pink eye shadow, upper lids done, lower rims just about. Someone rubs a fake tattoo of Snappy the Shark on my left pectoral while I smoke a cigarette then eat a couple of Twizzlers that I wash down with a Snapple an assistant hands me while someone inspects my belly button, vaguely impressed, and someone else camcords the event – another modern moment completed.

Modeling Todd's new seventies-influenced punk/New Wave/ Asia-meets-East-Village line are Kate Moss paired with Marky Mark, David Boals with Bernadette Peters, Jason Priestley with Anjanette, Adam Clayton with Naomi Campbell, Kyle MacLachlan with Linda Evangelista, Christian Slater with Christy Turlington, a recently slimmed-down Simon Le Bon with Yasmin Le Bon, Kirsty Hume with Donovan Leitch, plus a mix of new models – Shalom Harlow (pared with Baxter fucking Priestly), Stella Tennant, Amber Valletta – and some older ones including Chloe, Kristin McMenamy, Beverly Peele, Patricia Hartman, Eva Herzigova, along with the prerequisite male models: Scott Benoit, Rick Dean, Craig Palmer, Markus Schenkenberg, Nikitas, Tyson. There will be one hundred eighty costume changes. My first walk: black swimsuit and black T-shirt. Second walk: bare-chested. Third walk: pair of slacks and a tank top. Fourth walk: bikini briefs and a tank top. But everyone will probably be gazing at Chloe, so in a way it's all kind of mooty. Todd recites his pre-show instructions: 'Big smiles and be proud of who you are.'

On the first walk Chloe and I head toward a multitude of long zoom lenses that go nuts when we approach. Under the TV floodlights models glide by each other, each foot swinging effortlessly around the other. Chloe's hips are swaying, her ass is twisting, a perfect pirouette at the runway's end, both our stares unflinching, full of just the right kind of attitude. In the audience I'm able to spot Anna Wintour, Carrie Donovan, Holly Brubach, Catherine Deneuve, Faye Dunaway, Barry Diller, David Geffen, Ian Shrager, Peter Gallagher, Wim Wenders, Andre Leon Talley, Brad Pitt, Polly Mellon, Kal Ruttstein, Katia Sassoon, Carrie Otis, RuPaul, Fran Lebowitz, Winona Ryder (who doesn't applaud as we walk by), René Russo, Sylvester Stallone, Patrick McCarthy, Sharon Stone, James Truman, Fern Mallis. Music selections include Sonic Youth, Cypress Hill, Go-Go's, Stone Temple Pilots, Swing Out Sister, Dionne Warwick, Psychic TV and Wu-Tan Clan. After the final walk with Chloe I back off slightly and Todd grabs her by the waist and they both bow and then she pulls away and applauds him and I have to resist the impulse to stand back next to her and then everyone jumps on to the runway and follows everyone else backstage to Will Regan's after-show party.

Backstage: Entertainment Tonight, MTV News, A. J. Hammer from VH-1, 'The McLaughlin Group', 'Fashion File' and dozens of other TV crews push through the tents, which are so clogged no one can really move, overhead microphones towering over the crowd on long poles. It's freezing backstage even with all the lights from the video crews, and huge clouds of second-hand smoke are billowing over the crowd. A long table is covered with white roses and Sky Martinis and bottles of Moët and shrimp and cheese straws and hot dogs and bowls of jumbo strawberries. Old B-52 records blare, followed by Happy Mondays and then Pet Shop Boys, and Boris Beynet and Mickey Hardt are dancing. Hairstylists, make-up artists, mid-level transvestites, department store presidents, florists, buyers from London or Asia or Europe, are all running around, being chased by Susan Sarandon's kids. Spike Lee shows up along with Julian Schnabel, Yasmeen Ghauri Nadege, LL Cool J, Isabella Rossellini and Richard Tyler.

I'm trying to meet the vice-president of casting and talent at Sony but too many retailers and armies of associates and various editors with what seems like hundreds of cameras and microphones hunched over them keep pushing through the tents, relegating me to the boyfriends-and-male-models-sitting-around-slack-jawed   corner, some of them already lacing up their Rollerblades, but then I'm introduced to Blaine Trump's cook, Deke Haylon, by David Arquette and Billy Baldwin. A small enclave consisting of Michael Gross, Linda Wachner, Douglas Keeve, Oribe and Jeanne Beker is talking about wanting to go to the club's opening tonight but everyone's weighing the consequences of skipping *Vogue*'s dinner. I bum a Marlboro from Drew Barrymore.

Bret Easton Ellis, Glamorama, 1999

4. 'The British, alas, hate fashion'*: British Style

*Quoted in Anne Scott-James, *In the Mink*, 1952

Nearer our own time two English duchesses were turned away from Christian Dior. The people at the entrance considered them too dowdy to be admitted. In England if you are a duchess you don't need to be well dressed – it would be thought quite eccentric.

Nancy Mitford, 'Chic – English, French and American',
Atlantic Monthly, 1951

'I say, Titmuss. I say old boy,' Kempenflatt shouted as he approached. 'Who's your tailor?'

John Mortimer, *Paradise Postponed*, 1985

The themes of class and rebellion run through British dress. For the non-English reader or observer, Britain is a country dominated by the London season, Ascot, Henley, hunting and shooting. This kind of Britishness is reflected in the style of the English gentleman, described by P. G. Wodehouse, Evelyn Waugh and latterly by William Boyd – a classic look, worn by one generation of men to another – and the style of the English 'thoroughbred' woman described by Cecil Beaton, Evelyn Waugh and Elizabeth Bowen and epitomized both by Lady Diana Cooper and the late Princess of Wales. For other observers, Britain is the home of oddity and eccentricity, as illustrated by Ronald Firbank in his short stories and Wyndham Lewis in *The Apes of God*, and this kind of Britishness has also been reflected in dress.

For much of the century, British women have been regarded as badly dressed in comparison with their French counterparts, preferring decoration to severity of cut. However, though women have been denigrated for not being chic, there have been women who have epitomized the 'eccentric' element of British style and run richly through real life and literature – such as Lady Ottoline Morrell in *Women in Love*, depicted as Hermione Roddice by D. H. Lawrence 'in a dress of stiff old greenish brocade', and Edith Sitwell, described by Cecil Beaton as a 'tall graceful scarecrow' – and who might now be described as style leaders, constructing their own images just as Elfine dresses in a parody of Arts and Crafts style in Stella Gibbons' *Cold Comfort Farm*. This recreation of the self into something extraordinary is a significant element of British style, and can be seen today in the person of promoter of young designers and stylist Isabella Blow.

In this chapter some writers criticize British women's lack of fashion sense – Anne Scott-James and Nancy Mitford in particular; the latter notes the chintz New Look of England that horrified M. Dior. Mentioning designers' names, as in Bill Naughton's *Alfie*, in which Ruby displays invitations to Paquin, Worth and Hartnell, suggests one's class and aspirations. Clothes and the way they are worn by characters illustrate the wearers' place in the British caste system. In *Vile Bodies*, Evelyn Waugh describes as typical of aristocratic style the dress of the eldest daughter of the Duchess of Stayle, dressed in a garment 'enriched with old lace at improbable places'. Paul Pennyfeather's error in Waugh's *Decline and Fall* is to have his old school tie mistaken for that of another; and that ties denote social backround is described by the Duke of Windsor and Joe Orton. Others who acknowledge the British class system in terms of dress include George Orwell in his remark on Old Etonian Marxists who keep the bottom waistcoat button undone (a traditional mark of the gentleman); John Mortimer in his excruciating account in *Paradise Postponed* of wearing hired black tie at a 1950s ball;

E. M. Forster in his calling European costume in India 'leprosy'.

'British style' was not confined to the upper classes. Recalling the 1930s and time spent in a pub in Wapping, Elsa Schiaparelli noted that the 'simplicity and inventiveness of what used to be called in England the "lower working classes" was inspiring.'[1] Her comment was deeply perceptive, for by the 1950s' working-class youths were inventing themselves as fashion leaders for the first time: Teds in bootlace ties and mods in Italian bum-freezer jackets, and, as Nancy Mitford observes, even Etonians turned Ted. The 'British look' of the 1960s was an amalgam of youth from different backgrounds challenging almost every traditional sartorial rule, following the lead of pop groups, all made accessible by television, and purchasable at men's boutiques like His Clothes in Carnaby Street or Hung on You in the King's Road, also the home of Mary Quant's shop Bazaar. Quant overturned the Englishness of chintz and a twin-set and pearls by wearing and promoting the mini-skirt. Another kind of 'Britishness' was that of Mick Jagger and Nicky Haslam, who flouted convention in lace, black leather and Anello and Davide boots, as Andy Warhol recalls.

Despite such extremes of British style, at the end of the century the British 'thoroughbred' stereotype holds true, captured in the images of the late Princess of Wales, post Sloane-Ranger, in figure-hugging Versace and Galliano, and Isabella Blow romping in the ancestral grounds for *Vanity Fair*. In the case of the latter, her role as designer-detector and promoter continues to be of value, not only in providing the substance for media stories, such as the satirization of her in the *Guardian*, but also in identifying new designers to fuel the legend of British fashion.

That wonderful creature's eyes moreover readily met them – she ranked now as a wonderful creature; and it seemed a part of the swift prosperity of the American visitors that, so little in the original reckoning, she should yet appear conscious, charmingly, frankly, conscious, of possibilities of friendship for them. Milly had easily and, as a guest, gracefully generalized: English girls had a special, strong beauty, and it particularly showed in evening dress – above all when, as was strikingly the case with this one, the dress itself was what it should be.

Henry James, *The Wings of the Dove*, 1902

Chic is inimitable, so we have been told by fashion writers. But I am not so sure that they are entirely right, for some of us have acquired it without being born with it. Very few Englishwomen, in fact, possess this quality as a birthright. They may boast of their style, but their style differs from chic as widely as the scent of patchouli from the aroma of old rose leaves. Chic, indeed, is that subtle and indefinable air of good taste that only the best bred can attain to. It is a quality so impalpable and subtle that the ordinary British woman neither understands nor desires it. But she makes the greatest mistake, for with chic the ugliest woman can be made not only presentable but irresistible, while the professional beauty, with all her style, may be unattractive without chic.

Mrs E. Pritchard, *The Cult of Chiffon*, 1902

'In the afternoon [of 8 July 1900] Ella Pollock and I [Dorothy Gwynne] went to Bobo's [Violet Gordon Woodhouse's] room and she showed us some of her lovely clothes, what exquisite ones she has, her taste is wonderful . . . Bobo gave me such a lovely opera cloak of hers tonight, it is what I wanted more than anything, as my old blue one is hardly fit to wear and has got so shabby, and this came like an answer to a wish; it is a pale sort of heliotrope, long and has sleeves, it is much trimmed with chiffon and fits me fine, it is so nice to have a decent cloak, I like long cloaks infinitely better than capes. She first gave me a brocade cape, and then much to my joy she gave me this instead. She also gave me a little red dressing jacket, and a little bit of brown lace for a collar.

More than anything, Violet paid attention to her accessories – her gloves, belts and shoes, her velvet-lined hats rimmed in silk and banded in satins; and her parasols, some so finely embroidered that on dark backgrounds the patterns appeared like pale transfers. In summer, cream silk shades, stitched with blue – or red-flowered borders and a spray of coloured dots – opened from their slim bamboo shafts which had satin bows threaded through their handles, allowing a glimpse of a silk lining of the palest blue. There were other parasols for darker dresses – white appliqué lacework on black silk, or plain shot silk in blue and ochre – the shafts of ebony, the knobs and handles tipped with mother-of-pearl, silver, china or ivory. Instead of bows, silken tassels or plaited braids were threaded through the handles to fall gracefully down the wrist.

Jessica Douglas-Home, *Violet*, 1996

As regards the Fortuny gowns, we had at length decided upon one in blue and gold lined with pink which was just ready. And I had ordered, at the same time, the other five which she had relinquished with regret, in favour of this one. Yet with the coming of spring, two months after her aunt's conversation with me, I lost my temper with her one evening. It was the very evening on which Albertine had put on for the first time the indoor gown in blue and gold by Fortuny which, by reminding me of Venice, made me feel all the more strongly what I was sacrificing for her, who felt no corresponding gratitude towards me. If I had never seen Venice, I had dreamed of it incessantly since those Easter holidays which, when still a boy, I had been going to spend there, and earlier still, since the Titian prints and Giotto photographs which Swann had given me long ago at Combray. The Fortuny gown which Albertine was wearing that evening seemed to me the tempting phantom of that still invisible Venice. It was covered with Arabic ornamentation, like the Venetian palaces hidden like sultan's wives behind a screen of pierced stone, like the bindings in the Ambrosian Library, like the columns from which the oriental birds that symbolize alternatively life and death were repeated in the shimmering fabric, of an intense blue which, as my eyes drew nearer, turned into a malleable gold, by those same transmutations which, before an advancing gondola, change into gleaming metal the azure of the Grand Canal. And the sleeves were lined with a cherry pink which is so peculiarly Venetian that it is called Tiepolo pink.

Marcel Proust, *Remembrance of Things Past: The Guermantes Way II*, 1920

Fashion had come round to us. Gone were the buttoned boots, the curves, the boned collars, the straight-fronted stays, the hennaed hair and hairnets. We subscribed to a fashion paper called *L'Art et la Mode*, with drawings by a then little-known artist called Drian. It was everything my mother had always stood for – 'le vague' and lines of the body slinkily followed into the feet, loosely knotted hair, willowy and dependent, not armed for merciless conquest. I became an inspired dressmaker. A 'fit' was no longer necessary. I suppose I made a guy of myself, and soon worse was to come. Henry Bernstein came to Belvoir. He was, I suppose, young and very noble-looking. He smothered my mother in red roses, which we thought was a French custom. With him came Princess Murat, a fascinating surprise and totally different from anything we knew. She brought to us, Gentiles where fashion was concerned, the glad tidings of the rising star Poiret, an eccentricity, a new word and a new mania. She herself wore the first of those tanagra-esque garments, later sold by thousands (many to me over twenty years), made by Fortuni [sic] of Venice – timeless dresses of pure thin silk cut severely straight from shoulder to toe, and kept wrung like a skein of wool. In every crude and subtle colour, they clung like mermaid's scales. I think she must have had in her luggage a Poiret invention. It was a chiffon shirt worn in the evening over a skirt. It was cut like an Eastern djibbah and edged at hem and Eastern neckline with braid. I elaborated the design, even putting fur instead of braid, and made them by the dozen for friends and friends of friends. They cost me about fifteen shillings and I charged two guineas. I made over a hundred pounds, all of which I spent on books – editions de luxe and first editions, the Edinburgh Stevenson, Meredith, Wilde, Conrad and Maupassant. I owed a lot to Poiret and made him ridiculous, no doubt, by my base imitations.

Lady Diana Cooper, *The Rainbow Comes and Goes*, 1958

'Vere!' said Lady Dolly dreamily, at length, 'I am trying to think what one can do to get you decent clothes. My maid must run up something for you to wear by tomorrow. It is a pity to keep you shut up all this beautiful weather, and a little life will do you good after that prison at Bulmer. I am sure those three days I was last there I thought I should have yawned till I broke my neck, I did indeed, dear. She would hardly let me have breakfast in my own room, and she *would* dine at six! – six! But she was never like anybody else; when even the duke was alive she was the most obstinate, humdrum, nasty old scratch-cat in the county. Such ideas, too! She was a sort of Wesley in petticoats, and, by the way, her gowns were never long enough for her. But I was saying, dear, I will have Adrienne run up something for you directly. She is clever. I never let a maid *make* a dress. It is absurd. You might as well want Rubinstein to make the violin he plays on. If she is inferior, she will make you look a dowdy. If she is a really good maid she will not make, she will arrange, what your tailor has made, and perfect it – nothing more. But still, for you, Adrienne will go out of her way for once. She shall combine a few little things, and she can get a girl to sew them for her. Something to go out in they really must manage for tomorrow. You shall have brown holland if you are so fond of it, dear, but you shall see what brown holland can look like with Adrienne.

Ouida, Moths, 1919

7 March 1904
Davray gave me a new instance of politeness. At some English house a foreigner (nationality obscure, I forget, something small) wearing what looked like an overcoat. The hostess urged him to take it off; said it was the custom etc. He took it off, and appeared in his shirtsleeves. Consternation of the hostess, especially as other guests were expected. Presently Laurence Houseman came in and was advised privately of the situation. Houseman took off his coat, and sat down also in his shirtsleeves; then complained of the cold, and demanded from his hostess permission to resume his coat; the foreigner followed his example. '*C'était très fin*', commented Davray.

Arnold Bennett, The Journals of Arnold Bennett 1921–1928,
edited by Norman Fowler, 1933

At Oxford I was a bit of a dandy, wearing my hat at a rakish angle, tying my bow tie with care ... All my life, hitherto, I had been fretting against the constrictions of dress which reflected my family's world of rigid social convention. It was my impulse, whenever I found myself alone, to remove my coat, rip off my tie, loosen my collar and roll up my sleeves ... [later] I was 'produced' as a leader of fashion ... the middleman was the photographer ... employed by the trade ... with an especial eye for what I was wearing. A selection of these photographs, together with patterns [and] samples of ties, socks, waistcoats and so forth, was immediately rushed to America.

The Duke of Windsor, A Family Album, 1960

With her mass of chestnut hair falling on each side of her face, with her emphatic features, and wearing a yellow gown with a very wide skirt, she resembled a rather over-life-size infanta of Spain, and there was something, too, in her appearance that recalled the portraits of her remarkable ancestress Margaret, Duchess of Newcastle, the poet. I recall being amused when one night, oblivious, plainly, even of the name of the kind of theatre in which she now found herself, she gazed with an air of considerable disapprobation at one of the turns, and then sighed in her very individual voice, muffled but distinct for all that, 'Rather music hall, I'm afraid!' Though Lady Ottoline had been one of the earliest supporters of the ballet, when first it came to London, her personal distinction, her individual style, her way of looking, talking, thinking, her magnificent manner of dressing, her brocades and silks, as natural to her as tweeds to the owner of a fox terrier, made her seem as much out of place at Covent Garden as at the Coliseum.

Osbert Sitwell, *Laughter in the Next Room*, 1949

Hermione came down to dinner strange and sepulchral, her eyes heavy and full of sepulchral darkness, strength. She had put on a dress of stiff old greenish brocade, that fitted tight and made her look tall and rather terrible, ghastly. In the gay light of the drawing room she was uncanny and oppressive. But seated in the half-light of the dining room, sitting stiffly before the shaded candles on the table, she seemed like a power, a presence ... The party was gay and extravagant in appearance, everybody had put on evening dress except Birkin and Joshua Mattheson. The little Italian Contessa wore a dress of tissue, of orange and gold and black velvet in soft wide stripes, Gudrun was emerald green with strange network, Ursula was in yellow with dull silver veiling, Miss Bradley was of grey, crimson and jet, Fraulein Marz wore pale blue. It gave Hermione a sudden convulsive sensation of pleasure, to see these rich colours under the candlelight.

D. H. Lawrence, *Women in Love*, 1921

Glyn Philpot asked me to stay with him for it [Frank Schuster's fancy dress ball, Christmas 1918], which resulted in my being elaborately rigged-out as a Tartar prince in a gold turban. By the time he had finished I scarcely knew myself, for he insisted on painting two black curls and round pink spots on my cheeks and chin. Needless to say, this made me feel delightfully dissociated from my normal self. He himself was an Elizabethan Spaniard in black velvet. His face powdered dead white, white spur straps on long black boots, and large green gem rings on his fingers, he had transformed himself immeasurably away from the accomplished painter of Academy portraits. He had escaped into that imaginative environment for which he had a self-defensive predilection, and looked more suitable for a canvas in the Prado than for Schuster's elegant house in Old Queen Street, Westminster. There we found about thirty guests assembled, and soon afterwards I was sitting at the dinner table between Madame Vandervelde, the vivacious red-haired wife of the eminent Belgian politician-patriot, and a lady of no particular period who was plentifully adorned with tricolour ribbons and rosettes, from which I inferred that she impersonated La Belle France. This was Mrs Sturgis, Meredith's daughter, to whom Schuster had presented me in characteristically opulent style. (His introductions were always apt to be rather florid and effusive.) Next to her was 'Dodo' Benson, an Apache with a stubbly grey moustache. Opposite us, Lady Randolph as a Holbein Duchess in black velvet, was an appropriate partnership with Glyn Philpot. Our host was in ordinary evening clothes, over which he afterwards donned a hooded cloak. There were a good many young people, wearing the motley disguises of jesters, harlequins, pierrots, Dresden shepherdesses, and suchlike. In this atmosphere of masquerade it felt rather inept to be so eager to talk about the author of *Love in the Valley* and *The Ordeal of Richard Feverel.*

Siegfried Sassoon, *Siegfried's Journey*, 1945

On the night of my coming-out party in 1923 . . . was I calcimined that night! I was whiter than white. My dress was white, naturally. And then the reds were something. I had velvet slippers that were lacquer red. I carried red camellias . . . My mother disapproved. 'You should know,' she said, 'that red camellias are what the *demi-mondaines* of the nineteenth century carried when they had their periods and thus weren't available for their man. I don't think they're quite . . . suitable.'

I carried the camellias anyway. They were so beautiful. I had to assume that no one else at the party knew what my mother knew.

I doubt that my mother thought my dress was particularly suitable, either, but there was nothing she could do about it. It was copied from Poiret – white satin with a fringed skirt to give it *un peu de mouvement* and a pearl-and-diamond stomacher to hold the fringe back before it sprang. It looked like the South Sea Islands – like a hula skirt.

Diana Vreeland, *D. V.*, 1984

'It's positively pitiable,' the Duchess of Cavaljos commented, 'how the Countess of Tolga is losing her good looks; she has the air tonight of a tired businesswoman!'

'She looks at other women as though she would inhale them,' the Archduchess answered, throwing back her furs with a gesture of superb grace, in order to allow her robe to be admired by a lady who was scribbling busily away behind a door, with little nervous lifts of the head. For *noblesse oblige*, and the correspondent of the *Jaw-Waw*, the illustrious Eva Schnerb, was not to be denied.

'Among the many balls of a brilliant season,' the diarist, with her accustomed fluency wrote, 'none surpassed that which I witnessed at the English Embassy last night. I sat in a corner of the Winter Garden and literally gorged myself upon the display of dazzling uniforms and jewels. The Ambassadress Lady Something was looking really regal in dawn-white draperies, holding a bouquet of the new mauve malmaisons (which are all the vogue just now), but no one, I thought, looked better than the *Archduchess*, etc. . . . Helping the hostess, I noticed Mrs Harold Chilleywater, in an "aesthetic" gown of flame-hued Kanitra silk edged with Armousky fur (to possess a dear woolly Armousk as a pet is considered chic this season), while over her brain – an intellectual caprice, I wonder? – I saw a tinsel bow . . . She is a daughter of the fortieth Lord Seafairer of Sevenelms Park (so famous for its treasures) and is very artistic and literary, having written several novels of English life under her maiden name of Victoria Gelly-bore Frinton: she inherits considerable cleverness also from her mother. Dancing indefatigably (as she always does!), Miss Ivy Something seemed to be thoroughly enjoying her father's ball: I hear on excellent *authority* there is no foundation in the story of her engagement to a certain young Englishman, said to be bound ere long for the ruins of Sodom and Gomorrah. Among the late arrivals were the Duke and Duchess of Varna – *she* all in golden tissues: they came together with Madame Wetme, who is one of the new hostesses of the season, you know, and they say has brought the Duke of Varna's palatial town house in Samaden Square—'

'There,' the Archduchess murmured, drawing her wraps about her with a sneeze: 'She has said quite enough now I think about my *toilette!*'

Ronald Firbank, *The Flower Beneath the Foot*, 1923

If one is a greyhound, why try to look like a Pekingese? I am as stylized as it is possible to be – as stylized as the music of Debussy or Ravel.

Edith Sitwell, quoted in Victoria Glendinning, *Edith Sitwell:*
A Unicorn Among Lions, 1981

The carding was succeeded by the ritual of the construction of the bun. The bold wattlework was effected in swift-fingered in-and-out of human basket-making. The bun was completed. Twenty minutes had elapsed. Bridget now moved to the right-hand side of the vast chair, tongs in hand, in order to address herself to the manufacture of the curls.

As the curls were being laid down, beside each other, in stiffened cylinders, the eyes of her ladyship blazed. She began to pooh with a soft whistling pout. This was a nap upon which the solitary mason of this quick monument, so sharp-tongued a monolith, counted. Bridget put the finishing touches to the beldam, her mighty mistress, point by point, stepping about the passive purring skull that was her cult and old single-woman's bachelor passion.

Her ladyship awoke as the last touches ceased. She raised her head with slumberous majesty and she perceived that the curls were there. She was now at eye practice for a spell after the glooms of sleep. At present she moved her gums, upon which the teeth hung, in and out, preparatory to a dialogue.

'I think we will have the cap, now we will have the cap.'

The first uncertain whinny after the doze was thick.

'Milady.'

'The cap. The cap.'

'Yes your ladyship the cap is here. Will your ladyship have it?'

'Have it? Certainly. The cap.'

It was the cap, modelled upon that of Mrs Hennessey, of the finest reticella.

Lady Fredigonde lifted from her knees a hand mirror, her hand grasping it as a diver's flexible masked paw might mechanically seize some submarine object. She held it steadily before her and examined the curled but capless bust.

What a decadent emperor! Bridget crowned her with the cap. Gingerly held on high, she lowered it, breathing through her ears, down upon the crown of the head. The sea green of the hair, the formal surf of the cap, coalesced.

'A little more over the left eye: no a thought forward and up, forward and then up, over my left eye – my left one. You're not tall enough really are you to attend to me, you are too short by half a foot.'

The reticulated eaves were poked up from the green margin of hair by two forked fingers with their lustreless plates of copper skin.

'Dear me, my head one would say has grown: how very odd that would be if it were the case.'

She rocked her headpiece as if it had been a pumpkin and the surface of the vegetable's mother-earth had extended just beneath her chin.

'It's not so big as I thought. An alternative to my head having grown is I suppose that the cap may have shrunk in the wash.'

'Your ladyship will pardon me, I think it is the same as it was before.'

'Which? The cap or the head?'

'The cap, your ladyship.'

'I think you are mistaken, I should certainly say that it is a quarter of an inch out quite that – I am very familiar with this landscape garden.'

Wyndham Lewis, *The Apes of God*, 1930

27 August 1926

The journalists wanted to watch the dress rehearsal for the pageant [the Baroness D'Erlanger's costume ball, Venice]. An ungainly party, we trooped into the Princess's *palazzo*. Poor Mrs Whish looked her worst, hot and sticky in dusty black. There were screams when she appeared, and Mrs Robin d'Erlanger let fly at her in the most surprising manner. It seems that Mrs Whish was responsible for Mrs d'Erlanger's costume being lost. Mrs Whish looked thunderstruck. Messengers were sent off in every direction. We sat soddenly apart, ignored while the scarlet-haired Baroness plopped about on flat feet. By degrees, self-conscious young Frenchmen and Italians put in an appearance, dressed as Tritons in bright blue and green sequins. A press photographer waited about, eyeing me and my Kodak with suspicion.

Mrs Whish regained her journalistic ardour as soon as the lost costume was found. She gushed at a social lion who had no forehead or chin but impressively protruding teeth. He seemed brainless and quite forty-five! Mrs Whish said, 'Do let me introduce you to Mr Beaton. He wants to photograph you!'

The lion showed more of what was already showing. 'Oh well, I'm afraid . . .'

I thought, So should I be, if I'd got a face like yours!

Lady Wimborne appeared, wearing a crinoline of wheat sheaves embroidered in gold. She wagged her hips, pranced about, 'talking common', and shouted to the Duc de Verdura, ''allo, dearie.' Mrs Evelyn Fitzgerald glided in, wearing a poison-green sequinned crinoline. But the best was Princess Baba Lucigne, who really looked the part of 'Water' in a flowing armour made of hundreds of strips of tin and a *casquette* of florin-sized sequins.

The ball took place in the gilded La Fenice Theatre.

Mrs Settle was having difficulty with her borrowed fancy-dress skirt and train. Mrs Whish, wearing her inevitable black, looked like a Holbein creation. I felt self-conscious as a medieval page in stencilled tunic and tights.

Since the Crown Prince was expected, there could be no dancing before he arrived. A blatant band blared, while people wandered about aimlessly, growing tired of looking at one another. Some began to yawn.

At long last the Crown Prince took his place in the most royal royal box. He bowed formally from the hips and the pageant unfolded. The d'Erlanger 'elements' hobbled in, trashy as a *Folies Bergère* revue (but, of course, none of the group could do right for me!). Towards the end came Lady Cunard in a highly unsuitable Spinelly outfit of pink ostrich feathers and top hat to match. She looked surprised. Lady Diana Cooper was to have been part of a group of Porcelain Figures. But her prepared costume, a white mackintosh dress with mask, had to be abandoned: Italian etiquette forbids wearing a mask in front of royalty. Home she went, returning in a crinoline and Turkish turban. She looked furiously beautiful now, sitting in a box energetically picking her nose. Lady Abdy and an old Princess San Faustino were a study in dramatic contrast. Lady A., like a huge lioness with her mane of oatmeal-coloured hair, wore a black-and-white velvet dress. The bread-stick Princess looked a religious curio in her abbess's habit and wimple.

Cecil Beaton, *The Wandering Years*, 1961

Whilst in Paris Stephen went to a party given by Elsie Mendl at her Villa Trianon at Versailles. Here Lady Mendl — another of those seemingly interchangeable society interior decorators thrown up by the twenties' enthusiasm for the art — and her 'Bachelors' (her two female companions) reigned, in immaculate good taste, she with her gilded capes and clothes from the best Parisian designers, her hair dyed blue to match her poodles'. These were the last of the great parties, extravagant fêtes designed by Stephane Boudin. Stephen saw his hostess 'in chalk white Greek chiffon – gold cracker jewellery on her head, & a crinkled watered ravishing Schiaparelli cloak'.

Philip Hoare, *Serious Pleasures: A Life of Stephen Tennant*, 1990

1922

A short while after the contract for *The Young Idea* had been signed, I was invited by Lady Colefax to Oxford, where she had taken a house for a week, to entertain a party of young people for the Bullingdon dance. I knew her then only slightly, but we have been friends ever since . . .

There, beneath aged sycamores, were spread tea tables, cushions, wicker chairs, 'Curate's Comforts', and large bowls of strawberries and cream, the latter to be devoured by the returning game-players who were so much, much more suitably attired for the country than I. Their shirts and flannels were yellow and well used, against which mine seemed too newly white, too immaculately moulded from musical comedy. Their socks, thick and carelessly wrinkled round their ankles, so unlike mine of too thin silk, caught up by intricate suspenders.

Noël Coward, *Present Indicative*, 1937

The men were the flowers in these mysterious forests, sleek and orchidaceous in their hunt coats, the facings and collars pale, thin gold watch-chains crossing meagre stomachs, white ties as exact as two wings on a small bird's back, long legs black as cypripedium stems, hands sometimes gloved, eyes focused distantly, as if a fox stealing away from its covert was still the thought in mind. They would look over my shoulder and away, and they never listened to a word I said. If they spoke it was about the day's hunting.

There was something daring and men-only about that little party. Drenched in Richard's scent and wearing my older flowered crêpe de Chine, I felt very privileged to be there. I liked to watch the boys as they finished dressing. There was a quick, hard grace about their movements, in the way they put links quickly into the cuffs of evening shirts, such a different tempo from a girl's considered gesture. They wore narrow braces and their black trousers were taut round waists and bottoms. I seemed to join in the violent tact of hairbrushing – each hair into place and no nonsense. I felt easier, more part of them as the minutes passed. How dear they were. Spoilers of girls.

Molly Keane, *Good Behaviour*, 1981

Now it so happened that the tie of Paul's old school bore a marked resemblance to the pale blue and white of the Bollinger Club. The difference of a quarter of an inch in the width of the stripes was not one that Lumsden of Strathdrummond was likely to appreciate.

'Here's an awful man wearing the Boller tie,' said the Laird. It is not for nothing that since pre-Christian times his family has exercised chieftainship over unchartered miles of barren moorland.

Evelyn Waugh, *Decline and Fall*, 1928

'There is no time, sir, at which ties do not matter.'

P. G. Wodehouse, 'Jeeves and the Impending Doom',
from *Very Good, Jeeves!*, 1930

'. . . in the summer before I [Charles Ryder's father, speaking to him before he goes up to Oxford] was going up, your cousin Alfred rode over to Boughton especially to give me a piece of advice. And do you know what that advice was? "Ned," he said, "there's one thing I must beg of you. *Always* wear a tall hat on Sundays during term.

It is by that, more than anything else, that a man is judged." And do you know,' continued my father, snuffling deeply, 'I *always did?* Some men did, some didn't. I never saw any difference between them or heard it commented on, but I *always wore mine*. It only shows what effect judicious advice can have, properly delivered at the right moment. I wish I had some for you, but I haven't.'

My cousin Jasper made good the loss . . .

'Clothes. Dress as you do in a country house. Never wear a tweed coat and flannel trousers – always a suit. And do go to a London tailor; you get a better cut and longer credit . . .' I put more coal on the fire and turned on the light, revealing in their respectability his London-made plus fours and his Leander tie.

Evelyn Waugh, *Brideshead Revisited*, 1945

30 April 1926

But my mind is wandering. It is a question of clothes. This is what humiliates me – talking of compliments – to walk in Regent St, Bond Str etc: & be notably less well dressed than other people.

Virginia Woolf, *Diaries: Volume III 1925–1930*,
edited by Anne Olivier Bell, 1980

As a debutante, she [Unity Mitford] began to apply this talent to her selection of clothes. She shone like an enormous peacock in flashing sham jewels, bought at a theatrical costumers, and immense brocade evening dresses. To my mother's consternation, she bought a sham tiara, resplendent with rubies, emeralds and pearls, and insisted on wearing it to dances. She was generally out to shock – to '*épater les bourgeois*', as my mother disapprovingly put it – and in this she succeeded. Boud's dissatisfaction with life mirrored my own. I applauded her outrages, roared when she stole some writing paper from Buckingham Palace and wrote to all her friends on it, cheered when she took her pet rat to dances.

Jessica Mitford, *Hons and Rebels*, 1960

She went up to London and chose new clothes at a West End tailor's; the man in Malvern who had made for her father was getting old, she would have her suits made in London in future. She ordered herself a rakish red car; a long-bodied, sixty-horse-power Métallurgique. It was one of the fastest cars of its year, and it certainly cost her a great deal of money. She bought twelve pairs of gloves, some heavy silk stockings, a square sapphire scarf pin and a new umbrella. Nor could she resist the lure of pyjamas made of white crêpe de Chine which she spotted in Bond Street. The pyjamas led to a man's dressing gown of brocade – an amazingly ornate garment.

Radclyffe Hall, *The Well of Loneliness*, 1928

What is this curious object? But of course . . . it is a piece of monkey fur. This starts a whole train of memories. Very few women wear monkey fur today; in the twenties it was 'terribly smart'. I remember it on people like Baba Lucinge [Princess Faucigny-Lucinge], who was as thin as a rake, with antennae eyebrows and a face like a small, beautiful wasp. The Dolly Sisters used to wear a great deal of it too.

Fur fashions have altered radically. If you were rich, and if you had no aversion to advertising the fact, you wore sables, just as in the Edwardian days you would have worn ermine. (The ermine cloaks of the Edwardian ladies really were the most barbaric garments, fit only for savages, with all the tails of those nice little animals hanging round their necks like so many scalps. The day will come, one hopes, when a civilized woman will regard a coat made from the skins of animals with the same horror as she would regard a lampshade made from the skins of men, but that is not likely to be in my time.)

Beverly Nichols, The Sweet and Twenties, 1958

Next morning [Christmas weekend 1927] a brilliant sun was shining on the snow, and a transparent blue sky without a cloud stretched from horizon to horizon. Surely any psychological cloud should have disappeared, melted by so much beauty. Certainly a good many did. Lytton, who had an assignation with Roger in London, was boyishly eager to get away in spite of all difficulties, and a procession set out to walk to Hungerford, since there was no possibility of a car getting through the drifts. Lytton in a fur coat and waders, Ralph in top boots, a rucksack and a crimson hat trimmed with monkey fur, James with his head enveloped in a scarf – we must have looked a bizarre collection . . . At Hungerford the world suddenly became ordinary again, people stepped into the train wearing bowler hats, and gaped to see a troupe of performing Bulgarian peasants, headed evidently by the Prime Minister in his fur coat.

Frances Partridge, Memories, 1981

My mother had married Ross the furrier, not Sydney Ross the Cohen in his socks, dressed up in a white sheet, wailing.

Inside Ross the furrier's on Bold Street was enchantment, my father's principle distraction. The frozen wastelands of north America brought us mink, beaver, muskrat, opposum, ermine, silver fox, blue fox, red fox, white fox, raccoon, otter, sable, lynx, seal and wolverine. There were muskrats, marmots and martens from Siberia, the steppes of Tartary and the Pribolov Islands. Kolinsky came from the plains of China, ocelots from India, leopard from Ceylon, flying squirrel from Japan, chinchilla from the wilds of Peru, Persian lamb from Asia Minor. My mother and I did not drape animal skins around our shoulders like Neanderthals shivering in their caves. Far from it. My father's belief was that these were primitive, dumb creatures that willingly laid down their lives for us and not only to make us beautiful. They gave up their wildness and in death we civilized them, they became extensions of our humanity when we put them on . . .

Linda Grant, *The Cast Iron Shore*, 1996

Edward Throbbing stood talking to the eldest daughter of the Duchess of Stayle. She was some inches taller than him and inclined slightly so that, in the general murmur of conversation, she should not miss any of his colonial experiences. She wore a frock such as only duchesses can obtain for their elder daughters, a garment curiously puckered and puffed up and enriched with old lace at improbable places, from which her pale beauty emerged as though from a clumsily tied parcel. Neither powder, rouge nor lipstick had played any part in her toilet and her colourless hair was worn long and bound across her forehead in a broad fillet. Long pearl drops hung from her ears and she wore a tight little collar of pearls round her throat. It was generally understood that now Edward Throbbing was back these two would become engaged to be married.

Evelyn Waugh, *Vile Bodies*, 1930

The Englishwoman never, as long as she lives, gets rid of the idea of uniform in her clothes. The love of uniform in its purest form is inculcated into the spick and span Girl Guides. As smart, as neat, as glossy, and as well groomed as a six-weeks' recruit, the young Girl Guide struts proudly along in her long black stockings, blue skirt, and blue uniform blouse, with badges of rank or proficiency in shooting, etc. One can form an idea of how they pull off their shoes and stockings in camp and romp about like unruly flappers only if one manages to cast a surreptitious glance at one of the little tent settlements of these young guards. But one must seize a lucky moment, for in a trice the word of command rings out from the middle-aged female officer, and the young flock falls in again, obedient to all the accepted rules of military life.

Only a uniform can be smart. That is why the Englishwoman is smart and the Frenchwoman chic. At an English garden party, at Ascot, at the Wimbledon Lawn Tennis Tournament, and at the Ranelagh polo matches a battalion could easily be formed of the wearers of flowered or chiffon frocks.

That is why it is so exceedingly simple to be well dressed in England, provided one has anything like the necessary cash. For uniforms can be made only by tailors, who rule the sartorial order of society just as the military tailors rule the dress of the Army. The lady who wishes to be correct and is content to be smart cannot possibly go wrong. With a certain number of evening dresses, a few summer frocks, tea gowns, a tweed coat, and some tailor-mades a woman is certain to get through the Season satisfactorily.

The girl who can lay claim to a father in the City, three fine dogs, a horse, a Bentley sports car, and a young man to take her about in the evening is, of course, beautifully dressed. Although she may allow a touch of Paris for the evening, her daytime attire is entirely the creation of London. The 'cape' which the Berlin woman, inspired by the *demi-monde* of Paris, sometimes affects is quite out of the question. The tailor-made, the sober, perfectly simply, closely fitting tweed coat, and a number of evening dresses made to measure all run away with an enormous amount of petty cash. It is all too expensive for the office girl, who in Berlin can buy these things for a quarter of the price.

That is why the crowds of both men and women to be seen walking about Berlin during the day look much better dressed than similar crowds in London – that is to say, if one looks at the general effect and not at the sprinkling of incomparably well-dressed people who go riding in Rotten Row in the morning. But it is the latter who are regarded as 'typically English'. The ideal is regarded as typical and the exception as the rule.

Karl Silex, John Bull at Home, 1933

I first met her [Wallis Simpson] when I was running a little lingerie business near Berkeley Square. It was my first job. It was in a mews where a friend of mine kept his cars. Above the cars there was nothing doing, and that's where I started the shop and supervised all the work. I was always in Paris finding fabrics, finding designs ... We had some women who sewed in the shop, but the most beautiful work was done in a Spanish convent in London, and that's where I spent my time. There was a brief period of time when I spent *all* my time in convents. I was never not on my way to see the mother superior for the afternoon. 'I want it rolled!' I'd say. 'I don't want it hemmed, I want it *r-r-r-rolled!*' . . .

One day Wallis Simpson came into the shop. I didn't really know her then. I'd met her at a party at the embassy when we first arrived in London. She wasn't very well dressed then. She wasn't in what you'd call the smart set – at all. We didn't become great friends then. But one day she invited me to lunch and I went. And I've never eaten a meal like I had that day for lunch. All the people at the table that day said that they'd never had such a lunch. She gave other luncheons like this, always with the most remarkable food, and that's what really established her as a hostess in London, which she was by the time she walked into my shop.

She knew *exactly* what she wanted. She ordered three nightgowns, and this is what they were: first, there was one in white satin copied from Vionnet, all on the bias, that you just pulled down over your head. Then there was one I'd bought the original of in Paris from a marvelous Russian woman. All the great *lingères*, the workers of lingerie, were Russian, because they were the only people who really knew luxury when luxury was in fashion. The whole neck of this nightgown was made of petals, which was too extraordinary, because they were put in on the bias, and when you moved they rippled. Then the third nightgown was a wonderful crêpe de Chine. Two were pale blue, another in white – three pieces in all.

By this time she had left her husband, Ernest Simpson. She was on her own then. She didn't have anyone to support her, so this was a big splurge for her. The nightgowns were for a very special weekend. The Prince of Wales had discovered Wallis Simpson.

She gave our shop three weeks to do the job. 'This is the date!' she said. 'This is the deadline!' So then a week went by and she called again: 'How are those nightgowns getting on?' Then, in the third week, she called every day.

She was on her way to her first weekend alone at Fort Belvedere with her Prince.

Diana Vreeland, *D. V.*, 1984

A friend of mine from the eastern seaboard, a tall upstanding gentleman whom I have always regarded as more British than the British both in his apparel and in his accent, was in a London club one day, waiting for a member who had invited him for lunch. As he stood at the bar he overheard three young men speculating as to whether he was an American or Englishman. He could not resist approaching them with the question, 'Which do you really think I am?'

Two of them replied that they thought he was British. But the third dubbed him an American . . . 'Because of your tie.'

'You have ruined my life!' my friend exclaimed. He had thought this tie to be the discreetest and most British design. Now, whenever he goes to London he finds himself looking curiously at every man's tie before he looks at his face, trying in bewilderment to discover just how he went wrong.

However formally they may be dressed, Americans do tend to wear brighter ties than the British do. They also wear, rather more often, their own versions of the old school and club ties. There are many, of course, who wear those gaily painted ties, on which it is possible to have anything portrayed, from a skull and crossbones to the image and name of a sweetheart. But these are not, on the whole, numbered among my friends.

The Duke of Windsor, A Family Album, 1960

E. M. Forster appeared to dress himself carefully to look like 'the man in the street', in impossibly dull grey suits, a woolly waistcoat, perhaps a cloth cap, yet there was no mistaking him for one of his similarly attired fellows. Was it the curious shape of his head – large at the top and tapering to neck and chin – or the disconcerting gaze of his light blue eyes? I have run into him at unexpected places, like the quay at Dover or emerging from the caves at Lascaux, and recognized him instantly from afar.

Frances Partridge, Memories, 1981

'But these people – don't imagine they're India.' He pointed to the dusky line beyond the court, and here and there it flashed a pince-nez or shuffled a shoe, as if aware that he was despising it. European costume had lighted like a leprosy.

E. M. Forster, A Passage to India, 1924

We were going to Thika . . . a bit of El Dorado my father had been fortunate enough to buy in the bar of the Norfolk hotel from a man wearing an Old Etonian tie.

While everyone else strode about Nairobi's dusty cart-tracks in bush shirts and khaki shorts or riding breeches, Roger Stilbeck was always neatly dressed in a light worsted suit of perfect cut, and wore gold cuff links and dark brogue shoes. No bishop could have appeared more respectable, and his wife, who looked very elegant, was said to be related to the Duke of Montrose.

Elspeth Huxley, *The Flame Trees of Thika*, 1959

Comrade X, it so happens, is an old Etonian. He would be ready to die on the barricades, in theory anyway, but you notice that he still leaves his bottom waistcoat button undone.

George Orwell, *The Road to Wigan Pier*, 1937

Elsie Titmuss was a maid at Picton House, in the employment of Doughty Strove, when George Titmuss, already a clerk in the Brewery, met her at a Skurfield church outing and they entered into a prolonged engagement and a ferocious programme of saving money. This culminated in marriage and the birth of their only child, the young hopeful, Leslie. Elsie was a surprisingly beautiful young woman with a calm and untroubled expression which survived her long and demanding life as a wife and mother in the Titmuss household. On the evening of the Young Conservatives' dinner-dance she was fussing round her son with obvious pride, dabbing at him with a clothes-brush and arranging a white handkerchief in his top pocket, as he stood in his hired dinner jacket in front of the mirror over their sitting-room mantelpiece, his hair neatly combed and slicked down with brilliantine, his face industriously shaved and slightly dusted with his mother's talc.

'You use the handkerchief for display purposes only, Leslie,' his mother instructed him. 'Don't go and blow your nose on it, will you?'

'Mother. I do know.'

'Stop finicking with the boy, Elsie.' George Titmuss sat under a relentless overhead light at the dinner table, his jacket hung on the back of his chair, and he wore sleeve-grips to keep his cuffs high and his bony wrists free. The green velvet cloth was spread with files and papers. He was working late on the Simcox Brewery accounts.

'Or you can have it in your sleeve.' Elsie took the handkerchief from her son's top pocket. 'When I was in service a lot of the gentlemen carried the white dinnertime handkerchief in the cuff.'

'I'll have it in the display pocket.' Leslie, who was always firm with his mother, returned the handkerchief to its previous position.

'I don't know why the boy has to be sent out looking like a tailor's dummy,' George grumbled as he added up a column of figures.

'When I was in service with Mr Doughty Strove at Picton House. Pre-war, when I was in service . . .'

'Yes, Elsie,' George said. 'I think we've all had our fill of when you were in service.' Neither of the men in her life wished to hear about Elsie's past in the Stroves' kitchen.

'It was dress for dinner every night,' Elsie continued happily.

'Except Sundays. Sundays it was casual dress and cold cuts, naturally, with beetroot and a lettuce salad. But any other day of the week it was one gong for dressing and then half an hour later the second gong for dinner.'

'Yes, Elsie. We do know all about it.'

'Can I borrow the Prefect?' Leslie asked his father over his mother's head.

'Oh, go on, George. All the other Young Conservatives'll be there with their own transport.' As always Mrs Titmuss supported her son.

'I suppose it'll stop people talking.' Mr Titmuss gave the matter the careful consideration he bestowed on the agenda at the Parish Council. 'At least you won't be hanging round the bus stop dressed like a waiter.'

'He looks handsome.' Elsie stood back in admiration. 'Doesn't our Leslie look handsome, George?'

'I'd rather see him looking handsome at eight thirty in the morning when we've got our annual audit at the Brewery,' George grumbled.

Elsie, giving the collar of her son's jacket a final brush, noticed his ready made bow tie clipped on to the front of his starched white collar. With the knowledge she had gained in service she was shocked. 'Oh, Leslie. They didn't give you one of them!'

'One of what?'

'Ready made! They ought to have given you a tie-your-own. They always wore tie-your-owns when I was in service.'

'It doesn't matter.' Not for the first time Leslie found his mother irritating. 'No one's going to know, are they?'

'I suppose not.' Elsie was doubtful.

'I bet it cost enough, whatever sort of tie it is.' George was still muttering over his columns of figures.

'Well, you didn't have to pay. I said you didn't have to pay, did you, George?' Elsie asked as she gave the spotless dinner jacket its last brush.

'I say, Titmuss, I say, old boy,' Kempenflatt shouted as he approached. 'Who's your tailor?'

'Like your tie, old fellow.' Magnus steered alongside. 'Bet it took simply hours to get such a perfect butterfly.'

Leslie looked at them puzzled. Holding the solid, embarrassed Charlie he came to a slow halt as Magnus's hand snatched the clip-on tie from his collar. He gazed after it and saw it settle, a black bow in Jennifer's hair.

'You old cheater!' Magnus's voice was high-pitched, accusing. Leslie seemed to be surrounded by young men, healthy-faced, loud-voiced, and Charlie had abandoned him as the music stopped.

'Where did you get that suit, Titmuss?' Kempenflatt asked, and Magnus was pulling open Leslie's jacket, searching for the label.

'Savile Row, is it? Huntsmans?'

'Better than that,' Magnus announced. 'Please see this garment is returned to Henry Pyecroft, Gents Outfitter, River Street, Hartscombe.'

'Lovely bit of schmutter, isn't it?' Kempenflatt said in a stage-Jewish accent, feeling the cloth between his finger and thumb, and Magnus went on reading the label to announce, '"All clothing impeccably clean." Ugh!'

'Look here. I know it's just a bit of fun but . . .' Leslie smiled round at the strange faces, anxious to enjoy the joke. As he did so he felt a jerk behind him and Kempenflatt was pulling off the jacket. Magnus was saying persuasively, 'Take it off, Titmuss. You don't know where it's been.' Leslie began to panic, wondering where this unsolicited undressing was going to end.

'"Impeccably clean"! Strong smell of mothballs.' When it was off, Kempenflatt sniffed the jacket and chucked it to Magnus, who said, 'As last worn at the Municipal Sewerage Workers' Ball,' and did a quick pass to Jennifer, who held it uncertainly in front of her in a dark bundle.

As they stared at him Leslie said, 'Can I have it back, please?' After that the silence seemed endless and then Fred, who had been watching with interest from behind his drum set, started to whistle and tap out the rhythm of 'Always'. The other Stompers joined in. Jennifer looked at Magnus and then handed the jacket back to Leslie. He thanked her and turned away towards the glass doors that opened on to the hotel garden, walking as quickly as he could, but he still heard Kempenflatt boom, 'I say, Magnus. Do you actually know that fellow?' And the answer, 'Of course I know him. His mother was our skivvy.'

John Mortimer, *Paradise Postponed*, 1985

For some time Mother had greatly envied us our swimming, both in the daytime and at night, but, as she pointed out when we suggested she join us, she was far too old for that sort of thing. Eventually, however, under constant pressure from us, Mother paid a visit into town and returned to the villa coyly bearing a mysterious parcel. Opening this she astonished us all by holding up an extraordinary shapeless garment of black cloth, covered from top to bottom with hundreds of frills and pleats and tucks.

'Well, what d'you think of it?' Mother asked.

We stared at the odd garment and wondered what it was for.

'What is it?' asked Larry at length.

'It's a bathing costume, of course,' said Mother. 'What on earth did you think it was?'

'It looks to me like a badly skinned whale,' said Larry, peering at it closely.

'You can't possibly wear that, Mother,' said Margo, horrified. 'Why, it looks as though it was made in 1920.'

'What are those frills and things for?' asked Larry with interest.

'Decoration, of course,' said Mother indignantly.

'What a jolly idea! Don't forget to shake the fish out of them when you come out of the water.'

'Well, I like it anyway,' Mother said firmly, wrapping the monstrosity up again, 'and I'm going to wear it.'

'You'll have to be careful you don't get waterlogged, with all that cloth around you,' said Leslie seriously.

'Mother, it's *awful*, you can't wear it,' said Margo. 'Why on earth didn't you get something more up to date?'

'When you get to my age, dear, you can't go around in a two-piece bathing suit . . . you don't have the figure for it.'

'I'd love to know what sort of figure that was designed for,' remarked Larry.

'You really are *hopeless*, Mother,' said Margo despairingly.

'But I *like* it . . . and I'm not asking you to wear it,' Mother pointed out belligerently.

'That's right, you do what you want to do,' agreed Larry; 'don't be put off. It'll probably suit you very well if you can grow another three or four legs to go with it.'

> Gerald Durrell, *My Family and Other Animals*, 1956

To Violet Hammersley   7 rue Monsieur, VII
                                              6 July 1948

I saw Rosamund L[ehmann] on a station in England, running, hadn't the energy to run after her. Oh the dowdiness of English women – has it always been the same or are they worse now – I can't remember. It is so fundamental that I suspect the former. The London New Look made me die of laughing – literal chintz crinolines. Apparently Dior went over 'and when he realized that it was he who had started it all, he was ready to commit suicide'.

> Nancy Mitford, *Love From Nancy: The Letters of Nancy Mitford*,
> edited by Charlotte Mosley, 1993

'I can't lend you any soap this month,' Selina said. Selina had a regular supply of soap from an American Army officer who got it from a source of many desirable things, called the PX. But she was accumulating a hoard of it, and had stopped lending.

Anne said, 'I don't want your bloody soap. Just don't ask for the taffeta, that's all.'

By this she meant a Schiaparelli taffeta evening dress which had been given to her by a fabulously rich aunt, after one wearing. This marvellous dress, which caused a stir wherever it went, was shared by all the top floor on special occasions, excluding Jane who it did not fit. For lending it out Anne got various returns, such as three clothing coupons or a half-used piece of soap . . .

[The dress is saved by Selina from a fire at the May of Teck club at the end of the novel; risking life and limb, she plunges back through the bathroom window to bring it out safe and sound.]

She was carrying something fairly long and limp and evidently light in weight, enfolding it carefully in her arms. He thought it was a body . . . It was the Schiaparelli dress. The coathanger dangled from the dress like a headless neck and shoulders.

Jane went back to her brainwork and shut the door with a definite click. She was rather tyrannous about her brainwork, and made a fuss about other people's wirelesses on the landing, and about the petty-mindedness of these haggling bouts that took place with Anne when the taffeta dress was wanted to support the rising wave of long-dress parties.

'You can't wear it to the Milroy. It's been twice to the Milroy . . . it's been to Quaglino's, Selina wore it to Quags, it's getting known all over London.'

'But it looks altogether different on me, Anne. You can have a whole sheet of sweet-coupons.'

'Did Jack Buchanan get rid of you the moment you had finished your dinner?'

'Yes. He did. We had a row.'

She shook back her shining hair. For this evening, she had managed to borrow the Schiaparelli dress. It was made of taffeta, with small side panniers stuck out with cleverly curved pads over the hips. It was coloured dark blue, orange and white in a floral pattern as from the Pacific Islands.

He said, 'I don't think I've ever seen such a gorgeous dress.'

'Schiaparelli,' she said.

He said, 'Is that the one you swap amongst yourselves?'
'Who told you that?'
'You look beautiful,' he replied.
She picked up the rustling skirt and floated away up the staircase.
Oh, girls of slender means!

Muriel Spark, *The Girls of Slender Means*, 1963

The English, alas, hate fashion. The same Puritanical streak that ordains our licensing hours and countenances the Lord's Day Observance Society makes the island race despise clothes, fear personal beauty and feel shame in all colours but beige ... Think of those self-righteous (and usually ill written) letters which make a regular appearance in the daily papers ... 'Sir, the New Look is simply a racket devised by clever businessmen to make us spend money on clothes.' 'Sir, I have managed with two dresses and one apron for the past four years, and my husband says I am the best-dressed woman he knows.' 'Sir, willpower dresses ought to be stopped by law.' ... Sir, Sir, Sir, always protesting, hating, envying, with the same sort of destructive fury that slashes modern pictures and daubs unpopular statues ... the idea of fashion as a profession with an aesthetics, a vocabulary, a history, a technique, a discipline of its own would seem to them ridiculous.

And even the faithful frequently get stifled by the dead-weight of British indifference to colour, proportion and design – that same indifference that has made our artistic history so meagre. We needed to gulp the creative air of Paris from time to time, or take the oxygen treatment from New York.

Anne Scott-James, *In the Mink*, 1952

The Misses McAndrew were unlike any other buyers I had ever seen. They gave the impression that they had never stooped to anything as low as commerce. They were very quiet ladies with silver hair, beautifully dressed in rare tweeds and minimal quantities of excellent fur. They arrived on the first stroke of six and without delay settled down to work.

After ten minutes it was obvious that things were not going well. As I showed dress after dress with the Misses McAndrew looking grimly at them the quietness which I had first remarked in them as a lady-like quality now seemed to assume a more sinister significance.

'No, Mr Newby!'

'Not that, Mr Newby!'

'Our ladies would not wear such a garment, Mr Newby!'

'No, Mr Newby!'

'That is not at all the kind of thing we require, Mr Newby!'

Sometimes they said nothing at all but simply looked in eloquent silence.

I felt my nerve going. I was in the presence of twin intelligences of a sort that I had never before encountered. Intelligence that was linked with a highly developed and individual sense of style. Even now when I was showing them all the wrong things, I knew what they wanted – the difficulty was to provide it.

'Now this,' I said, holding up the last dress in the collection that I dared to show them, a wool georgette in a washed-out shade of green that everyone else had brought, 'is the sort of thing . . .'

'No, Mr Newby!'

Together they rose to their feet adjusting their pieces of sable.

'Lovely, aren't they?' said Mr Wilkins, choosing this inopportune moment to come forward and put his foot in it.

Both sisters gave him a withering look.

'Mr Willukins,' said the younger of the two who looked even more deceptively gentle than the other, 'how often do we have to tell you that our customers are not the sort who wear wool georgette?' She made it sound as though some stigma might result from contact with the stuff.

'For the most part they spend their time in outdoor pursuits. They need fine checks for indoors and really thick tweeds for the hills.'

There was not a moment to lose. It was obvious that she was pronouncing a funeral oration over my collection. I picked up one of Mr Wilkins's swatches of suit patterns. They were fine saxonies intended for men's suits and because of this they were three times as expensive as the materials I would normally have used for such a purpose.

'That's what we want, Mr Newby,' one of them said, instantly. 'Now all we need are three simple styles in which they can be made.'

I took the three simplest styles in the collection and said that they would be even more simple. I managed to convince them that what they would get would be little more than tubes of material which had four holes in them. I also said that they would be very expensive, which was true.

'To our customers,' the elder Miss McAndrew said, 'expense is a secondary consideration. The important thing, Mr Newby, is satisfaction. Satisfaction and quality.'

'We could also have the dresses made with jackets. Like that,' she indicated one of Mr Wilkins's suits, 'but no padding in the shoulders.'

'And horn buttons,' said her sister.

'Horn buttons and leather belts for the dresses. The belts must be of the finest quality. We want none of your *wholesale belts*.'

'Two-pieces,' said Mr Wilkins, waking up suddenly. 'I do the two-pieces.'

'They are too dressed-up for our ladies, Mr Wilkins,' one of them said firmly. 'They require them for shooting.'

For a moment I had an insane desire to ask what.

'This is the kind of material we need,' she went on, looking through a swatch of twenty-one-ounce tweeds intended for gamekeepers. 'For our ladies to wear on the hills. With horn buttons. Providing that they do not cost more than thirty guineas you can write the order.

You can confirm the price to us later. And remember – no padding in the shoulders.'

It was the biggest order I had had. They ordered the saxony dresses in three different styles and six different colours. They also ordered the two-pieces in a number of permutations of colour and style. I calculated that two thicknesses of the twenty-ounce tweed would be almost bulletproof. Perhaps that was what the Misses McAndrew intended.

Made amicable by having found what they wanted they then proceeded to order a surprisingly large number of black chiffon dinner dresses.

One of these dresses was so expensive that so far I had only succeeded in selling one to Miss Reekie and then only by agreeing to let her have the model at a reduced price. In fact I had already decided to withdraw it from the collection. Although extremely elegant its effect seemed to be too sepulchral for the wholesale.

It was an extraordinary order – the combination of the heavy tweeds and the funereally graceful chiffons. When not engaged in killing things the McAndrews' customers seemed to spend their evening dining in a family vault.

Eric Newby, *Something Wholesale*, 1962

[Nancy Mitford describes the Duchess of Windsor, *c.*1952] 'in a crocheted straw dress, utter knockout, saying "Just the sort of thing you pick up in a village, you know." *What village?*'

Sir Harold Acton, *Nancy Mitford: A Memoir*, 1975

She was wearing a fur-topped Cossack cap and big fur gloves and a full-skirted cashmere topcoat. Her eyes were sparkling and her cheeks fused a little and there was about her that clean smell – like baby powder mixed with new-mown hay – which I had noticed the first time I'd met her.

When I handed the tickets to the usher she caught sight of their price. 'Four and six,' she said. 'Golly. Isn't that frightfully expensive?'

I looked at her sharply; did she expect a box? But I saw that she was quite serious and I was astounded and delighted at her naïvety; the clothes she was wearing must have cost a good fifty pounds.

A young man and a girl got in at the next stop. At least, I thought she was about nineteen; her face, like the young man's, had a settled look, as if she'd decided what was the most respectable age to be, and wasn't going to change it in a hurry. She had a round flat face with lipstick the wrong shade and her silk stockings and high heels struck an incongruously voluptuous note, it was as if she were scrubbing floors in a transparent nylon nightie. The young man had a navy-blue overcoat, gloves, and scarf, but no hat; he was following the odd working-class fashion which seemed to me now, after Alice's tuition, as queer as going out without trousers. I felt a mean complacency; with that solid mass of brilliantined hair and mass-produced face, bony, awkward, mousy, the face behind the requests on Forces Favourites, the face enjoying itself at Blackpool with an open-necked shirt spread out over its jacket, the face which Wilfred Pickles might love but which depressed me intensely – Len or Sid or Cliff or Ron – he'd never have the chance of enjoying a woman like Susan, he'd never explore in another person the passion and innocence which a hundred thousand in the bank could alone make possible.

John Braine, *Room at the Top*, 1957

I saw three figures ambling towards me from the Arlington Street entrance. They were dressed as Teddy-boys, but there was no mistaking the species. With their slouching, insouciant gait, dead-fish hands depending from, rather than forming part of, long loose-jointed arms, slightly open mouths and appearance of shivering as if their clothes, rather too small in every dimension, had no warmth in them, they would have been immediately recognizable, however disguised, on the mountains of the moon, as Etonians.

Here were the chrysalises of the elegant, urbane Englishmen I so much longed for my sons to be; this was the look which, since I was familiar with it from early youth, I found so right, and which I had missed from the tough premature manliness of the other two boys. Charlie and Fabrice had changed their clothes but not yet their personalities; what a relief!

Nancy Mitford, *Don't Tell Alfred*, 1960

Dixon moved down the room through the company and leaned against the wall at the end by the door where the bookshelves were. Placed here, savouring his cigarette, he was in a good position to observe Bertrand's girl when she came in, slowly and hesitantly, a few seconds later, and stood unnoticed, except by him, just inside the room.

In a few more seconds Dixon had noticed all he needed to notice about this girl: the combination of fair hair, straight and cut short, with brown eyes and no lipstick, the strict set of the mouth and the square shoulders, the large breasts and the narrow waist, the premeditated simplicity of the wine-coloured corduroy skirt and the unornamented white linen blouse. The sight of her seemed an irresistible attack on his own habits, standards and ambitions: something designed to put him in his place for good. The notion that women like this were never on view except as the property of men like Bertrand was so familiar to him that it had long since ceased to appear an injustice. The huge class that contained Margaret was destined to provide his own womenfolk: those in whom the intention of being attractive could sometimes be made to get itself confused with performance; those with whom a too-tight skirt, a wrong-coloured, or no, lipstick, even an ill-executed smile could instantly discredit that illusion beyond apparent hope of renewal. But renewal always came: a new sweater would somehow scale down the large feet, generosity revivify the brittle hair, a couple of pints site positive charm in talk of the London stage or French food.

Kingsley Amis, *Lucky Jim*, 1954

Goldfinger had made an attempt to look smart at golf and that is the only way of dressing that is incongruous on a links. Everything matched in a blaze of rust-coloured tweed from the buttoned 'golfer's cap' centred on the huge, flaming red hair, to the brilliantly polished, almost orange shoes. The plus-four suit was too well cut and the plus-fours themselves had been pressed down the sides. The stockings were of a matching heather mixture and had green garter tabs. It was as if Goldfinger had gone to his tailor and said, 'Dress me for golf – you know, like they wear in Scotland.' Social errors made no impression on Bond, and for the matter of that he rarely noticed them. With Goldfinger it was different. Everything about the man had grated on Bond's teeth from the first moment he had seen him. The assertive blatancy of his clothes was just part of the malevolent animal magnetism that had affected Bond from the beginning.

Ian Fleming, *Goldfinger*, 1959

The tea room at the top of a Knightsbridge department store was the place appointed; the time, three forty-five of an afternoon by now some way on into September. The decor nicely estimated the patrons' likings: tables low, chairs sympathetic and carpet costly. Now and then a mannequin prowled through. There have been stranger places for a council of war.

A big woman wearing a tight black turban, and on the lapel of her dark suit a striking brooch, sat down, with all but no hesitation, opposite a woman already there at the table. The already-seated woman seemed in two minds as to whether to rise or not. She advanced a hand uncertainly, took it back again, slightly opened her mouth but did not speak. Given her almost excessively *mondaine* air, her look of being slightly too smart for London, her inadequacy was in itself dramatic. Her hat was composed of pink roses.

First, each drew a breath, summoning her forces. Then, as though at a signal, they looked straight across at each other, then away again. Having got that over, they simultaneously uttered a sort of titter. Black Turban, settling into her chair, bumped a leg of the table with her knee, whereat Pink Roses tittered: 'There you go again!' She added: 'Imagine seeing *you* again!'

'I'd been going to say, imagine seeing you!'

As airily as could be, Pink Roses hazarded: 'You'd never have known me, I suppose?'

The other grinned, but didn't commit herself. 'I don't say it wasn't a good idea to describe your hat.'

'That was my husband's idea,' said Pink Roses, in a tone which made plain that it was her rule to do that individual justice whenever possible. 'He said that as this was bound to be embarrassing enough for both of us, you and me I mean, it would be a mistake to start by going around staring at the wrong woman, inviting snubs. "So let her know what you'll wear," he said, "and be sure you wear it." He also hoped neither of us would be surprised if we got a shock. – No, I don't suppose I'd ever have spotted you if, in return, you hadn't described your brooch. – I *should* like to ask you: is it Italian?'

'Not my type, in a general way,' observed Black Turban, ducking a look at her lapel. 'Too much an eye-catcher. Still, it's served its purpose.'

Pink Roses narrowed her eyes, to continue to look at the brooch, gluttonously. 'Directly after I wrote to you,' she went on, 'I thought, whatever made me say *this* hat? Suppose it had rained? Coming up for the day, you never know. And it's rather a summery hat for this time of year . . .' Suddenly conscious of being studied, in a leisurely, neutral manner, across the table, she flamed up into suspicion, became defiant. 'Or perhaps *you* think——?'

'No,' decided the other (still cocking an eye, though). 'I don't. No, you can still get away with it.'

Elizabeth Bowen, *The Little Girls*, 1964

Where was I? Oh yes – Ruby. Another thing – she always has plenty of food and drink in, gins, whiskies, you name it and she has it, except perhaps Dimple Haig, but who wants that – whilst these young chicks can't even offer you a Lucozade. Comfort never enters a young bird's mind. Not unless she's a real fat lazy dope. And Ruby's got some beautiful clobber. She goes in mostly for what you call 'model' coats, and she's got some lovely fur coats as well, a real Persian lamb, she's even got a wild mink jacket for evenings. And you should see all the fashion cards she's got on her mantelpiece: 'Hardy Amies Ltd. request the pleasure of your company at the showing of their Spring Collection.' Then you get Worth requests it, Paquin, Norman Hartnell – I don't know how many of those fashion geezers request the pleasure of Ruby's company.

Bill Naughton, *Alfie*, 1966

1963

At Jane Holzer's dinner I'd noticed [David] Bailey and Mick [Jagger]. They each had a distinctive way of dressing: Bailey all in black, and Mick in light-colored, unlined suits with very tight hip trousers and striped T-shirts, just regular Carnaby Street sport clothes, nothing expensive, but it was the way he put things together that was so great – this pair of shoes with that pair of pants that no one else would have thought to wear. And, of course, Bailey and Mick were both wearing boots by Anello and Davide, the dance shoemaker in London.

Andy Warhol and Pat Hackett, *POPism: The Warhol '60s*, 1981

The girls in Chelsea had great legs and knew how to wear the skirts that we made shorter and shorter. Angry bowler-hatted men with rolled umbrellas beat on the shop window with rage. I didn't think of the mini as sexual but as an instrument of liberation. I wanted to make clothes that you could move in, skirts you could run and dance in, but, of course, wearing clothes like that made you feel and look sexy. Young men loved it and brought their girlfriends to buy. Actors from the Royal Court theatre, journalists, painters and sculptors all came – it was, at first, a very Chelsea thing. It became known as the mini.

Mary Quant, 'The Meaning of the Mini', *Daily Telegraph*, 1997

20 July 1967
... went to the record shop in Sicilian Arcade and bought a copy of the LP [*Sgt. Pepper's Lonely Hearts Club Band*]. Kenneth bought an old Etonian tie. He thinks it's funny but, as I pointed out, he's come full circle and the tie is most conventional. Unless you know it's an old Etonian it isn't funny. Still it looks a nice plain tie anyway.

22 July 1967
Went to Peter Willes for dinner. When we got there he stared at Kenneth in horror. 'That's an old Etonian tie!' he screeched. 'Yes,' Kenneth said, 'it's a joke.' Willes looked staggered and wrinkled up his face in an evil sort of way. 'Well, I'm afraid it's a joke against you then. People will imagine you're passing yourself off as an old Etonian. They'll laugh at you.' 'I'm sending up Eton,' Kenneth said.

'Oh, no!' Willes cackled with a sort of eldritch shriek. 'You're just pathetic! I mean it's disgraceful wearing that tie.' 'It's a joke!' Kenneth said, looking tight-lipped, a little embarrassed and angry. 'People will know.' 'Not the people I meet,' Kenneth said. 'They'll think it's funny.' 'You're making people angry,' Willes said. 'I don't care,' Kenneth said, laughing a little too readily. 'I want to make them angry.' 'But why?' Willes said, as we sat down. 'People dislike you enough already. Why make them more angry? I mean – it's permissible, although silly as a foible of youth, but you – a middle-aged nonentity – it's sad and pathetic.' I could see that the conversation had become impossible and that unless something were done the evening would begin in ruins. 'Now stop this both of you!' I said in a commanding voice. 'It's ridiculous to carry on in this way over a wretched tie.'

Joe Orton, *The Orton Diaries*, edited by John Lahr, 1986

Sloane Ranger clothes exactly reflect regimental values and solid background – conservative and reassuring. They are made to last, both in style (never high fashion, then never out of fashion) and in material – tweeds, wools, silks, cottons; natural and dateless fibres. (An exception is made for the dreaded nylon when it comes to the Husky.) Caroline is a walking example of what any Frenchwoman knows: one can't afford cheap clothes if one's not rich. Quality counts, but Sloane clothes also show the way the wind is blowing – literally. There is always a pennant substitute or an erstwhile windsock fluttering at Caroline's neck, bag, bodice or arms. The Sloane is the upper middle class on parade.

Glossy magazines, from time to time, make much of *le style anglais* or the Rich Girl Look, but to Caroline her sort of clothes are not a 'look'. They express her real values and her solid country roots. Rangers don't aim to look sexy, nor do they have to dress in an exotic Original to get attention.

The old **Ranger Brigade** (Knightsbridge Knotted era) looked like an endangered species at the end of the seventies. But when Diana Spencer hit the lenses she pepped up the Ranger wardrobe and boosted morale, reaffirming the Sloanes' looks and qualities but reaffirming them for the eighties, encouraging Sloanes everywhere to be a touch dressier, a little more dashing. Caroline, of course, looked natural in frilled high necks, not mutton dressed as lamb cutlets like many Princess-followers. Trad Romance has never been far beneath the Sloane surface: it appears again and again in the Victorian heroine evening dresses that epitomize Caroline's deepest feelings towards a ball (Ranger-speak: a bollock).

The principles underlying Caroline's dress code are: Quality, Conservatism, Classicism.

Henry knows the form, which means no fashion and limited self-expression in the kit. Sloane men's clothes are a uniform. There really *are* rules, still. Henry's clothes, like everything else, relate to What Really Matters. WRM has altered little in the last twenty years, except for the arrival of Guccis and jeans (currently worn with tweed jacket) and the departure of the bowler hat.

Everything is worn until it falls apart. Henry wears outerwear indoors, country wear in London, and many of his clothes closely resemble his old school uniform, thereby proclaiming him part of that invisible club of Rangerdom. SRMs [Sloane Ranger Men] are annoyed, subconsciously, that foreigners wear *le style anglais* as a look and not as a badge of faith.

Henry, though utterly predictable, is usually the most attractive man on any occasion. He wears the uniform of the City gent, country squire, penguin, as though he was born to it, which he was. The overall look is knowing the form (properly dressed) but not thinking about it (suspect). The aristocratic tradition means that business Rangers are allowed to look more dashing than their inhibited over-careful American cousins the Preppies. The basics of Ranger dressing are balanced by historically sanctioned flash. Real Ranger clothes, like Tory hair, look a bit *cavalier*. Henry adds colours and Sloane glamour which other classes wouldn't risk – foppish snuff handkerchief, rakishly tilted Herbie J cap, broad scarlet or mustard box-cloth braces.

Ann Barr and Peter York, *The Sloane Ranger Handbook*, 1982

[Suzy Menkes, fashion editor of the *International Tribune*, said] 'There's the thoroughbred look, which of course doesn't travel well. Look what happened to our poor Princess of Wales in Italy. And the other side is imaginative, exuberant, eccentric young London. One so longs for the two sides to come together in one wonderful flowering. But the tragedy of English street fashion is that we have no tailoring. The tailoring in England looks like it was put together with a knife and fork, and a blunt one at that.'

Nicholas Coleridge, *The Fashion Conspiracy*, 1985

In truth, it is not very intelligent to blame Anna Wintour for the wave of conservatism that has broken over British fashion this year – but what can you expect of an area of journalism that relies more on gut instinct than thorough analysis? Ms Wintour is in fact more symptom than cause, a new broom driving out what she considers to be the undesirable cobwebs of English eccentricity, nostalgia and lackadaisical diffidence. She is a woman on a clean-up mission whose editorship has been a platform to a higher proportion of American clothes of both the exec and glitzy type, not to mention a higher proportion of US journalist friends – André Leon Talley, Joan Juliet Buck and Marion McEvoy among them. The effect on fashion editorial has been mooted as 'very right wing', and a by-product looks to have been the resignation of Grace Coddington, long-time *Vogue* fashion director and visionary stylist, whose brilliant touch will be sadly missed . . .

Ms Wintour's new-look *Vogue* should be seen simply as a piece of apposite timing rather than a dominating and malign influence. After all, we're talking about the year in which Katharine Hamnett turned to cashmere twinsets; when the new star, Alistair Blair, turned out not to be a struggling young student, but a man who was trained in Paris to perfectionist standards; and when John Galliano started wearing suits.

The feeling in fashion imagery has been for disciplined, old-fashioned values, and a sometimes tongue-in-cheek plundering of the couture of the fifties. The collections shown in March for winter 1986–7 took the theme of establishment conservatism in its most literal form – turning out pinstripe suits for men and women alike.

Since then, for next spring, there's been an apparent backlash – in the form of the much vaunted puffball skirt, a plethora of frills and flounces and baby-doll frippery. This latest swing of the pendulum may be as valid as a visual change from all that strictness, but those old conservative values are still very much to the fore. The idea of trying to get all us big, strong, hard-headed females into dressing in feminine retro-froth surely has some symbolic meaning for the times. Some of us have even given ourselves a scare by detecting the re-emergence of thirties Aryan values in upcoming collections . . . metaphorically shooting us back to the bedroom, the crib and the kitchen. Don't say you haven't been warned.

Sarah Mower, 'Fashion', *The Face*, 1987

This morning he was a serious individual, representing Park Avenue and Wall Street. He wore a blue-gray nailhead worsted suit, custom-tailored in England for $1,800, two-button, single-breasted, with ordinary notched lapels. On Wall Street double-breasted suits and peaked lapels were considered a bit sharp, a bit too Garment district. He squared his shoulders and carried his long nose and wonderful chin up high.

*

For a start, there was Judy's dress. It was bare-shouldered but had short puffed sleeves the size of Chinese lampshades covering the upper arms. It had a fitted waist but was puffed up in the skirt to a shape that reminded Sherman of an aerial balloon. The invitation to dinner at the Bavardages' prescribed 'informal' dress. But this season, as *tout le monde* knew, women dressed far more extravagantly for informal dinners in fashionable apartments than for formal dances in grand ballrooms.

The women came in two varieties. First, there were women in their late thirties and in their forties and older (women 'of a certain age'), all of them skin and bones (starved to near perfection). To compensate for the concupiscence missing from their juiceless ribs and atrophied backsides, they turned to the dress designers. This season no puffs, flounces, pleats, ruffles, bibs, bows, batting, scallops, laces and darts, or shirts on the bias were too extreme. They were the social X-rays, to use the phrase that had bubbled up into Sherman's own brain. Second, there were the so-called Lemon Tarts. These were the women in their twenties or early thirties, mostly blondes (the Lemon in Tarts), who were the second, third, and fourth wives or live-in girlfriends of men over forty or fifty or sixty (or seventy), the sort of women men refer to, quite without thinking, as *girls*. This season the Tart was able to flaunt the natural advantages of youth by showing her legs from well above the knee and emphasizing her round bottom (something no X-ray had).

Tom Wolfe, *The Bonfire of the Vanities*, 1988

'I'd like to thank my father and mother for having me,' he said, 'and giving me such a wonderful party, and for my sister Taggie for doing all the work, and making this wonderful cake.' For a second Maud looked furious at the loudness of the cheers. 'Thank you all for coming, and for all your presents, which I'll open later when I get a moment.'

There were more loud cheers. Just then, as Caitlin finished lighting the candles, like the dark stranger coming over the threshold, Cameron Cook walked in. She was wearing an extremely tight-fitting, strapless, black suede dress, which came eight inches above her knees. Three-inch cross-laced gaps on either side from armpit to hem made it quite plain she was wearing nothing but Fracas and Mantan underneath. There was a heavy metal chain round her neck, and among the heavy silver bangles worn over her long black suede gloves gleamed Tony's diamond bracelet.

Anyone else would have looked tarty in that dress, but Cameron, with her marvellously lean, sinuous, rapacious beauty, succeeded in looking both menacing and absolutely staggering.

Jilly Cooper, *Rivals*, 1988

The Diana who finally fought her way through the sickness and deceit and cruelty and who came out the other side like a soldier emerging from a treacherous jungle swamp looked like the eighties; streamlined and strong, built to fight and win. A conspiracy between genetics and gym, Harvey Nichols and health club, diet and designers, she epitomized the healthy body clothed by a healthy credit card (the healthy mind could be put on hold, to attend to once the desk was cleared), that was the eighties' idea. Diana, after her Prim Period (dressed in frills) and her Pizzazz Period (dressed to thrill), took to power dressing like a halibut in H2O, forever striding towards the camera on her way to shake hands with yet another charity director in skyscraper heels and short-skirted, bright-coloured suits, and you could see why. She had been powerless for so long that even dressing the part must have felt like a step in the right direction.

Julie Burchill, *Diana*, 1998

Pass Notes: Isabella Blow

Profession: Fashion director of the *Sunday Times*; *de facto* godmother of British fashion; tireless promoter of the avant-garde.

Famous for: A wardrobe on the bonkers side of eccentric – she frequently stops the traffic.

Since when was wearing funny trousers a legitimate claim to fame? Since they were Alexander McQueen trousers.

McQueen, the self-styled bad boy of British fashion? That's the one. The same one who hit the headlines when he got the top designer's job at French fashion house Givenchy.

And he owes it all to Blow, right? Indeed. She 'discovered' him, buying up his entire graduation collection when he left Central Saint Martin's.

So when Blow comes to call . . . You become the future of fashion, darling. Blow's other protégés include super-milliner Philip Treacy, knitwear supremo Julien MacDonald and models Honor Fraser and Sophie Dahl. Oh, and fashion photographer Sean Ellis.

Who presumably has gone on to bigger and better things? Sure has. Ellis directed the Brit-winning video for the All Saint's single 'Never Ever'.

This being London Fashion Week, anyone Blow thinks we should keep an eye on? New designers with the Blow seal of approval include Deborah Milner, tipped, along with just about anyone you care to mention, as a future designer at Versace, and Tristan Webber.

Who he? A recent graduate of you-know-where, of course.

Huh? Central Saint Martin's, stupid.

Don't tell me. He's avant-garde. You're getting the hang of this fashion lark.

Blow on new talent: 'I'm passionate about fashion and about new talent. I'm like an animal foraging for truffles . . .'

Famous relatives: As notorious as her protégés. Grandfather Sir Henry John Delves Broughton was cleared of the murder of Lord Erroll in the 1941 'Happy Valley' trial in Kenya.

Not to be confused with: Anna Piaggi, famously eccentric doyenne from Italian *Vogue*; a flamboyant and none-too-healthy ostrich.

Don't say: 'Who's that prat in the hat? I wish she'd take it off – I can't see a thing.'

Believe her when she says: 'Darling, you'll be the toast of London Fashion Week.'

Least likely to say: 'Not another new designer! Think I'll skip this show and have a cup of tea.'

Pass Notes, Guardian, 1998

Lorimer held up the sleeves of his suit coat to show single-button cuffs that actually unbuttoned. Ivan had told him how he abominated the two-, three- or four-button cuff as pretentious and *arriviste*. A cuff was a cuff: it was there to allow you to fold up your sleeve, not as decoration.

'The shirt is first rate,' Ivan said. Lorimer had had them made to Ivan's design also, the collar deliberately miscut so that the point on one side rode over the revere a little awkwardly and untidily but, as Ivan pointed out, it was a defect that only arose with hand-made shirts, and what was the purpose of having hand-made shirts if they could not be recognized as such. 'Only people who have hand-made shirts themselves will recognize the problem,' Ivan assured him, 'but they're only people you want to notice.'

Lorimer lifted his trouser leg to show off his midnight blue socks.

'Shoes are only just passable,' Ivan said. 'Thank God you've got no tassles but I don't know if I like these American loafers. Very *nouveau*. Still.'

'I think they're right for this City crowd.'

'Just. Good God, what's that tie?'

'My school. Balcairn.' Actually it was a tie he had had his tailor make up for him. Navy blue with thin bands of mauve and an unidentifiable crest.

'Take it off at once. I'll lend you another. School ties are for schoolboys and schoolmasters. No grown man should be seen dead in a school tie. Same goes for regimental and club ties. Appalling bad taste.'

Ivan came back with a tie in lime green silk covered in a motif of tiny blue spiders. 'Bit of fun. It is an "At Home", after all.' Ivan looked him up and down in a kindly, almost proprietorial way, the old knight sending out his squire to joust in the lists of High Society.

'Very good, Lorimer. Even I can't find much fault.'

William Boyd, *Armadillo*, 1998

5. 'A fetishistic attachment': Fashion and Fetishism

But, for others, she wore drawers of Chantilly lace . . . her monogram embroidered in hair on all her lingerie, dear boy, in golden hairs from her own head . . . faery handicraft!

Colette, *The Last of Cheri*, 1926

If I wanted to use the longest words for the shortest thing I would say that I was a passive foot fetishist. My feet were smaller than an ordinary mortal's and I wanted everyone to know this.

Quentin Crisp, *The Naked Civil Servant*, 1968

'Ful fetys was hir cloke': the word 'fetys', or 'fetis', used by Chaucer to describe the skilful fashioning of the dress of the Prioress,[1] was already connected with clothing by the fourteenth century, the period in which tailoring evolved in Europe allowing for shaping and altering the body. '*Feitiço*' is a Portuguese word meaning sorcery in connection with a made object and the origin of the definition of a fetish as an object into which we project magic or spiritual properties; the fetish's magic is that it wards off or neutralizes fear.[2] Clothing as a powerful carrier of both body shaping and of spirit was already part of western culture before the word 'fetis' was further defined in the nineteenth and twentieth centuries. Sigmund Freud used the word 'fetish' to indicate forms of sexual activity in which desire is displaced on to a fetishized part of the body or adjunct to it. Today, 'fetish', when connected to dress, is often read as something sexual, items of clothing making ideal fetishes because they take on the spirit of the wearer, but fetishism in the context of dress is essentially about the wearer and observer's response to clothing.

Fashion uses the erotic appeal of certain physical characteristics that can be enhanced by clothes – the waist constricted, the foot elongated with heel elevated by stiletto – which attract 'normal' individuals as well as fetishists. Valerie Steele in her exhaustive study *Fashion and Eroticism* explores the difference between fetishism and erotic appeal, the latter, in her opinion, being more likely to apply to fashion. In his article 'Fetishism' Freud writes, 'The fetish is a substitute for the woman's [the mother's] penis that the little boy once believed in and . . . does not want to give up . . . for if a woman had been castrated, then his own possession of a penis was in danger.' The fetish represents an unconscious 'compromise' between the 'unwelcome perception' that the mother has no penis and the wish and earlier belief that she does. The ego defends itself by disavowing or repressing an unpleasant perception. 'Yes, in his mind the woman has got a penis . . . but this penis is no longer the same . . . Something else has taken its place.'[3] The 'something else' might be pieces of underwear, which symbolize the act of undressing, fur or velvet which represents pubic hair without the penis, or the foot representing the woman's missing penis. But as Steele points out, what is proposed is an almost entirely male phenomenon because most women do not fear castration. Very few men are real fetishists so pathological fetishism plays a very small part in fashion. Rather, fashion is often about erotic symbolism for both men and women – the way, for instance, high heels make the hips and buttocks sway, arch the back and push the bust forward.[4]

Throughout the twentieth century writers have discussed clothes in terms of sexual and non-sexual fetishism and eroticism: for example, the way constriction of some part of the body at the turn of the century was a normal adjunct of dressing, as in the tight gloves worn by Leon in Colette's *Claudine and Annie*: 'Not tight, only new,' which we now regard as fetishistic. The frou-frou rustle of petticoats and skirts was regarded as feminine, erotic as well as evocative; Mrs

E. Pritchard preaches that the 'invisible is more important than the visible' in 1902. Sixty years on, John Braine describes the erotic sound of a petticoat in *Life at the Top*, which made Joe Lampton understand a man's desire to rape; Daphne du Maurier, on the other hand, writes of the young Mrs de Winter imagining of the rustle of a gown to describe the spirit of the ever-present Rebecca. The clothes of the dead can be seen to still hold this energy and go beyond mere evocation of memories.

The idea of items of clothing as erotic is explored in literature by Anaïs Nin and Pauline Reage. Nin's 'Elena' not only uses Pierre's leather belt as a phallic symbol – 'it had been a heavy, strong leather belt with a silver buckle': the sound of the clicking buckle is an erotic moment for her. Dressing or undressing in front of a lover is made more exciting by what clothes reveal or conceal and Pierre's belt represents the beginning or end of sex, anticipation and regret. The belt also says something else: it was the symbol of the working man, for the middle or upper-class man wore braces. The belt is the symbol of rough trade. It not only holds a sexual fascination here: it symbolizes a world that Elena does not know.

Pauline Reage, in her erotic/pornographic novel, examines not only the power of fetishwear but, in passing, its relationship with fashion. In the first novel, *The Story of O*, the fetish dress Jacqueline wears is a gown similar to a Dior; in *The Story of O: Part Two*, the fetish dress has become 'fixed' in style and does not relate to the unconstricting womenswear of 1969. In 1970, Germaine Greer was to castigate the male 'fetishist' for placing women in bras and girdles.

The wearing of fur as both a symbol of luxury and a subconscious fetish is described by Dodie Smith in *The Hundred and One Dalmatians*. Cruella de Vil is young in the novel, but appears as a relic of the 1930s, a vamp for whom luxury and the wearing of colour-co-ordinated fur is everything: her madness is rapacious, her desire for the feel of puppy fur on her body obscene. Smith's young couple are fresh, post-war, new-generation Londoners for whom the wearing of fur belongs to the world of night-clubs and sin. Linda Grant in *The Cast Iron Shore* looks back to the 1930s and sees fur as erotic: a fur wrap, slipping from a woman's naked shoulders, provided by her man, is dress at its most primitive and within the novel provides a symbolic moment. Beverly Nichols, on the other hand, speaks out against the immorality of wearing fur, describing pieces of monkey fur from the 1920s, when it was very popular as a trimming for hems, collars and cuffs. As a luxury, however, fur has remained a symbol of status; despite the anti-fur campaign of the mid-1980s, it has returned to designer shows.

The cult of chiffon has this in common with the Christian religion – it insists that the invisible is more important than the visible.

Mrs E. Pritchard, *The Cult of Chiffon*, 1902

'What a crowd of people, Leon!'

'Yes. I recognized the Voronsoffs' carriage and the Gorkaus' and the . . . Be so kind as to button my glove, Annie . . .'

'Your gloves are terribly tight!'

'Not tight, Annie, only new. The woman at the glove shop always says to me "Monsieur's hands seem to get smaller and smaller" . . .'

I did not even smile at his childishness. Vain of his hands and feet, my poor brother-in-law endures a thousand small tortures but will not concede even a quarter of a size to his mangled fingers.

Colette, *Claudine and Annie*, 1903

Although she walked very short distances, Mrs Lydig possessed at least three hundred pairs of shoes, shoes that have never been seen before or since. These were made by Yanturini, the East Indian curator of the Cluny Museum, a strange individual with an extraordinary gift for making incredibly light footwear that was moulded like the most sensitive sculpture. The conditions under which he would supply a few favoured customers were somewhat unusual. Yanturini demanded a deposit of $1000 from which he would subtract the price of each shoe or boot supplied, though delivery often took two or three years. Once he had agreed to work for a customer, he made a plaster model of both feet, on which he would then work and mould his materials until they were as flexible as the finest silk. Mrs Lydig's shoes were fashioned from eleventh- and twelfth-century velvets, with variations in long pointed toes or square-ended toes and correspondingly square heels. Her evening and boudoir slippers utilized brocades or gold- and silver-metal tissue. Some were covered with lace appliqué and leather spats that fitted like a silk sock. Mrs Lydig collected violins expressly so that Mr Yanturini could use their thin, light wood for his shoe trees. With its tree inside, each shoe weighed no more than an ostrich feather. She preserved these shoes in trunks of Russian leather made in St Petersburg, with heavy locks and rich cream velvet lining.

Cecil Beaton, *The Glass of Fashion*, 1954

'I [Augustus John, writing to Alick Schepeler] would rather talk to you about your beautiful underclothing ... Tell me, Undine, how are your shoes wearing? It seems so fitting, that you – a soulless, naked immortal creature, come straight out of the water, should take to shoes with such a passion.'

Michael Holroyd, *Augustus John: A Biography*, 1977

But when a belief vanishes, there survives it – more and more vigorously so as to cloak the absence of the power, now lost to us, of imparting reality to new things – a fetishistic attachment to the old things which it did once animate, as if it was in them and not

in ourselves that the divine spark resided, and as if our present
incredulity had a contingent cause – the death of the gods.

Marcel Proust, *Remembrance of Things Past: Swann's Way*, 1913

To Edward Brittain   1st London General Hospital
                                       14 January 1916

All Roland's things had just been sent back from the front through
Cox's; they had just opened them and they were all lying on the
floor. I had no idea of the after-results of an officer's death, or what
the returned kit, of which so much has been written in the papers,
really meant. It was terrible . . . There were His clothes – the clothes
in which he came home from the front the last time – another set
rather less worn, and underclothing and accessories of various
descriptions. Everything was damp and worn and simply caked with
mud. And I was glad that neither you nor Victor nor anyone else
who may some day go to the front was there to see. If you had been
you would have been overwhelmed by the horror of war without
its glory. For though he had only worn the things when living, the
smell of those clothes was the smell of graveyards and the Dead.
The mud of France which covered them was not ordinary mud; it
had not the usual clean pure smell of earth, but it was as though it
were saturated with dead bodies – dead that had been dead a long,
long time. All the sepulchres and catacombs of Rome could not
make me realize mortality and decay and corruption as vividly as
did the smell of those clothes. I know now what he meant when he
used to write of 'this refuse-heap of a country' or 'a trench that
is nothing but a charnel-house'. And the wonder is, not that he
temporarily lost the extremest refinements of his personality as Mrs
Leighton says he did, but that he ever kept any of it at all – let alone
nearly the whole. He was more marvellous than even I dreamed.

There was his cap, bent in and shapeless out of recognition – the soft cap he wore rakishly on the back of his head – with the badge coated thickly with mud. He must have fallen on top of it, or perhaps one of the people who fetched him in trampled on it. The clothes he was wearing when wounded were those in which he came home last time. We discovered that the bullet was an expanding one. The hole where it went in in front – well below where the belt would have been, just beside the right-hand bottom pocket of the tunic – was almost microscopic, but at the back, almost exactly where his backbone would have been, there was quite a large rent. The underthings he was wearing at the time have evidently had to be destroyed, but they sent back a khaki waistcoat or vest (whatever that garment is you wear immediately below your tunic in cold weather) which was dark and stiff with blood, and a pair of khaki breeches also in the same state, which had been slit open at the top by someone in a great hurry – probably the doctor in haste to get at the wound, or perhaps even by one of the men. Even the tabs of his braces were bloodstained too. He must have fallen on his back as in every case the back of his clothes was much more stained and muddy than the front.

The charnel-house smell seemed to grow stronger and stronger till it pervaded the room and obliterated everything else. Finally Mrs Leighton said, 'Robert, take those clothes away into the kitchen, and don't let me see them again; I must either burn or bury them. They smell of Death; they are not Roland, they even seem to detract from his memory and spoil his glamour. I won't have any more to do with them.' And indeed one could never imagine those things the same as those in which he had lived & walked. One couldn't believe anyone alive had been in them at all. No, they were not Him.

Vera Brittain, *Letters From a Lost Generation*, edited by Alan Bishop and
Mark Bostridge, 1998

By roundabout ways he considered cunning, he would lead the Pal to speak of Lea, then he would clear the narrative of all bawdy asides that might retard it. 'Skip it! Skip it!' Barely bothering to enunciate the words, he relied on the initial sibilants to speed up or curtail the monologue. He would listen only to stories without malice in them, and glorifications of a purely descriptive nature. He insisted upon strict respect for documentary truth and checked his chronicler peevishly. He stocked his mind with dates, colours, materials and places, and the names of dressmakers.

'What's poplin?' he fired at her point-blank.

'Poplin's a mixture of silk and wool, a dry material . . . if you know what I mean; one that doesn't stick to the skin.'

'Yes. And mohair? You said "of white mohair".'

'Mohair is a kind of alpaca, but it hangs better, of course. Lea was afraid to wear lawn in the summer; she maintained it was best for underwear and handkerchiefs. Her own lingerie was fit for a queen, you'll remember, and in the days when that photograph was taken – yes, that beauty over there with the long legs – they didn't wear the plain underclothes of today. It was frill upon frill, a foam, a flurry of snow; and the drawers, dear boy! they'd have sent your head whirling . . . White Chantilly lace at the sides and black in between. Can't you just see the effect? But *can* you imagine it?'

Revolting, thought Cheri, revolting. Black Chantilly in between simply to please herself. In front of whose eyes did she wear them? For whom?

He could see Lea's gesture as he entered her bathroom or boudoir – the furtive gesture as she drew her wrap across her body. He could see the chaste self-confidence of her rosy body as she lay naked in the bath, with the water turned to milk by some essence or other.

Colette, *The Last of Cheri*, 1926

Beaming with confidence in both their futures, she disengaged herself from him, because there were stirring in her mind imperative commands about the dress she must buy for that night. It must be of white satin, because that is the one white stuff which does not seem poor when one thinks of real things. White velvet is like snow lying under a sober sky, but not so good, and all the white crêpes are like sunlit snow crisped by winds of different forces, but none of them so good, and the thinner weaves are not so white and fine as the filaments of frost. But white satin is a human idea, a human triumph. There is nothing like it in nature save the contented face of the cream in its broad bowl on the dairy shelf, and that is not so beautiful, for it looks not quite right, as it tastes not quite right, because of the greasiness which reminds you that the cow is a bit of a silly and does not answer as a horse does when you speak to it over the gate. Thick white satin is like light made solid for a woman's wearing when she wants to think of nothing but pure light, when colours are all wrong because they are stains which refer to passing moods, and there is nothing now on hand but a feeling that is going on for the rest of one's life. It should be simply made, for light takes simple forms, the path of the moon on the water is quite straight, the lightning through the cloud traces a pattern simpler than a branch. It was lovely that there were artists who attended to such things, who would make her a dress for tonight.

Rebecca West, *Sunflower*, 1986

RHINESTONES: NO THANK YOU!!!

We are tired of trying on stays!!!
We are going to stick them on drays!!!
We've sent dozens & dozens,
To poor country cousins,
A Kindness that nothing repays.

Black & Pink!! Black & Pink!!
Paris Corsets make you think
Lace and whalebone make you wink!!
Black & Pink! Black & Pink!!

Stephen Tennant, from 'Manual of Style', quoted in Philip Hoare,
Serious Pleasures: A Life of Stephen Tennant, 1990

Major Fosdick finished his second piece of cake. He sat for a few minutes, thinking. Then he got up from his chair and walked slowly out of the room. He had had enough of his sons for the moment. This was his hour. The time to please himself. A period of mental relaxation.

He went upstairs to his dressing room and when he had arrived there he locked the door. Then he turned to the bottom drawer of his wardrobe, where he kept all his oldest shooting suits. He knelt down in front of this and pulled it open. Below the piles of tweed was a piece of brown paper and from under the brown paper he took two parcels tied up with string. Major Fosdick undid the loose knots of the first parcel and took from out of it a large picture hat that had no doubt been seen at Ascot some twenty years before. The second parcel contained a black sequin evening dress of about the same date. Removing his coat and waistcoat, Major Fosdick slipped the evening dress over his head and, shaking it so that it fell down into position, he went to the looking-glass and put on the hat. When he had it arranged at an angle that was to his satisfaction, he lit his pipe and, taking a copy of *Through the Western Highlands with Rod and Gun* from the dressing table, he sat down. In this costume he read until it was time to change for dinner.

For a good many years now he had found it restful to do this for an hour or two every day when he had the opportunity. He himself would have found it difficult to account for such an eccentricity to anyone whom he might have happened to encounter during one of these periods and it was for this reason that he was accustomed to gratify his whim only at a time when there was a reasonable expectation that his privacy would be respected by his family. Publicly he himself would refer to these temporary retirements from the arena of everyday life as his Forty Winks.

Anthony Powell, *From a View to a Death*, 1933

Last night Gerald and I talked long and interestingly about the past, and also about a recent incident that has greatly disturbed him, although he is aware of its comic side.

Lytton lately took it into his head to go through his cupboards and wardrobes and get rid of things he no longer liked or wore. He discarded several suits and a great many ties and handkerchiefs. Carrington, knowing that Gerald was hard up at the moment, wrote and asked him if he would like some of them, without realizing (at any rate consciously) that she was presenting a red rag to a bull. Everything of Lytton's is so hallowed to her that she feels anyone ought to be delighted to be given it. The fact that Gerald *knew* she felt thus enraged him all the more. 'Lytton's old clothes! How would she like it if I sent her some of Winnie's disused garters?' [a prostitute friend of Brenan's]. He wrote refusing them coldly and with ironical politeness, adding a PS that he saw she had been giving away his presents; did this mean she was annoyed with him? The present in question was a silk handkerchief which Carrington had accidentally left behind at No. 41, and I (having no idea whose it was) had been wearing round my neck one evening when Gerald visited us. What a concatenation of circumstances! Gerald had roused my suspicions by the unnatural voice in which he asked me: 'Where did you get that nice handkerchief from, Frances?' and I, still uncertain of its provenance, merely said, 'It's not mine.'

This was all he was going on, but ironically enough, Carrington, who *had* given away some of his presents, was touched on a guilty spot and put up a frantic smokescreen. Yes, she had given away some of his presents, because (unlike him) she was so upset by these relics of the past that she couldn't bear to keep them.

'The little hypocrite,' said Gerald, 'when I know that half Ham Spray is furnished with my presents.' (A wild exaggeration.) But worst of all, with this letter she sent a parcel of Lytton's ties, 'and such awful ones,' said Gerald, 'especially chosen as an ironical comment on my clothes. One was knitted from that *shiny wood-silk*,' (here his voice rose to a scream); '*quite impossible to wear it*.'

Frances Partridge, *Memories*, 1981

It was Rose who brought her Papa's favourite pale tweed coat, gone at the elbows, frayed at the cuffs, for which he had an obstinate adoration. Mrs Brock spread the coat on the table, excited by his problem, and presently worked away in the haze of scents impregnating its stuff: turf smoke and burnt heather roots – it had been handwoven in a cottage. Through and beyond this rough base, other smells came faint and vaporous. Egyptian cigarettes stayed the most constant, defeating horses' sweat in the coat-tails and hair oil in the collar. As the coat warmed under her hands and on her knee, a masculine presence enveloped and pervaded her.

Papa noticed the miracle of repair performed on his old favourite. 'So you did remember to have a go at Rose about this old coat, bless you. You know I love it,' he said to Mummie. 'Good old Rose – I knew she had it in her. Never gives her running unless she's under the stick.'

'I don't know what you are talking about,' Mummie said.

'Of course you do – you told me to throw it away.'

'Yes, I wish you had. It's not your colour, really.' She looked into him, through him, lost in consideration.

'Extraordinary.' He lifted his arm, the wing of a jungle cock; he preened with pleasure in his old plumage. 'I shall give her half a sovereign for this job,' he said with firm intention.

It was more than I could bear. 'I know. I know who did it.'

Molly Keane, Good Behaviour, 1981

Blanche showed me the crêpe de Chine knickers trimmed with real lace that she had made. She said Mrs Buller only wore handmade underclothes, or if she did buy any ready-made, she took them to pieces and resewed them herself. 'Real people feel almost ill if they have a machine stitch anywhere near them, not only hems, tucks and embroidery, but everything,' she said with awe.

Barbara Comyns, A Touch of Mistletoe, 1967

Mrs Danvers came back and stood beside me. She smiled, and her manner, instead of being still and unbending as it usually was, became startlingly familiar, fawning even. 'Now you are here, let me show you everything,' she said, her voice ingratiating and sweet as honey, horrible, false . . .

'That was her bed. It's a beautiful bed, isn't it? I keep the golden coverlet on it always, it was her favourite. Here is her nightdress inside the case. You've been touching it, haven't you? This was the nightdress she was wearing the last time, before she died. Would you like to touch it again?' She took the nightdress from the case and held it before me. 'Feel it, hold it,' she said; 'how soft and light it is, isn't it?I haven't washed it since she wore it for the last time. I put it out like this, and the dressing gown and slippers, just as I put them out for her the night she never came back, the night she was drowned.' She folded up the nightgown and put it back in the case. 'I did everything for her, you know,' she said, taking my arm again, leading me to the dressing gown and slippers. 'We tried maid after maid but not one of them suited. "You maid me better than anyone, Danny," she used to say, "I won't have anyone but you." Look, this is her dressing gown. She was much taller than you, you can see by the length. Put it up against you. It comes down to your ankles. She had a beautiful figure. These are her slippers. "Throw me my slips, Danny," she used to say. She had little feet for her height. Put your hands inside the slippers. They are quite small and narrow, aren't they?'

She forced the slippers over my hands, smiling all the while, watching my eyes. 'You never would have thought she was so tall, would you?' she said. 'These slippers would fit a tiny foot. She was so slim too. You would forget her height, until she stood beside you. She was every bit as tall as me. But lying there in bed she looked quite a slip of a thing, with her mass of dark hair, standing out from her face like a halo . . .

'You would like to see her clothes, wouldn't you?' She did not wait for my answer. She led me to the little ante-room and opened the wardrobes, one by one.

'I keep her furs in here,' she said. 'The moths have not got to them yet, and I doubt if they ever will. I'm too careful. Feel that sable wrap. That was a Christmas present from Mr de Winter. She told me the cost once, but I've forgotten it now. This chinchilla she wore in the evenings mostly. Round her shoulders, very often, when the evenings were cold. The wardrobe here is full of her evening clothes. You opened it, didn't you? The latch is not quite closed. I believe Mr de Winter liked her to wear silver mostly. But of course she could wear anything, stand any colour. She looked beautiful in this velvet. Put it against your face. It's soft, isn't it? You can feel it, can't you? The scent is still fresh, isn't it? You could almost imagine she had only just taken it off. I would always know when she had been before me in a room. There would be a little whiff of her scent in the room. These are her underclothes, in this drawer. This pink set here she had never worn. She was wearing slacks of course and a shirt when she died. They were torn from her body in the water though. There was nothing on the body when it was found, all those weeks afterwards.'

Daphne du Maurier, *Rebecca*, 1938

He must have spent a considerable amount of money on his clothes; his suits were really beautiful and I sometimes stroked them when I had to go to his wardrobe. His pyjamas were real silk and his shirts and shoes were made-to-measure. He said his bootmaker had plaster casts of his feet and I was always meaning to see them, but never did.

Barbara Comyns, *A Touch of Mistletoe*, 1967

I decided to spend this buying a pair of shoes. This was always a difficult and dangerous mission for me. If I wanted to use the longest words for the shortest thing I would say that I was a passive foot fetishist. My feet were smaller than an ordinary mortal's and I wanted everyone to know this. As time went by I wore shorter and shorter shoes, not because the length of my feet decreased but because the amount of discomfort I could bear became greater. Finally I was able to endure footwear that was hardly visible to the naked eye. For me, as for Hans Andersen's little mermaid, every step was agony but as she had finally been rewarded by dancing with a prince, I never gave up. Almost as uncomfortable as wearing the shoes was buying them. Both I and the shop assistant needed all the fortitude we could summon. I would describe the shoes I had in mind and ask for a size four. The salesman or woman (according to what sex the management had decided I was) would measure my foot and bring me a shoe that fitted me perfectly. This immediately aroused my suspicion. When I ripped it off and looked at the sole, I found it to be a six. Moving down the scale in semitones, I would try on successive sizes until my toes were folded inside the shoe like the leaves of an artichoke. Then I would say, 'Now lift me up.' If I could stand in them, those were the shoes I bought. Tottering into the street, I screamed for a taxi. To this day my feet are two misshapen plinths of twisted bone.

*

Like Florrie Forde, I and most of the homosexuals whom I knew best wanted 'something in a uniform'. Any national dress or occupational outfit may be sexually stimulating and there are as many kinks as there are kinds of costume. Uniforms appeal to devotees of the fearless man of action. They also pander to the Cophetua complex so prevalent among homosexuals. When any of my friends mentioned that he had met a 'divine' sailor he never meant an officer. Women seem to feel differently about these things. They prefer airmen, by which they always mean the higher ranks. I used to sit in the window seat in a King's Road café discussing these matters with a certain Mrs Gardner. I should have guessed that she was a born murderee. She used to wear a leopardette coat.

When I was young the word 'soldier' meant one of the red-coated guardsmen who strutted up and down Knightsbridge in the evenings. These men were willing to go for 'a walk in the park' for as little as half a crown. This appeared to be what Berwick Street would call a desperate bargain at a never-again price but, had I accepted the offer, I have no doubt that I should have been beaten to a pulp with or without benefit of sex.

Sailors never asked for money but, on the contrary, had large sums of money to spend in short spasms of shore leave. They also never turned nasty. Perhaps the act of running away to sea was an abandonment of accepted convention and, after a sojourn in strange ports, they returned with their outlook and possibly their anus broadened.

The fabulous generosity of their natures was an irresistible lure – especially when combined with the tightness of their uniforms, whose crowning aphrodisiac feature was the fly flap of their trousers. More than one of my friends has swayed about in ecstasy describing the pleasures of undoing this quaint sartorial device. All that is ended now. Naval uniforms have been altered. With a vertical instead of horizontal opening to their trousers, sailors can

walk their shoes to the uppers without a single stranger asking them
for a light.

Quentin Crisp, *The Naked Civil Servant*, 1968

'I [Nancy Mitford, writing in 1947] saw Dolly Radziwell just now
and she told me the following story. Her vendeuse at Balmain had
a new client, a M. Lecomte, who chose about six dresses and said,
"My wife is not well, will you bring them round for her to see." So
round she goes – luxury flat, exquisite creature appears with a curtain
of gold hair, darling little waist, long elegant legs and so on and they
begin trying on the dresses. Suddenly the vendeuse becomes aware
that the pretty little bosoms are not quite real – looks again at the
face – horrors! M. Lecomte himself!! He sees that she is very much
put out and says, "*Jusqu'à present je me suis habillé chez Jacques Fath, vous
n'avez qu'à lui telephoner pour des reseignements sur moi.*" So as soon as
she gets back Balmain himself gets through to Fath who says, "*Vous
êtes vraiment veinard, c'est un client comme il n'y en a peu, doux, gentil et riche
à milliards.*" The end of it is he has ordered several dresses including
a shell pink ball dress—!! The hair was a wonderful WIG. Do
admit—!!'

Sir Harold Acton, *Nancy Mitford: A Memoir*, 1975

Oh dear, oh dear, isn't it annoying about Truman getting in again.
There I went and ordered a sumptuous dress from Hattie Carnegie
specially to wear at the White House and now I shan't be *going* to
the White House. It's all very vexing. Oh, and don't let Hattie talk
you into one of those willpower dresses. I had one all beautifully
fitted and boned and everything was fine until I *ate*. Then, oh my
Gawd, I seemed to swell and swell and the bones cut into my flesh
and I thought I'd bust. I had to rush to the powder room and tear

the dress off and go straight home in my wrap. You never knew such agony.

Anne Scott-James, In the Mink, 1952

Pierre was sitting at the edge of the bed and had slipped his pants on and was fastening the buckle of his belt. Elena had slipped on her dress but was still coiled around him as he sat. Then he showed her his belt. She sat up to look at it. It had been a heavy, strong leather belt with a silver buckle but was now so completely worn that it looked about to tear. The tip of it was frayed. The places where the buckle fastened were almost as thin as a piece of cloth.

'My belt is wearing out,' Pierre said, 'and it makes me sad because I have had it ten years.' He studied it contemplatively.

As she looked at him sitting there, with his belt not yet fastened, she was sharply reminded of the moment before he unfastened his belt to let his pants down. He never unfastened it until a caress, a tight embrace of their bodies against one another, had aroused his desire so that the confined penis hurt him.

There was always that second of suspense before he loosened his pants and took out his penis for her to touch. Sometimes he let her take it out. If she could not unbutton his underwear quickly enough, then he did it himself. The little snapping sound of the buckle affected her. It was an erotic moment for her, as was, for Pierre, the moment before she took down her panties or loosened her garters. Though she had been fully satisfied a moment before, she was aroused again. She would have liked to unfasten the belt, let his pants slip down and touch his penis once more. When it first came out of the pants, how alertly it straightened itself to point to her, as if in recognition.

Then suddenly the realization that the belt was so old, that Pierre had always worn it, struck her with a strange, sharp pain. She saw him unfastening it in other places, other rooms, at other hours, for other women.

She was jealous, acutely jealous, with this image repeating itself. She wanted to say, 'Throw the belt away. At least do not carry the same one that you wore for them. I will give you another.'

It was as if his feeling for the belt were a feeling of affection for the past that he could not rid himself of entirely. For her, the belt represented the gestures made in the past. She asked herself if all the caresses had been the same.

Anaïs Nin, 'Elena', from *Delta of Venus*, 1978

Over a whalebone bodice which severely constricted the waist, and over a starched linen petticoat, was worn an ample gown, the open neck of which left the breasts, raised by the bodice, practically visible beneath a light film of gauze. The petticoat and gauze were white, the bodice and gown a sea-green satin.

She'd bend her head ever so slightly towards her left shoulder, leaning her cheek against the upturned collar of her fur . . . O caught her once that way,* smiling and sweet, her hair faintly lifted as though by some gentle breeze, and her soft but hard cheek grazing silver-fox, as grey and delicate as fresh firewood ash. Her lips were parted, her eyes half-closed. Under the cool brilliance of glossy paper one would have thought this the picture of some blessed victim of drowning; pale, so very pale.

Jacqueline . . . was wearing an immense gown of heavy silk brocade, red, like what brides wore in the Middle Ages, going to within a few inches of the floor, flaring at the hips, tight at the waist, and whose armature sketched her breasts . . . it was what couturiers called a show gown.

Pauline Reage, *The Story of O*, 1954

*O works as a fashion photographer, taking pictures of girls modelling couturier's show gowns.

Main character, Humbert the Hummer. Time: Sunday morning in
June. Place: sunlit living room. Props: old, candy-striped davenport,
magazines, phonograph, Mexican knick-knacks (the late Mr Harold
E. Haze – God bless the good man – had engendered my darling
at the siesta hour in a blue-washed room, on a honeymoon trip to Vera
Cruz, the mementoes, among these Dolores, were all over the place).
She wore that day a pretty print dress that I had seen on her once
before, ample in the skirt, tight in the bodice, short-sleeved, pink,
chequered with darker pink, and, to complete the colour scheme, had
painted her lips and was holding in her hollowed hands a beautiful,
banal, Eden-red apple. She was not shod, however, for church.

Lola the bobby soxer, devouring her immemorial fruit, singing
through its juice, losing her slipper, rubbing the heel of her slipper-less
foot in its sloppy anklet, against the pile of old magazines . . . between
my gagged, bursting beast and the beauty of her dimpled body in
its innocent cotton frock.

Vladimir Nabokov, *Lolita*, 1959

At that moment, the peace was shattered by an extremely strident
motor horn. A large car was coming towards them. It drew up at a
big house just ahead of them and a tall woman came out on to the
front-door steps. She was wearing a tight-fitting emerald satin dress,
several ropes of rubies, and an absolutely simple white mink cloak,
which reached to the heels of her ruby red shoes. She had a dark
skin, black eyes wth a tinge of red in them, and a very pointed nose.
Her hair was parted severely down the middle and one half of it was
black and the other white – rather unusual.

'Why, that's Cruella de Vil,' said Mrs Dearly. 'We were at school
together. She was expelled for drinking ink.' . . .

'What's your married name, Cruella?' asked Mrs Dearly, as they
walked through a green marble hall into a red marble drawing room.

'My name is still de Vil,' said Cruella. 'I am the last of my family so I made my husband change his name to mine.'

Just then the absolutely simple white mink cloak slipped from her shoulders to the floor. Mr Dearly picked it up.

'What a beautiful cloak,' he said. 'But you'll find it too warm for this evening.'

'I never find anything too warm,' said Cruella. 'I wear furs all the year round. I sleep between ermine sheets.'

'How nice,' said Mrs Dearly, politely. 'Do they wash well?'

Cruella did not seem to hear this. She went on: 'I worship furs, I live for furs! That's why I married a furrier.'

Then Mr de Vil came in. He was a small, worried-looking man who didn't seem to be anything besides a furrier. Cruella introduced him and then said: 'Where are those two delightful dogs?'

Pongo and Missis were sitting under the grand piano feeling hungry. The red marble walls had made them think of slabs of raw meat.

'They're expecting puppies,' said Mrs Dearly, happily.

'Oh, are they? Good!' said Cruella. 'Come here, dogs!'

Pongo and Missis came forward politely.

'Wouldn't they make enchanting fur coats?' said Cruella to her husband.

'For spring wear, over a black suit. We've never thought of making coats out of dogs' skins.'

Dodie Smith, *The Hundred and One Dalmatians*, 1956

A woman is not a woman without her furs, my father said. A man in evening dress slips a sable from a woman's back and they drink cocktails together. Taking off a fur is a sexual undressing. Under the fur, satin or crêpe de Chine, cut on the bias. Emeralds. Diamond clips.

Linda Grant, *The Cast Iron Shore*, 1996

Roy Johnson and I walked in the drizzle; I went to Eddie's girl's house to get back my wool plaid shirt, the shirt of Shelton, Nebraska. It was there, all tied up, the whole enormous sadness of a shirt.

Jack Kerouac, *On the Road*, 1957

1963

In those days I didn't have a real fashion look yet. I just wore black stretch jeans, pointed black boots that were usually all splattered with paint, and button-down-Oxford-cloth shirts under a Wagner College sweatshirt that Gerard [Malanga] had given me. Eventually I picked up some style from Wynn [Chamberlain], who was one of the first to go in for the S&M leather look.

1964

The theme of the party was going to be 'Mods vs. rockers', so on the night of the party, to make it look authentic, Nicky went over to an S&M leather bar on 33rd Street and Third Avenue called the Copper Kettle, where he'd just taken his friend Jane Ormsby Gore dressed as a boy (she was the daughter of the British ambassador to Washington) and invited all the leather boys to come by later on but to really bust their way in to make it look like a real confrontation between mods and rockers. The leather boys did come, but since nobody even tried to stop them, they just wandered in with no problem – and no impact.

Andy Warhol and Pat Hackett, *POPism: The Warhol '60s*, 1981

Monique was wearing a dress cut roughly the same as the long dresses that O remembered, but Monique's was more severe, more staid, an effect which doubtless stemmed from the material – a very dark grey-blue wool – and the shawl which covered her head, shoulders and bosom. When O had donned the same clothing and

saw herself in the mirror beside Monique, she realized what it was
that had surprised her when she had seen Monique. It was an outfit
which oddly resembled those worn in women's prisons, or by
servants in convents. But not if you really looked closely at them.
The wide, full skirt, lined with taffeta of the same colour, was sewed
on to a band with large, open, unpressed pleats that fastened over
the corset, exactly like certain evening gowns do. And although it
appeared closed, it was open in the middle of the back from the
waistline down to the feet. Unless you deliberately pulled the dress
to one side or the other, however, you would never have noticed it.
O noticed it on hers only after they had put on her skirt, and she
had failed to remark it earlier on Monique's. The blouse, which
buttoned in the back, had short, scalloped peplums which covered,
for about the width of a person's hand, the onset of the pleats. It
was fitted with darts and two elastic panels. The sleeves were cut
out but not sewed on, with a seam on the upper part of the arm
that extended to the shoulder seam and ended at the elbow in a
wide, flared bias. A similar bias piped the *decolleté* neckline which
tightly followed the curve of the corset. But a large scarf of black
lace covered her head, one corner of which hung down in the middle
of her forehead, like a kerchief, while the other corner extended
down her back, falling between her shoulder blades. It was fastened
by four snaps, two on the shoulder seams and two on the bias of
the low-cut neckline, just at the rise of the breasts, and crossed
between them, where a long steel pin held it taut to the corset. The
lace, held in the hair by a comb, framed the face and completely
concealed the breasts, but was supple and transparent enough so
that you could make out the nipples, as you knew that the breasts
were bare beneath the shawl. Besides, all you had to do to make
them completely bare was to remove the pin, as, in the back, all you
had to do was spread the two folds of the skirt to bare the backside.

Before she undressed her again, Monique showed O how, with
two straps that raised the two sections of the skirt and then tied in

front at the waist, it was a simple matter to keep them open. It was while she was demonstrating this that, in effect, Anne-Marie answered the question raised by O:

'It's the uniform of the community,' she said.

Pauline Reage, *The Story of O: Part Two*, 1969

She was complete in that room, surrounded by her souvenirs and her relics, the epiphenomena of a life: the fluffy toys won for her by some former boyfriend at a coastal fair years ago, the strata of cosmetics (above the washstand) that dated back to the original Body Shop and then, finally, the bottom line – the row of twenty pairs of shoes, spread out like a crescendo on a creased sheet of music. The spoils of a thousand shopping trips, the evidence of a thousand rainy afternoons in bad-tempered shops. From the plimsolls rebelliously worn to school, to the court shoes worn once to a friend's wedding, to the scuffed and despised work shoes, to the final sad lustre of the catalogue bridal slippers – white shells in a rockpool of tissue paper. Her fiancé was marrying a collection of shoes, scorched by hot pavements and frozen by bus-stop sleet.

Michael Bracewell, *The Crypto-Amnesia Club*, 1988

TIES

The dark green Tootal with white spots he wore
in the first photograph of him I saw –
the tie he lent me for my first date

and later told me I could keep,
the matching scarf too. So 1930s,
I might as well have been in the war.

Two autumn-coloured, large check ties
that gave me, so I thought, the air
of a schoolmaster out of Evelyn Waugh.

Then the red houndstooth, a bracing affair
with a dash of gin-and-it or *Brighton Rock*,
a lounge-lizard's whiff of the paddock.

The last, that I've worn once, I took
because I had to: a sort of crêpe
he bought for funerals, and hated.

Alan Jenkins, from *In The Hot-House*, 1988

Thank God it's over, or at least until next spring. Fashion Show
Fever, that is. Because if I read more about women asserting their
sexuality through provocative, crotch-hugging designs, or about
such-and-such a designer exposing acres of cleavage in order to
celebrate the new femininity, I may puke all over someone's Pucci
tights.

What is it with these people? If I pay fifteen nubile women in
street-walking clobber to expose the gussets of their underwear to
an audience in a Soho nightclub, I'm a sleaze merchant, a social
pariah. But if I send the same fifteen women in the same clothes
down a catwalk, tart the whole thing up with a bit of jazz-rap, and
throw my post-show party at the same Soho club, then it's odds-on
some half-wit Windsor will be double-kissing me by Christmas.
Confused? Me too.

Maybe I'm missing the point, but as a heterosexual follower of
fashion I find sluttish clothes for women a very poor joke. Maybe
the irony is too refined for me. Sluttish clothes are for sluts, and
sluts get hurt. After putting out, that's their primary function in life.

In case you'd forgotten this, Dolce e Gabbana have created a catalogue to remind you. It has 'super-model' Linda Evangelista in anguished slut mode, photographed in loving monochrome for that hint of realism, being abused and intimidated by some jerk who still thinks designer stubble is hip. The subtext is this season's fashionable in-joke: 'Look at her, dancing on the bar, wearing slut garb. She's asking for it!'

Shortly after finding the catalogue in a Knightsbridge boutique, I was confronted by photo-reports of Thierry Mugler's latest collection, featuring vinyl S&M outfits that would look clichéd in the small ads of *Bondage* magazine. I don't expect much of Mugler, but I was disturbed to see his cheap gimmickry echoed by other younger (and, one would think, more intelligent) designers in Milan, London and Paris. Worse still, air-headed fashion hacks have bent backwards to excuse this camp chauvinism as 'liberating' and 'adventurous'. Others say it doesn't matter that women are being patronized with trashy, trivializing designs because politics and aesthetics don't mix. I'm sure that Magda Goebbels, patron of Nazi Germany's Institute of Fashion, would have agreed . . .

Bad bitches are nothing new and as long as that is acknowledged, we're on reasonably safe ground. The problem occurs when designers present good old-fashioned titillation as post-feminist advancement, and fashion journalists take this rubbish at face value. If only the perpetrators of smutty slutty garb would come clean, if only they'd say: 'Look, we're in the midst of a conservative and neurotic period of British history. Our careers are threatened by recession, our personal liberties eroded, our concept of sexuality compromised by the threat of Aids. We'd like to present you with a vision of the future but we honestly can't get it together. Meanwhile, we've picked over the past and jazzed it up a bit. What do you think?'

If only. But fashion dare not admit that it doesn't know the way forward. There are too many threads being unravelled already: a couple more and the whole macramé catsuit will come undone. The

designer's mystique is disappearing fast and, for many, only the hype
remains . . .

Alix Sharkey, 'Slut style: going too far?', Guardian, 1992

Fashion, art, sex and the club scene are all cohering into a new
expression of sexuality. We are barely aware, when we buy a
Wonderbra, that we are taking part in a revival of corsetry and
tight-lacing, banished since the sixties to the pages of pin-up magazines . . . Three years ago, sado-masochism began to emerge out of
a furtive, shame-ridden underworld. From being a sexual subculture,
it has become part of nineties' style, via post-Aids gay safe sex. In
the nineties, the dominatrix has become the icon of the sexual
woman; the message she is giving out is one of power over herself
and over men . . .

Jane Wildgoose, a lecturer at the Royal College of Art, is currently
working on a book, *The World, the Flesh and the Dress Designer*, which
brings together such phenomena as pierced bodies on the catwalk
and artists like Damien Hirst and Kiki Smith who are rejecting
precious or durable materials in favour of blood, body parts and
biodegradable materials . . . [In the book she says:] 'The idea that
one can take on a role through clothes is very important, but what
do these images really mean? The dominatrix is a completely male
fantasy, albeit one many women are happy to share. Why does
everything have to be so black and white? Why do there have to be
good women and bad women?' Perhaps the dominatrix on the one
hand and Kate Moss on the other are only part of the old, old
contrast between the devouring woman and innocence just about
to be sullied . . .

There is another issue that most commentators are reluctant to
verbalize, though it has been articulated to some extent by Susan
Faludi in *Backlash*. 'This is very difficult to say, but male homosexual
designers, artists and film-makers all have a tremendous influence

over the shape of women's bodies,' Wildgoose argues. 'Homosexual expressions are moving into the mainstream and influencing the way women's bodies are portrayed.'

It is a woman designer, Coco Chanel, who has had the most enduring influence on clothes for women that are both practical and elegant. When Karl Lagerfeld took over the house, Wildgoose points out, his designs satirized and caricatured the legacy he had inherited. It is predominantly gay male designers who have restored the stiletto and Wonderbra. In other words, male designers are requiring their models to have not only the bodies those designers desire in boys, but also the bodies they would, in their secret fantasies, like to have themselves. To gay men, women don't look like Jean Muir but RuPaul in high heels and false eyelashes.

Linda Grant, 'Cut and Thrust', *Guardian*, 1996

'Ursula!' cried Mearns, the greenmailer. 'How lovely to see you; you look quite, quite marvellous.' He rose and went to meet her. Richard unstuck his head from his hands and blinked. She was standing in the doorway, bracing herself with both hands held above her head. She had one thigh raised up and half-crossed over the top of the other. She was wearing some sort of golden, spangled top, the spangles scattered over a fine mesh that exposed as much as it concealed her magnificent embonpoint. And Ursula wasn't just wearing a short skirt, she was wearing a pelmet – a little flange of thick, green, brocaded material that hung down, barely covering her lower abdomen. To either side of this lappet, flaring curtains of material descended. If Ursula had been straight-legged, ordinarily disposed, this would have presented a decorous enough picture. However, given the attitude she had struck, the longer drapes of cloth fell away, making an arch that framed the very juncture of her thighs. Richard let fly with a deep, glottal groan.

This was ignored by the others, who all rose and went over to

Ursula. One by one they all kissed the air some inches in front of her cheek, as exemplary an acknowledgement as possible of the fact that they would rather be some inches *inside* her body.

Will Self, *The Sweet Smell of Psychosis*, 1996

6. 'We do not dress for ourselves alone': The Well-dressed Man

Give a naked man a coat, and he will be more a man than before and therefore more a gentleman.

Eric Gill, *Clothes*, 1931

I prefer the secretiveness of suits that aren't featured in reams of fashion magazines. I felt like moving into a finer art of disguise, where I can cross frontiers and not feel like a marked man.

Malcolm McLaren, 'Hype-Allergic', *Details*, 1992

If Paris was the centre of women's fashion, then London was the centre for men's style: the role of tailoring in creating the image of the English gentleman in a suit was essential. It shaped what J.C. Flugel called the 'Great Masculine Renunciation' of 1789: 'the magnificence and elaboration of costume which so well expressed the ideals of the *ancien regime*' were 'distasteful to the new social tendencies and aspirations that found expression in the French Revolution'[1] and the example set in early nineteenth-century England by dandy 'Beau' Brummell of wearing a suit of dark cloth of the finest quality and exquisite cut with clean linen was followed in Europe, in North America and the European colonies. The rules and regulations of men's dress and what made – and makes – a well-dressed man are reflected in many examples in literature, from the work of P. G. Wodehouse to that of Bret Easton Ellis, as this chapter demonstrates.

By the end of the nineteenth century a gentleman's wardrobe might contain white ties and tailcoat for formal wear, black tie and dinner jacket for the evening; suits in brown or tweed for the country, grey or blue for town, and occasionally black, though this was deemed more appropriate for funerals; and old school or regimental ties if one had the right, with woven ties following these colours as an option. Brown shoes in town never; and suede was the mark of the homosexual. Which both allowed a lot of room for deviation and created a code of dress so firmly fixed it was 'classic' rather than fashionable.

The years following 1918 were ones of huge social upheaval in Britain and America as elsewhere. The decimation of young men of marriageable age obviously affected women, and the young Prince of Wales became a romantic figure on both sides of the Atlantic, contrasting favourably with his more formal father, George V. 'At Oxford I was a bit of a dandy,' he wrote, 'wearing my hat at a rakish angle, tying my bow tie with care . . . [later] I was "produced" as a leader of fashion . . . the middleman was the photographer . . . employed by the trade . . . with an especial eye for what I was wearing. A selection of these photographs, together with patterns [and] samples of ties, socks, waistcoats and so forth, was immediately rushed to America.'[2] He found the role constricting: 'All my life, hitherto, I had been fretting against the constrictions of dress which reflected my family's world of rigid social convention. It was my impulse, whenever I found myself alone, to remove my coat, rip off my tie, loosen my collar and roll up my sleeves.'[3]

The formality imposed on him made him favour sportswear: he introduced the sleeveless pullover for hunting, popularized plus fours, launched the Fair Isle sweater as a fashion item when he wore one to play golf at St Andrews and introduced the soft formal shirt. The growing mode for wearing sports clothes in town, which he popularized, led to the lounge suit replacing the frock coat in the City,[4] and the gradual acceptance of the suit as formal and informal wear for men.

By the 1930s, British and American fashions were moving away from each other. *Vanity Fair*'s 'London Letter', which had been a fixed item since the magazine's launch in 1913, became less frequent, with editorial concentrating on American menswear style – and the stars of Hollywood. As the style of each country evolved, the difference between the well-dressed American and British man became more marked. In Britain, there were calls for the reform of men's clothes. The artist Eric Gill had called for beauty and colour to be brought back to men's clothes, with open-necked shirts, shorts and sandals for the day, and black knee breeches and a silk blouse for evening.[5] In 1929, Dean Inge of St Paul's Cathedral and Walter Sickert founded the Men's Dress Reform Party, with the aim of converting the public to a more comfortable, rational and attractive dress. The Russian designer Erté had already expressed the need to bring back 'beauty' to men's dress in interviews in Hollywood in 1925; but with Erté, the question of sexuality hovered over the debate, and Inge and Sickert were faced with preconceptions, summed up by a (conventional) tailor at a Dress Reform dinner debate in 1932, who stated that those men who wore unusual or exotic attire were 'sexually abnormal' and that 'soft, sloppy clothes are symbolical of a soft and sloppy race'.[6] Open-necked shirts and shorts were worn anyway by hikers celebrating the outdoor life, part of a movement for health and vigour that was growing increasingly popular in Nazi Germany; George Orwell identified them as the Socialist uniform with disgust at its ugliness. Faced with such opposition in 1936, the MDRP closed down.

Gill believed that the dominance of the tailored suit, and the convention that demanded that men should look the same, was a mark of a predominantly Calvinist/Protestant society. The European view of men's style was different, in that *fashion* for men was acceptable. The 1920s French magazine *Monsieur* had high-quality illustrations in the tradition of the *Gazette du Bon Ton* and whimsical features on dandyism. Doucet in the 1920s, Schiaparelli in the 1930s, Dior and Fath in the 1950s all produced menswear ranges.

In Britain, high-street shops catered for the mainstream, Savile Row to the 'gentleman' and small tailors and outfitters to youth or the gay customer looking for colour and style. After the Second World War, Guards officers, nostalgic for the Edwardian glamour of the 'man about town', began to wear ornate brocaded waistcoats, and, by 1948, long and narrow single-breasted jackets and narrow trousers, turned-back velvet cuffs and velvet collars on overcoats, topped with a carnation and a silver-topped cane.[7] The style was a reaction against the drabness of demob and a move to establish the style of the upper-class Englishman in ascendancy over a growing American influence. It was soon adopted by older men – predominantly homosexual – such as Cecil Beaton and Bunny Roger; most importantly, it was copied by the new youth group, the Teds (discussed further in Chapter Eight).

The idea that men in general enjoyed wearing clothes, and that the potential market was huge, took hold, and in 1959 Hardy Amies was invited by Hepworth's to design a menswear range for its high-street shops. *Man About Town* magazine, which included fashion spreads, was launched in the same year, running a seminal article on the mod – named after the followers of American Modernist jazz stars – street-dandies Mark Feld (Marc Bolan) and friends in September 1962. In 1957, John Stephen had opened a boutique, His Clothes, just off Carnaby Street and John Michael Ingram opened his first John Michael shop in the King's Road; both served the new youth market. From November 1965 the new magazine *Men in Vogue* featured the grander men of style: Cecil Beaton, Christopher Gibbs, Julian Ormsby-Gore and Brian Jones.

In 1969 Beaton was listed as one of the best-dressed men in the world, which he found farcical, noting in his diary on 13 January, 'If only people knew! I spend comparatively little on clothes, an occasional good suit but most of my suits are made in Hong Kong or Gillingham Dorset, or bought on quaysides during my travels abroad . . .'[8] The same year, Mick Jagger was nominated the best-dressed man in Britain by Professor Janey Ironside of the Royal College of Art; he had just appeared wearing a dress designed by Mr Fish at a Hyde Park concert.

A year later, in 1970, Paul Smith opened his first menswear shop in Nottingham, offering an alternative to the blue shirts, blue suits and blue ties that most of the men in the provinces were condemned to wearing, despite the fashion revolution taking place in London.[9] Aware of the expanding designer label market for men, in 1974 Yves Saint Laurent expanded into menswear, and in 1975 Giorgio Armani followed. His unstructured jacket, which demanded complex cut and construction, was perfect for the 'less is more' look that became popular by the late 1970s. By the mid-1980s, men were demanding designer labels which conferred identity – what Malcolm McLaren has called the 'designer suit club'.[10]

American anxiety over getting the 'right' label or patronizing the 'right' tailor in London, illustrated in the early issues of *Vanity Fair*, satirized by Tom Wolfe, Bret Easton Ellis and Jay McInerney, is an insecurity which dates back to the British culture of class-as-dress. It has continued unabated in some quarters and still attracts a xenophobic snobbery which is not entirely justified; to view men's style as the story of good-if-not-best tailoring is to ignore other elements which go to make a man 'well dressed'. What is true, however, is that in a reaction against urban street culture, the traditional notion of being a 'well-dressed' man has returned in the 1990s, with a desire once again for suits that are individually crafted to a high quality.

Dressed in a suit of white flannel, with a blue shirt and handkerchief bought at Doucet's, and with his head, that resembled an actor's, crowned with a straw boater, he flitted about talking excellent French. Harry's [Melvill] dancing, his bridge playing, his polo and tennis and golf were all astonishing; he was a fashionable comedian, a traveller who felt at home in Paris, in Venice and Florence, in Vienna and Madrid.

J. E. Blanche, *Portraits of a Lifetime*, 1937

Malcolm is a tittsy-pootsy man! Not as tall as I am, and thin as a rail, with a look of his knees being too near together. He must be awful in a kilt, and I am sure he shivers when the wind blows, he has that air. I don't like kilts, unless men are big, strong, bronzed creatures who don't seem ashamed of their bare bits. I saw some splendid specimens marching once in Edinburgh, and they swung their kilts just like the beautiful ladies in the Bois, when Mademoiselle and I went out of the allée Mrs Carruthers told us to try always to walk in.

Elinor Glyn, *The Vicissitudes of Evangeline*, 1905

Fashions in men's clothes find their origin with the gentlemen of England; the makers there are simple artisans who execute the orders of their betters. To understand the requirements of your world, you must live *in* it. This first-hand knowledge of social conditions is essential to create any proper change in dress. The brothers of these British artisans on this side of the water have not always an equal sense of their limitations. They frequently intrude boldly with attempts to improve or to accentuate. The result is those against which every man of sense rebels. Costume, like every other incidental phase of life, is an expression of evolution with a constant tendency to recurrent types. The student will perceive that what may be called a new fashion from England is more often merely a modified return, for this commercial day, to details of some fashion that had grace and value yesterday.

The English and American fashion plates of men's clothes for the coming autumn and winter have been out for some weeks. I find no *tout-ensemble* among them indicative of the better dressed men either here or in Europe. There are certain public places –

hotels in New York – where one may see the Well-Dressed Man, either by day or in the evening; and even though he is yet in his summer apparel. I should advise following the style seen on him now – in preference to most of the advance professional advice and published illustrations of men's attire.

'The Well-Dressed Man', *Vanity Fair*, 1913

He was walking along with a light step, stimulated by the rathe spring, perceptible in the moist gusty wind and the exciting earthy smells of squares and private gardens. Every now and again a fleeting glimpse in a glass would remind him that he was wearing a becoming felt hat, pulled down over the right eye, a loose-fitting spring coat, large light-coloured gloves, and a terracotta tie. The eyes of women followed his progress with silent homage, the more candid among them bestowing that passing stupefaction which can be neither feigned nor hidden.

Colette, *Cheri*, 1920

Denis woke up next morning to find the sun shining, the sky serene. He decided to wear white flannel trousers – white flannel trousers and a black jacket, with a silk shirt and his new peach-coloured tie. And what shoes? White was the obvious choice, but there was something rather pleasing about the notion of black patent leather. He lay in bed for several minutes considering the problem.

Before he went down – patent leather was his final choice – he looked at himself critically in the glass. His hair might have been more golden, he reflected. As it was, its yellowness had the hint of a greenish tinge in it. But his forehead was good. His forehead made up in height what his chin lacked in prominence. His nose might have been longer, but it would pass. His eyes might have been blue and not green. But his coat was very well cut and, discreetly padded, made him seem robuster than he actually was. His legs, in their white casing, were long and elegant. Satisfied, he descended the stairs.

Aldous Huxley, *Crome Yellow*, 1921

I think a truly honest person would never wear a hat. Except in arctic weather a hat wears no purpose. The mitre, the Easter bonnet, the helmet, they function as an insignia of power.

W. H. Auden, from Charles Osborne, *W. H. Auden*, 1982

There was a group of tall young men at the entrance [the Loyalty Club, Mayfair], maybe waiting for their women from the cloakroom, maybe waiting for sirens to come to them from the night, maybe waiting for taxicabs, maybe only waiting for the next minute, as young men will. Admirably formal they looked, admirably toned to the dress coats of Davies, the trousers of Anderson and Sheppard, the hats of Lock, the waistcoats of Hawes and Curtis, the ties of Budd. Handkerchiefs by Edouard and Butler. The glory to God.

Michael Arlen, *The Green Hat*, 1924

I went to many parties in my new tail suit, savouring to the full the sensation of being well dressed for the first time. The days of twirling anxiously before Moss Bros's looking-glasses were over. No more hitching of the armpits to prevent sleeves from enveloping the hands altogether. No more bracing of outgrown trousers to their lowest, with the consciousness that the slightest movement of the arms would display a mortifying expanse of shirt between waistcoat and flies. All that belonged to the past. Now I could dance and dine securely, feeling smart and *soigné*, and very very smooth . . . Michael Arlen was also just beginning to blossom about this time. We used to wave languidly to each other across dance floors, shedding our worldliness later, in obscure corners. He was very dapper, and his Hawes and Curtis backless waistcoats aroused envy in me, which I soon placated, by ordering some for myself, but his exquisite pearl and platinum watch-chain was beyond competition, and all I could do was to admire it bravely, and hope, in my heart, that perhaps it was just a little bit ostentatious.

It was in the midst of this misguided splendour that I was unwise enough to be photographed in bed wearing a Chinese dressing gown and an expression of advanced degeneracy. The last was accidental and was caused by blinking at the flashlight, but it emblazoned my unquestionable decadence firmly on to the minds of all who saw it. It even brought forth a letter of indignant protest from a retired Brigadier-General in Gloucestershire.

Noël Coward, *Present Indicative*, 1937

'Clothes need reformation, but the reformation should begin with the man, not the woman,' according to Roman de Tirtoff-Erté.

'Women,' he says, 'may make many mistakes in dress, they may be exploited and imposed upon by unscrupulous dealers, but at least they make an attempt to express beauty in their clothes and to emerge from the commonplace and the deadly dull. Men don't even attempt to escape from the ugliness of line and material that characterizes the garments they have adopted as their uniform. Apparently they are satisfied . . . [Men's evening clothes are] entirely out of keeping with everything beautiful. Picture the modern homes, clubs and restaurants, with artistic decoration, subdued colors, shaded lights and flowers. A woman enters in shimmering cloth of gold or silver or delicate chiffon. With her is a man in a stiff black uniform that is an entirely discordant note and ruins the picture.' (Hortense Saunders, *NEA*, 11 March 1925)

Erté, *Things I Remember*, 1975

30 April

So Dorothy said we might as well go out to Fountainblo with Louie and Robber if Louie would take off his yellow spats that were made out of yellow shammy skin with pink pearl buttons because, Dorothy said, 'Fun is fun but no girl wants to laugh all of the time.' So Louie is really always anxious to please, so he took off his spats but when he took off his spats, we saw his socks and when we saw his socks we saw that they were Scotch plaid with small-size rainbows running through them. So Dorothy looked at them a little while and she really became quite discouraged and she said, 'Well Louie, I think you had better put your spats back on.'

Anita Loos, *Gentlemen Prefer Blondes:*
The Illuminating Diary of a Professional Lady, 1926

15 May 1924

Tailor, Collins, came to try on yesterday. Of the overcoat he said: 'It's a beautiful back on you, sir.' And of another coat: 'It's a lovely run, sir.' Also of the same coat: 'This is a *young* coat, sir,' meaning it made me look young. He also said, when I said I liked the pattern of the new suit: 'One mustn't always wear dark clothes, sir. Makes you look morbid. This plum colour is a pleasant change.'

20 October 1924

Collins the tailor, trying on new trousers on Saturday, asked me whether I wanted a 'break' at the foot. As I hesitated he said, 'Just a shiver.' I said yes. Shiver is a lovely word for this effect.

Arnold Bennett, *The Journals of Arnold Bennett*,
edited by Norman Flower, 1933

[Bertie Wooster:] 'But lots of fellows have asked me who my tailor is.'
[Jeeves:] 'Doubtless in order to avoid him, sir.'

P. G. Wodehouse, 'Jeeves Takes Charge', from *Carry on, Jeeves*, 1926

'It would kill me to live in New York,' he went on, 'to have to share the air with six million people! To have to wear stiff collars and decent clothes all the time! To—' He started. 'Good Lord! I suppose I should have to dress for dinner in the evenings. What a ghastly notion!'

I was shocked, absolutely shocked.

'My dear chap!' I said reproachfully.

'Do you dress for dinner every night, Bertie?'

'Jeeves,' I said coldly. 'How many suits of evening clothes have we?'

'We have three suits of full evening dress, sir; two dinner jackets—'

'Three.'

'For practical purposes two only, sir. If you remember, we cannot wear the third. We also have seven white waistcoats.'

'And shirts?'

'Four dozen, sir.'

'And white ties?'

'The first two shallow shelves in the chest of drawers are completely filled with our white ties, sir.'

I turned to Rocky.

'You see?'

The chappie writhed like an electric fan.

'I won't do it! I can't do it! I'll be hanged if I'll do it! How on earth can I dress up like that? Do you realize that most days I don't get out of my pyjamas till five in the afternoon, and then I just put on an old sweater?'

> P. G. Wodehouse, 'The Aunt and the Sluggard', from
> *Carry On, Jeeves*, 1926

[Madame Sarbecoff to Mr Hewetson:] 'I was so glad your trousers were so tight. Where do you get such wonderful material to stand such a terrible strain?'

Compton Mackenzie, *Extraordinary Women: Theme and Variations*, 1928

Adam also attempted in an unobtrusive way to exercise some influence over the clothes of his readers. 'I noticed at the Café de la Paix yesterday evening,' he wrote, 'that two of the smartest men in the room were wearing black suede shoes with their evening clothes – one of them, who shall be nameless, was a Very Important Person indeed. I hear that this fashion, which comes, like so many others, from New York, is likely to become popular over here this season.' A few days later he mentioned Capt. Stuart-Kerr's appearance at the embassy 'wearing, of course, the ultra-fashionable black suede shoes'. In a week he was gratified to notice that Johnny Hoop and Archie Schwert had both followed Captain Stuart-Kerr's lead, while in a fortnight the big emporiums of ready-made clothes in Regent Street had transposed their tickets in the windows and arranged rows of black suede shoes on a silver step labelled 'For evening wear'.

His attempt to introduce a bottle-green bowler hat, however, was not successful; in fact, a 'well-known St James's Street hatter', when interviewed by an evening paper on the subject, said that he had never seen or heard of such a thing, and though he would not refuse to construct one if requested to by an old customer, he was of the opinion that no old customer of his would require a hat of that kind (though there was a sad case of an impoverished old beau who attempted to stain a grey hat with green ink, as once in years gone by he had been used to dye the carnation for his buttonhole).

Evelyn Waugh, Vile Bodies, 1930

To begin with, we are second to none in our respect for a well-tailored suit – the Bond Street young man has our sincere admiration. He may, to the eye of enlightenment, appear rather comic, and it is indisputable that it is funnier to have trousers than Bond Street trousers – just as, to quote an immortal contemporary, 'it is funnier to have a nose than a Roman nose'; but the comic is not ugly. Again, we have a special love for the modern evening-dress suit. Even in its worst period, about twenty years ago, it was a very becoming rig-out, and now it has regained very great and real beauty.

Eric Gill, *Clothes*, 1931

2 December 1930

To Arnold Bennett: 'You have all the clothes you want, I suppose,' I said. 'And baths – and beds. And a yacht.' 'Oh yes, my clothes cdnt be better cut.'

Virginia Woolf, *Diaries: Volume III 1925–1930*,
edited by Anne Olivier Bell, 1980

His bedroom was the simplest room of all – except where the dresser was garnished with a toilet set of pure dull gold. Daisy took the brush with delight, and smoothed her hair, where upon Gatsby sat down and shaded his eyes and began to laugh . . .

Recovering himself in a minute he opened for us two hulking patent cabinets which held his massed suits and dressing gowns and ties, and his shirts, piled like bricks in stacks a dozen high.

'I've got a man in England who buys me clothes. He sends over a selection of things at the beginning of each season, spring and fall.'

He took out a pile of shirts and began throwing them, one by one, before us, shirts of sheer linen and thick silk and fine flannel, which lost their folds as they fell and covered the table in many-coloured disarray. While we admired he brought more and the soft rich heap mounted higher – shirts and scrolls of plaids in coral and apple-green and lavender and faint orange, with monograms of Indian blue. Suddenly with a strained sound, Daisy bent her head into the shirts and began to cry stormily.

'They're such beautiful shirts', she sobbed, her voice muffled in

the thick folds. 'It makes me sad because I've never seen such –
such beautiful shirts before.'

F. Scott Fitzgerald, *The Great Gatsby*, 1926

'Jeeves,' I said, when he came back, 'you don't read a paper called
Milady's Boudoir by any chance, do you?'

'No, sir. The periodical has not come to my notice.'

'Well, spring sixpence on it next week, because this article will
appear in it. Wooster on the well-dressed man, don't you know?'

'Indeed, sir?'

'Yes, indeed, Jeeves. I've rather extended myself over this little
bijou. There's a bit about socks that I think you will like.'

He took the manuscript, brooded over it, and smiled a gentle,
approving smile.

'The sock passage is quite in the proper vein, sir,' he said.

'Well expressed, what?'

'Extremely, sir.'

I watched him narrowly as he read on, and, as I was expecting,
what you might call the love-light suddenly died out of his eyes. I
braced myself for an unpleasant scene.

'Come to the bit about soft silk shirts for evening wear?' I asked
carelessly.

'Yes, sir,' said Jeeves, in a low, cold voice, as if he had been bitten
in the leg by a personal friend.

'And if I may be pardoned for saying so—'

'You don't like it?'

'No, sir. I do not. Soft silk shirts with evening costume are not
worn, sir.'

'Jeeves,' I said, looking the blighter diametrically in the centre of
the eyeball, 'they're dashed well going to be. I may as well tell you
now that I have ordered a dozen of those shirtings from Peabody

and Simms, and it's no good looking like that, because I am jolly well adamant.'

'If I might—'

'No, Jeeves,' I said, raising my hand, 'argument is useless. Nobody has a greater respect than I have for your judgement in socks, in ties, and – I will go farther – in spats; but when it comes to evening shirts your nerve seems to fail you. You have no vision. You are prejudiced and reactionary. Hidebound is the word that suggests itself. It may interest you to learn that when I was at Le Touquet the Prince of Wales buzzed into the Casino one night with soft silk shirt complete.'

'His Royal Highness, sir, may permit himself a certain licence which in your own case—'

P. G. Wodehouse, 'Clustering Round Young Bingo',
from *Carry on, Jeeves*, 1926

It was about eleven o'clock in the morning, mid-October, with the sun not shining and a look of hard wet rain in the clearness of the foothills. I was wearing my powder-blue suit, with dark blue shirt, tie and display handkerchief, black brogues, black wool socks with dark blue clocks on them. I was neat, clean, shaved and sober, and I didn't care who knew it. I was everything the well-dressed private detective ought to be. I was calling on four million dollars.

Raymond Chandler, *The Big Sleep*, 1939

Slim quiet Negroes passed up and down the street and stared at him with darting side glances. He was worth looking at. He wore a shaggy borsalino hat, a rough grey sports coat with white golf balls on it for buttons, a brown shirt, a yellow tie, pleated grey flannel slacks and alligator shoes with white explosions on the toes. From his outer breast pocket cascaded a show handkerchief of the same brilliant yellow as his tie. There were a couple of coloured feathers tucked into the band of his hat. But he didn't really need them. Even on Central Avenue, not the quietest-dressed street in the world, he looked about as inconspicuous as a tarantula on a slice of angel cake.

Raymond Chandler, *Farewell My Lovely*, 1940

As for his suit, it was a chocolate brown in colour, with a broad, white, stripe; his shoes were dappled white and chocolate. He looked every inch a pimp, but one who had risen to the top of his profession.

Angela Carter, *Wise Children*, 1991

What else is there to add? The small extravagances of his dress were hardly noticeable in one whose fortune had always seemed oddly matched against a taste for old flannel trousers and tweed coats. Now in his ice-smooth sharkskin with the scarlet cummerbund he seemed only what he should always have been – the richest and most handsome of the city's bankers: those true foundings of the gut. People felt that at last he had come into his own. This was how someone of his place and fortune should live. Only the diplomatic corps smelt in this new prodigality a run of hidden motives, a plot perhaps to capture the King, and began to haunt his drawing room with their studied politenesses. Under the slothful or foppish faces one was conscious of curiosity stirring, a desire to study Nessim's motives and designs, for nowadays the King was a frequent visitor to the great house.

Lawrence Durrell, *Justine*, 1957

The afternoon before he had had to admit to a certain degree of Americanization at the hands of the FBI. A tailor had come and measured him for two single-breasted suits in dark blue lightweight

worsted (Bond had firmly refused anything more dashing) and a
haberdasher had brought chilly white nylon shirts with long points
to the collars. He had to accept half-a-dozen unusually patterned
foulard ties, dark socks with fancy clocks, two or three 'display
kerchiefs' for his breast pocket, nylon vests and pants (called T-shirts
and shorts), a comfortable lightweight camel-hair overcoat with
over-buttressed shoulders, a plain grey snap-brim fedora with a thin
black ribbon and two pairs of hand-stitched and very comfortable
black moccasin 'casuals' [and] . . . a 'Swank' tie-clip in the shape of
a whip.

Ian Fleming, Live and Let Die, 1954

Cecil was considered a fastidious dresser and his name appeared
frequently in lists of best-dressed men. In 1952 he was in *The Tailor
and Cutter*'s first eleven along with four-year-old Prince Charles. He
was always entertained by this as he considered it a myth. He only
had a second bath in the day if he was really tired. When he was not
seeing anyone he wore old clothes and did not shave. If his first
engagement was lunch then he shaved just before going out, so that
he looked as fresh as possible. Eddie Sackville-West, now a neighbour
at Long Crichel, was astonished at this, declaring: 'My dear, I dress
just as carefully if I'm going to see no one. I dress for my own
satisfaction, not for the doubtful pleasure of others.' Cecil liked to
vary his guise from the scruffy to the ultra chic. Sometimes he
appeared at dinner at Reddish in a London suit. At other times he
wore outrageous clothes, so that his collaborator Waldemar Hansen
said: 'It was embarrassing to be seen with him.' And at about this
time Evelyn Waugh joked to Nancy Mitford about Teddy boys, who
dressed like Cecil in 'braided trousers and velvet collars'. He wrote
with more hope than truth: 'Poor Cecil is always being stopped now
by the police and searched for knuckle dusters.' Cecil himself joked

in speeches that a Teddy boy had approached him and said: 'The job's on tonight with razors.'

Hugo Vickers, *Cecil Beaton*, 1985

My clothes were my Sunday best: a light grey suit that had cost fourteen guineas, a plain grey tie, plain grey socks and brown shoes. The shoes were the most expensive I'd ever possessed, with a deep, rich, nearly black lustre. My trenchcoat and my hat, though, weren't up to the same standard; the coat, after only three months, was badly wrinkled and smelled of rubber, and the hat was faintly discoloured with hair oil and pinched to a sharp point in front. Later, I learned, among other things, never to buy cheap raincoats, to punch the dents out of my hat before I put it away, and not to have my clothes match too exactly in shade and colour. But I looked well enough that morning ten years ago, I hadn't then begun to acquire a middle-aged spread and – whether it sounds sentimental or not – I had a sort of eagerness and lack of disillusion which more than made up for the coat and hat and the ensemble like a uniform. The other evening I found a photo of myself taken shortly after I came to live at Warley. My hair is plastered into a skullcap, my collar doesn't fit, and the knot of my tie, held in place by a hideous pin shaped like a dagger, is far too small. That doesn't matter. For my face is, not innocent exactly, but *unused*. I mean unused by sex, by money, by making friends and influencing people, hardly touched by any of the muck one's forced to wade through to get what one wants.

When she'd left the room I opened my suitcase and unfolded my dressing gown. I'd never had one before; Aunt Emily thought not only that they were an extravagance (an overcoat would serve their purpose) but that they were the livery of idleness and decadence. As I looked at it I seemed to hear her voice. 'I'd sooner see someone naked,' she'd say. 'Working people look daft in dressing gowns, like

street women lounging about the house too idle to wash their faces
. . . spend your money on something sensible, lad.' I smiled; there
was certainly nothing sensible about the garment. Its material was,
I remember, a very thin rayon and the shop assistant had used the
term shot silk, which meant that, according to the light, it looked
either garish or drab. The stitching was poor and after one washing
it became a shapeless rag. It was a typical example of the stuff turned
out for a buyer's market in the early post-war period and I rather
think that I was drunk when I bought it.

For all that, it gave me far more pleasure than the dressing gown
I have now, which was bought from Sulka's in Bond Street. Not
that I don't like the Sulka; it's the best, and I always wear the best.
But sometimes I feel uncomfortably aware that I'm forced to be a
living proof of the firm's prosperity, a sort of sandwich-board man.
I've no desire to be ill dressed; but I hate the knowledge that I
daren't be ill dressed if I want to. I bought the cheap rayon garment
to please myself; I bought the expensive silk garment because always
to wear clothes of that quality is an unwritten term of my contract.
And I shall never be able to recapture that sensation of leisure and
opulence and sophistication which came over me that first afternoon
in Warley when I took off my jacket and collar and went into the
bathroom wearing a real dressing gown.

John Braine, *Room at the Top*, 1957

So there was I, in fact, crossing it in my new Roman suit, which was
a pioneering exploit in Belgravia, where they still wore jackets hanging
down over what the tailors call the seat. And around my neck hung
my Rollieflex, which I always keep at the ready, night and day,
because you never know, a disaster might occur, like a plane crashing
in Trafalgar Square . . .

Colin MacInnes, *Absolute Beginners*, 1959

I pull myself out of the glass and go and have a wash in the bathroom. Then I decide to go and borrow Jim's new tie, the blue knitted one with the horizontal stripes. There's a light showing under his door and I find him sitting up in bed with the exercise book on his knee and a pencil in his hand.

I pick up the tie off the drawers. 'Lend me this?'

He mumbles something. I don't suppose he could care less.

I start to put the tie on in the glass. Another glass.

'I've never seen anybody make so much fuss over tying a tie,' he says in a minute.

'What fuss?'

'All that twisting and turning and threading through. Why don't you tie a knot an' have done with it?'

'That's the Windsor knot,' I tell him. I pull it into place and smooth my collar down. 'When you tie a tie like that it makes a neat knot and it stays put.'

'It'll be all creased up now when I want it.'

'What do you care?'

'Hmm,' he says, and goes back to his books.

'It's a nice tie.'

He says nothing.

'Like to flog it?'

'Eh?'

'The tie. Would you like to sell it?'

'I didn't buy it. Me mother bought it.'

I look in the glass. It really is a smart tie; too good for Jim who doesn't care about clothes anyway. 'I'll give you half a crown for it.'

'It cost more than that.'

'You didn't buy it.'

'No, and how can I sell it when I didn't buy it?'

'You'd like the half-crown better, though, wouldn't you?' I say, looking at him through the glass. He's always broke, Jim is, because he's always buying something or saving up to buy something, like guinea pigs or rabbits to keep in the shed, or stamps for his collection, or something.

He's watching me, turning something over in his mind. 'I'll tell you what,' he says, 'I'll let you wear it whenever you like at threepence a time. And you owe me threepence now for tonight.'

Stan Barstow, *A Kind of Loving*, 1960

What about those fellows waiting still and silent there on the platform, so still and silent they clash with the crowd in their very immobility, standing noisy in their very silence; harsh as a cry of terror in their quietness? What about these three boys, coming now along the platform, tall and slender, walking with swinging shoulders in their well-pressed, too-hot-for-summer suits, their collars high and tight about their necks, their identical hats of black cheap felt set upon the crowns of their heads with a severe formality above their conked hair? It was as though I'd never seen their like before: walking slowly, their shoulders swaying, their legs swinging from their hips in trousers that ballooned upward from cuffs fitting snug about their ankles: their coats long and hip-tight with shoulders far too broad to be those of natural western men. These fellows whose bodies seemed – what had one of my teachers said of me? – 'You're like one of those African sculptures, distorted in the interest of design.' Well, what design and whose?

Ralph Ellison, *The Invisible Man*, 1964

1964
Mark [Lancaster] had fallen in love with Bloomingdale's; he bought all his clothes there, but everyone in Provincetown, as soon as they heard his accent, kept complimenting him on his 'fantastic English clothes'. One Monday afternoon at the Factory, he told me that Mailer had walked over to him at a party over the weekend and punched him in the gut.

I was impressed. 'Norman Mailer actually punched you?' I said. 'How great . . . Why?'

'That's what I asked *him*. He said it was for wearing a pink jacket.'

Norman Mailer was one of the few intellectuals that I really enjoyed.

Andy Warhol and Pat Hackett, *POPism: The Warhol '60s*, 1981

In his new boots, Joe Buck was six-foot-one and life was different. As he walked out of that store in Houston something snapped in the whole bottom half of him: a kind of power he never even knew was there had been released in his pelvis and he was able to feel the world through it. Brand-new muscles came into play in his buttocks and in his legs, and he was aware of a totally new attitude toward the sidewalk. The world was down there, and he was way up here, on top of it, and the space between him and it was now commanded by a beautiful strange animal, himself, Joe Buck. He was strong. He was exultant. He was ready.

'I'm ready,' he said to himself, and he wondered what he meant by that.

Joe knew he was no great shakes as a thinker and he knew what thinking he did was best done looking in a mirror, and so his eyes cast about for something that would show him a reflection of himself. Just ahead was a store window. Ta-click ta-click ta-click ta-click, his boots said to the concrete, meaning power power power power, as he approached the window head on, and there was this new and yet familiar person coming at him, broad-shouldered, swaggering, cool and handsome. Lord, I'm glad I'm you, he said to his image – but not out loud – and then, Hey, what's all this ready crap? What are you ready for?

And then he remembered.

When he arrived at the H tel, a hotel that not only had no name but had lost its O as well, he felt the absurdity of anyone so rich and hard and juicy as himself ever staying in such a nameless, no-account place. He ran up the stairs two at a time, went to the second-floor rear and hurried into the closet, emerging seconds later with a large package. He removed the brown paper and placed on the bed a black-and-white horsehide suitcase.

He folded his arms, stood back and looked at it, shaking his head in awe. The beauty of it never failed to move him. The black was so black and the white so white and the whole thing so lifelike and soft, it was like owning a miracle. He checked his hands for dirt, then brushed at the hide as if it were soiled. But of course it wasn't, he was merely brushing away the possibility of future dirt.

Joe set about removing from their hiding place other treasures purchased in recent months: six brand-new Western-cut shirts, new slacks (black gabardines and black cottons), new underwear, socks (a half-dozen pair, still in their cellophanes), two silk handkerchiefs to be worn at his neck, a silver ring from Juarez, an eight-transistor portable radio that brought in Mexico City without a murmur of static, a new electric razor, four packs of Camels and several of Juicy Fruit chewing gum, toilet articles, a stack of old letters, etc.

Then he took a shower and returned to the room to groom himself for the trip. He shaved with his new electric razor, cleaning it carefully before placing it in his suitcase, splashed his face and armpits and crotch with Florida Water, combed a nickel-sized glob of Brylcreem into his brown hair, making it appear almost black, sweetened his mouth with a fresh stick of Juicy Fruit and spat it out, applied some special leather lotion to his new boots, put on a fresh, seven-dollar shirt (black, decorated with white piping, a shirt that fit his lean, broad-shouldered frame almost as close and neat as his own skin), tied a blue handkerchief at his throat, arranged the cuffs of his tight-thighed whipcord trousers in such a way that, with a kind of stylish untidiness, they were half in and half out of those richly gleaming black boots so you could still see the yellow sunbursts at the ankles, and finally he put on a cream-colored leather sport coat so soft and supple it seemed to be alive . . .

On this day of the trip, Joe liked especially what he saw: liked the sweet, dark, dangerous devil he surprised in the dirty mirror of that H tel room. Beyond his own reflection he could see the splendid suitcase lying on the bed, and in his hip pocket he could feel the flat-folded money, two hundred and twenty-four dollars, more than he'd ever at any one time owned before. And he felt most of all the possession of himself, inside his own skin, standing in his own boots, motivator of his own muscles and faculties, possessor of all that beauty and hardness and juice and youngness, box-seat ticket holder to the brilliant big top of his own future, and it was nearly overwhelming to him.

James Leo Herlihy, *Midnight Cowboy*, 1966

Charlie was lying on his back on the attic floor. I took the joint from him, removed my boots and lay down.

'Come and lie beside me,' he said. 'Closer.' He put his hand on my arm. 'Now, you're not to take this badly.'

'No, never, whatever it is, Charlie.'

'You've got to wear less.'

'Wear less, Charlie?'

'Dress less. Yes.'

He got up on to one elbow and concentrated on me. His mouth was close. I sunbathed under his face.

'Levis, I suggest, with an open-necked shirt, maybe in pink or purple, and a thick brown belt. Forget the headband.'

'Forget it.'

I ripped my headband off and tossed it across the floor.

'For your mum.'

'You see, Karim, you tend to look a bit like a pearly queen.'

I, who wanted only to be like Charlie – as clever, as cool in every part of my soul – tattooed his words on to my brain. Levis, with an open-necked shirt, maybe in a very modest pink or purple. I would never go out in anything else for the rest of my life. While I contemplated myself and my wardrobe with loathing, and would willingly have urinated over every garment, Charlie lay back with his eyes closed and real sartorial understanding in his mind. Everyone in the house but me was practically in heaven.

I didn't want to go home right away, so Allie took me to a new club in Covent Garden designed by a friend of his. How London had moved on in ten months. No hippies or punks: instead, everyone was smartly dressed, and the men had short hair, white shirts and baggy trousers held up by braces. It was like being in a room full of George Orwell lookalikes, except that Orwell would have eschewed earrings. Allie told me they were fashion designers, photographers, graphic artists, shop designers and so on, young and talented.

Hanif Kureishi, *Buddha of Suburbia*, 1990

I no longer want to be a member of the designer-suit club. I don't want to be locked in what's being brand-imaged and sold around the world, because I don't like the people who wear those clothes. I've seen them and they're not going anywhere, except maybe to the local wine bar. I don't want to be branded with those Madison Avenue or West End advertising-executive suits – with guys whose only way of trying to be like me is being trendy. I want out of the fashion victim brigade. I no longer wish to be recognized as a grand image that sprang from someone else's brain. I am not here to expand the coffers of Christian Dior or Jasper Conran.

Why pay all that money for some hallmark approved by *GQ*? How boring! Who cares? Fashion doesn't have that power any more. It reached its peak when all those designers became orators and philosophers, when they began to believe they could design their customers' lives as well as their clothes. Everybody waited for them to say something significant, but they never did. I prefer the secretiveness of suits that aren't featured in reams of fashion magazines. I felt like moving into a finer art of disguise, where I can cross frontiers and not feel like a marked man.

So now I love the idea of having suits specifically made for me, with my own quirks, fancies, and desires. Designers don't know any secrets, and they aren't doing anything a Savile Row tailor can't do a hundred times better. And cheaper. If I buy a Romeo Gigli suit, it costs me £900. If I go to Savile Row, it costs me £700, in the cloth of my choice, and I can order it by telephone. And I love the idea of a genuine relationship with a tailor. I love the idea of personal clothing.

Of course, Savile Row has been on the endangered list for years. But there's always a rise of interest in something that's falling apart. While it might take another year, there's going to be an avalanche of tailors again. People just have to learn what it's about. Instinctively, we already know what it's about. It's a reaction against the homogenization of everything else around us.

It started with Levis in the fifties. America has been marketing the workwear look – denim, dungarees, T-shirts, and work shirts – ever since. But it doesn't impart any sophistication or individualism, any mystery or romantic notion, and ultimately it puts you on the production line with everybody else. It's irrelevant and boring, and worst of all, it makes girls look boring. We live in such an ersatz world. If we can wear something handmade and individual, it's a touch closer to reality, to roots. And this will be the beginning of a turnaround not only in fashion but in all of culture.

Malcolm McLaren, 'Hype-Allergic', *Details*, 1992

This morning, as the blue BMW purred into the yard, a couple of white youths in baseball jackets and caps turned and fled, both with a couple of the boxes they had been helping themselves to, under each arm. They ran, anxiously squeezing their way out of the narrow yard through the even narrower gap between the BMW and the wall.

It clicked with Leroy immediately that something was going down and he killed the engine and jumped out of the car all in one go and gave chase instinctively, shouting 'Stop thief!' as he did.

The youths legged it swiftly down Portobello Road with their shirt backs full of wind and still clutching tight to their booty. Leroy had little chance of catching them.

Leroy had been very fortunate to get the deal on the hundred pairs of Nike sneakers. It was rare that street traders like himself ever got a good deal on top of the range training shoes, so this was something of a coup, an irresistible business opportunity. And he had snapped the hundred pairs up almost as soon as Terry, his regular wholesaler, called him on the mobile to tip him off.

'You'll love this stuff, mate,' Terry had insisted, '. . . top of the range stuff . . . sell 'em anywhere . . . selling like hot patties all over the place . . .'

Terry assured Leroy that the training shoes, a consignment of Nike seconds, would fetch a good price on the open market.

'They're in perfect condition,' his voice crackled down the line. 'I can't understand why they're seconds. I'm wearing a pair myself. Trust me Leroy, they're going to go like hot batties.'

'Batties! You mean patties, innit?'

'Yeah man, that's what I said, hot patties.'

'Well, as long as they're not as *hot* as hot patties,' Leroy teased.

'Oh come on, man, you know me Leroy, me nah inna dat, star. Strickly legal runnings.'

'So watcha dealin'-dealin?' Leroy asked, getting back to the business at hand.

'A hundred pairs at £10 a pair, a cool grand, I can't take nothing less.'

'Well, I'm talking £5 a pair,' Leroy told Terry. 'I can't offer nothing more.'

'You've got to be joking, star,' came the anxious reply. 'This is good stuff Leroy, or I wouldn't be calling. You'll be able to get thirty quid a pair for them down the high street, maybe more.'

Leroy paused, making some quick mental calculations.

'They'd better be good . . .' he said.

'Take my word for it.'

Leroy smiled as he pulled a pair of the trainers out of the box. A good line in trainers would go down very well on the street level, he knew that. Everybody wanted Nikes, they would definitely be easy to sell. With any luck they might be the popular new Air Darwins . . . Then he caught sight of the label on the sturdy black training shoes.

'What the fuck is this?!' he cried aloud, both in shock and dismay.

'Mike'? What the raas was Mike? He had paid a grand for a hundred pairs of Nike trainers and he had got a hundred pairs of Mike delivered! What the raas was going on?!

Leroy jerked his mobile from his breast pocket and dialled furiously.

Monica Grant, *The Ragga & the Royal*, 1994

Civilization means a respect for law and order; an appreciation of invention and of beauty; a desire for love and friendship. It upholds the tradition of primogeniture in the family and of acceptance of loyalty to a ruler, be it a king, queen or president.

To the Romans, the most desirable way of life was that in a villa, with baths and garden. In direct descent from that we have the English country house – probably the most satisfactory of all – going down in scale to the country cottage and second home.

Latin should be taught intelligently and interestingly in every school. We should honour our true forebears.

The whole of the English-speaking world wears a suit; so does the whole of Europe. America does, of course. The gents who sat in Philadelphia in 1776 and decided to go their own way wore British suits even if they were made in Boston. Today, the American gentleman dresses like an Englishman. Dark-skinned Americans wear suits. They choose the shirts and ties to wear with them with an accurate eye. They wear hats with the brim well over their eyes, like guards officers, with a mixture of amusement and arrogance.

Sir Hardy Amies, *The Englishman's Suit*, 1994

SARTORIAL AID

At seven fifteen the town car arrives, glistening with sleety rain. The driver, a taciturn Irishman, hands me a garment bag and tells me he'll wait in the car. At least she didn't send someone to dress me.

I emerge stylishly from my apartment in my John Bartlett suit with navy-on-navy shirt-and-tie ensemble.

We drive uptown to pick up Jillian at her building off Madison. The doorman calls her while I stand in the lobby admiring the neoclassical architectural prints.

'You look wonderful,' I say, admiring her tight, lime-green pants and black turtleneck.

She examines me, loosens my tie, shakes her head. 'Lose the tie,' she advises. 'Always underdress a little, if only to make others worry that they are overdressed.'

Satisfied, she takes my arm. 'Anyway, we're going to the *West* Side.'

POLITE CONVERSATION AT THE MAJESTIC

This remarkable talent of mine for showing embarrassment is remarked upon as I am introduced to the other guests, including my host, looking very much at home in jeans and a cashmere sweater; James Croydon, the editor of *Beau Monde*, in full Savile Row armor, who appears to be doing a Tom Wolfe imitation, and Todd Fulham, the decorator, in basic downtown black, who tells me he did the apartment, a ten-million-dollar penthouse disguised as an Adirondack hunting lodge.

Jay McInerney, *Model Behaviour*, 1998

7. 'Knights of the Bracelet': Aesthetes and Dandies

Show me a dandy and I'll show you a hero.

Diana Vreeland, *D. V.*, 1984

[He] chose his best black one, a lounge suit which had caused almost a sensation among his acquaintances because of its elegance, then selected another shirt and began to dress with great care.

Franz Kafka, *The Trial*, 1925

The aesthete and the dandy are two male nineteenth-century stereotypes who defined themselves through appearance: the former an effete with a question over his sexuality, the latter a man for whom exquisite simplicity is perfection, an aristocrat of the spirit in the modern era. Both the dandy and the aesthete run through the pages of twentieth-century writing, often merged into a hybrid to describe a *poseur* or latent homosexual.

In the autumn of 1884, Oscar Wilde, lecturing on dress, told his audience, 'One should either be a work of art or wear a work of art.' Wilde was prominent in the aesthetic movement of the 1880s, wearing velvet knee breeches and cape in reaction to the ugliness of the age; the aesthete first as effeminate then as homosexual was defined by Wilde's career. When Harold Acton writes of styling himself at Oxford and starting Oxford bags, or Evelyn Waugh presents Anthony Blanche, they are describing the aesthete – the connoisseur or dilettante - who is sexually ambiguous, satirized for the same reasons as the 'macaronis' of 1760s and 1770s England. They reflected foreign – French or Italian – manners and notions of men's dress which involved colours of the hothouse, not the hunting field. Such a style was – and still is – anathema to John Bull's xenophobic view of English masculinity.

A dandy, ironically, is far more of a narcissist than the aesthete but has never been as disliked. He emerged in England during the years immediately preceding the French Revolution, when the style of the gentleman, not the aristocrat, was regarded as epitomizing the new spirit of democracy. 'Beau' Brummell, the first – and greatest – dandy identified the style: 'No perfumes . . . but very fine linen, plenty of it and country washing. If John Bull turns round to look after you, you are not well dressed; but either too stiff, too tight or too fashionable.'[1] The true dandy was obsessed by self-image; he did not follow fashion, nor did he care if he led it.

In 1863, in an essay in *Le Figaro* on 'The Painter in Modern Life', Baudelaire argued that dandyism is modern, appearing in periods of transition: 'Dandyism is the last spark of heroism amid decadence . . . first and foremost the burning need to make oneself something original.' The perfect dandy was a kind of artist, who created himself.[2] Thus the dandy was re-defined by writers as an outsider made visible through dress. Comte Robert de Montesquieu, the dandy-homosexual-poet who was the model for J.-K. Huysmans' *A Rebours* (1884) as well as Proust's M. de Charlus,[3] originally wore white suits with a bunch of violets in place of a tie. By 1897, he 'favoured grey suits whose harmonies and exquisite draperies made him even more noticeable than ever'.

The perceived affectation of Montesquieu and Wilde led to a backlash. Just as Brummell had led a transition in dress from decadent *ancien régime* to neo-classical democratic, modernist theorist Adolf Loos advised his readers in *Ornament and Crime* to reject the 'degenerate aristocrats', the dandies and aesthetes of the *fin de siècle* who had confused life with art. 'I am preaching to the aristocrats. Whoever goes about in a velvet suit nowadays is not an artist but a fool or a house-painter.'[4]

Kafka heard Loos lecture on ornament in 1911. As a student he had played the role of fop or elegant littérateur, dressing with the refined elegance that was then common for an aspiring writer, and frequenting the popular literary clubs, cafés and cabarets of Prague; 'I merely try casually and in a hit-and-miss way to dress well,' he said, drawing a line between this style and the affectation of other writers 'who paint their fingernails'.[5] After he heard Loos, he changed to dandy. The pose as a dandy suited him, as he saw himself as an outsider, being Jewish in an anti-Semitic culture. He insisted on being well dressed and had his suits made by a very good tailor; before going out, he would observe himself critically for a long time in the mirror, not from vanity but from a desire to be 'correct' – so correct he would not stand out.[6]

Chanel's modernist aesthetic (explored in Chapter Three) was reflected in her adoption of the dandy's notion of being well dressed. 'It was the identification with women's emancipation which gave such an anti-decorative uniform its appeal to women. In the hands of Chanel the look was also glamorous. In borrowing from the male wardrobe Chanel drew on the way in which men's clothes, within the terms of classical male dandyism, could signify personal independence within a rigid order.'[7]

The artists who illustrated Lucien Vogel's de luxe fashion magazines *Gazette du Bon Ton* and *Journal des Dames et des Modes* called themselves 'Beaux Brummells', or 'Knights of the Bracelet' because they affected a bracelet. They were linked to ornament-loving Paul Poiret and the 'decadent' style of the Orient rejected by Loos. The Knights included Bernard Boutet de Monvel, Pierre Brissaud, Georges Barbier, Jean Besnard, A. E. Marty, Charles Martin, Paul Iribe and Georges Lepape. Their age limit was thirty and although most had 'comfortable' incomes, to support their way of life, they had to work.[8]

An article in *Vogue* at the time – although it did not point out that a bracelet wasn't in the Brummellian tradition, nor that Max Beerbohm claimed that no dandy would demean himself by daubing with a paintbrush – described a foreign dandyism, an effete affectation that was to colour the perception of many men involved in fashion. A notable example was the designer and illustrator Erté, who is reflected in Evelyn Waugh's description of the 'wholly exotic' Anthony Blanche. 'I don't know what I expected of Monsieur Erté, but I was entirely unprepared for the thin, willowy little Russian who appeared,' wrote the Hollywood costume designer Howard Greer in his autobiography recalling their meeting in Cannes in 1920. 'His slippers had very high heels and square, silver buckles, and his suit was cut with an exaggeratedly waspish waist . . . He was wearing lounging pyjamas which I suspected were made of ermine.'⁹ In 1925, Hollywood journalists noticed Erté wore a bracelet.

The Duke of Windsor as Prince of Wales, promoted as a dandy ideal by the press and fashion industry, was also a healthy British antidote to the dandy-aesthete, by now personified by Cecil Beaton, Stephen Tennant, Oliver Messel and Harold Acton, homosexuals all. In literature writers described the difference: Nancy Mitford's Cedric Hampton is clearly an aesthete; F. Scott Fitzgerald's Dick Diver a dandy; MacInnes's Billy Whispers a dandy-king of the street. Social changes after 1945 saw different identities emerge. The neo-Edwardians – Norman Parkinson, Bunny Roger – sought to return to the elegance of the Edwardian era and, in the popular imagination, were like the dandies of old fashion plates, followed, in this case, by the working-class youth of London. In 1965, when *Men in Vogue* was launched, London was seen as a centre for a new dandyism, the dandy now being a dedicated follower of fashion. Carnaby Street's dandyism was ersatz besides that of Christopher Gibbs, Julian Ormsby Gore, Mick Jagger and Tara Browne; Gibbs, writing a shopping column for *Men in Vogue*, most certainly combined the aesthete with the dandy. Mark Lancaster was punched by Norman

Mailer for wearing a pink jacket, and Bill Naughton created Alfie, who has all the fastidiousness of a Brummell in dress and in regards to women.

The dandyism of Christopher Gibbs stood starkly apart from the dressed-down inelegance of the late 1960s hippy. The extract from Richard Allen's *Suedehead* included in this chapter illustrates the democracy of true dandyism, exemplified also by Tom Wolfe's description of the urban African Americans as 'Brummells and Gentlemen of Leisure'. The New Romantics, the subculture personified by Steve Strange and Boy George, were the dandies manqué of the early 1980s, with their individualistic theatricality and narcissism, soon to be replaced by the fashion-conscious man choosing anonymity in a designer suit.

In the 'lad' culture which has characterized the 1990s, dandyism today is misunderstood as overdressed or effeminate, or appearing in fashion editorials inspired by Byron featuring men in long hair, velvet coats and cravats. Paraphrasing Adolph Loos, Bunny Roger said disparagingly, 'Anyone who wears a cloak and floppy bow tie is considered a dandy; I think they look like fools. Someone terribly smart isn't a dandy, either.'[10] Perhaps there is always a confusion between a dandy and an aesthete, invariably in vaguely historical dress: Donna Tarrt and Amanda Craig both describe the hybrid well. To be a dandy requires a narcissism and an obsession with the niceties of image that few men either have or can afford; John Galliano is one, Prince another. Interestingly – the dandy perhaps no longer interesting to writers – neither have yet appeared adequately described in literature.

Essentially an aristocrat, in person dainty, neat, fastidious, Cherry-Marvel's art was essentially democratic, for it abhorred all imitation and exacted from him its complete display on every occasion ... Eager, exquisite, always prepared, always with a handkerchief fluttering between his breast pocket and the corner of his eye, you must imagine him against the tapestry of wasted time, a figure of ancient, aesthetic dandysme, on immaculate lawns, in drawing rooms, up and down terraces of palazzos, in clubs and cabarets.

Michael Arlen, *The Green Hat*, 1924

[K.] lifted a coat from a chair and held it up for a little while in both hands, as if displaying it to the warders for their approval. They shook their heads. 'It must be a black coat,' they said. Thereupon K. flung the coat on the floor and said – he did not himself know in what sense he meant the words – 'But this isn't a capital charge yet.' The warders smiled, but stuck to their 'It must be a black coat.' 'If it's to dispatch my case any quicker, I don't mind,' replied K. opening the wardrobe, where he searched for a long time among his many suits, chose his best black one, a lounge suit which had caused almost a sensation among his acquaintances because of its elegance, then selected another shirt and began to dress with great care.

On the evening before K.'s thirty-first birthday – it was about nine o'clock, the time when a hush falls on the streets – two men came to his lodging. In frock coats, pallid and plump, with top hats that were apparently uncollapsible . . . Without having been informed of their visit, K. was sitting also dressed in black in an armchair near the door, slowly pulling on a pair of new gloves that fitted tightly over the fingers, looking as if he expected guests.

Franz Kafka, *The Trial*, 1926

Dandyism offers the possibility of social mobility on one's own, albeit restricted, terms. Within dandyism the whole idea of social marginality becomes dynamic. But the marginalization of women cuts across class and excludes the deliberate play on social marginality which dandyism offers. Furthermore, dandyism flirts with the conventionally feminine areas of narcissism, artificiality and fashion. The dandy demonstrates his control by the way in which he survives trivialization, the way in which he is not emasculated by it. For women, the construction of femininity prescribes triviality, making it less easy to flirt with . . . One could argue that the spirit in which the so-called New Woman took up the values of purpose and ambition, of self-control, inflexibility and even respectability, and her [Chanel's] espousal of the rigidities of the male wardrobe (shirts, ties and the 'tailor-made' suit), were entirely reactionary were it not for the progressive politics of women's emancipation that went with them.

Caroline Evans and Minna Thornton, *Women and Fashion*, 1989

I bought a grey bowler, wore a stock and let my side-whiskers flourish. Instead of the wasp-waisted suits with pagoda shoulders and tight trousers affected by the dandies, I wore jackets with broad lapels and broad pleated trousers. The latter got broader and broader. Eventually they were imitated elsewhere and were generally referred to as 'Oxford bags'.

Harold Acton, *Memoirs of an Aesthete*, 1948

'Erté's own appearance might be taken for an illustration of his theory . . . He had chosen gray and red as color notes and carried them through his entire costume. His suit, tailored by Larsen of Paris, was gray with double stripes of dull red. With neither pocket flaps nor vent, his jacket was slightly shaped to follow the lines of his body, and was cut out in a single-breasted, two-button model with wide peaked lapels. He expressed himself as also extremely partial to double-breasted models as suiting his slim figure. His attached silk collar, which he wore plain, with basket-weave tie in a gray and red zig-zag pattern, was pale gray with a darker quarter-inch stripe around the middle, with fine dull red stripes on either side. His trousers were cut medium width and did not hide pale gray socks. Here Erté declared his fondness for distinctive footwear (he admits to over twenty pairs of shoes) in an unusual modification of the Deauville sandal. These Oxfords had wing-tips and heels of soft calf which met low on the sides and extended up the eyelets. The remainder of the shoe was made of closely woven thin leather stripes of grayish glint.' (*Daily News Record*, 23 March 1925)

Erté, *Things I Remember*, 1975

There was a new suit, which he had not worn yet, rather daring, for the trousers, dark fawn, were distinctly of Oxford cut, and he felt quite boyish as he looked at them. He had ordered them in a moment of reckless sartorial courage, and a quiet tea with Daisy Quantock, followed by a quiet dinner with Lucia, was just the way to make a beginning with them, far better than wearing them for the first time at church on Sunday, when the whole of Riseholme simultaneously would see them. The coat and waistcoat were very dark blue, they would look blue at tea and black at dinner; and there were some grey silk socks, rather silvery, and a tie to match them . . .

And the coat buttoned beautifully, just the last button, leaving the rest negligently wide and a little loose. Georgie put on an amethyst tiepin in his grey tie, which gave a pretty touch of colour, brushed his hair back from his forehead, so that the toupée was quite indistinguishable from his own hair, and hurried downstairs to go out to tea with Daisy Quantock.

E. F. Benson, *Lucia in London*, 1927

'Who are the young men of today? Or rather, who are the models on whom they are bidden to mould their personalities? Let us take the Hon. Stephen Tennant, who cut so dashing a figure at his brother's bottle and pyjama party: and his friend, Mr Cecil Beaton. Both these young men are in their very early twenties, are slender, with a most definite artistic sense which their predecessors in the rough old days might envy.' (*Sphere*, 16 June 1928)

Philip Hoare, *Serious Pleasures: The Life of Stephen Tennant*, 1990

When the eggs were gone and we were eating the lobster Newburg, the last guest arrived.

'My dear,' he said, 'I couldn't get away before. I was lunching with my p-p-preposterous tutor. He thought it was very odd my leaving when I did. I told him I had to change for f-f-footer.'

He was tall, slim, rather swarthy, with large saucy eyes. The rest of us wore rough tweeds and brogues. He had on a smooth chocolate-brown suit with loud white stripes, suede shoes, a large bow tie and he drew off yellow, wash-leather gloves as he came into the room; part Gallic, part Yankee, part, perhaps, Jew; wholly exotic.

This, I did not need telling, was Anthony Blanche, the 'aesthete' *par excellence*, a byword of iniquity from Cherwell Edge to Somerville. He had been pointed out to me often in the streets, as he pranced along with his high peacock tread; I had heard his voice in the George challenging the conventions; and now meeting him, under the spell of Sebastian, I found myself enjoying him voraciously.

Evelyn Waugh, *Brideshead Revisited*, 1945

Lord and Lady Montdore got up and stood together in front of the fireplace as the butler opened the door and announced 'Mr Cedric Hampton'.

A glitter of blue and gold crossed the parquet, and a human

dragonfly was kneeling on the fur rug in front of the Montdores, one long white hand extended towards each. He was a tall, thin young man, supple as a girl, dressed in rather a bright blue suit; his hair was the gold of a brass bed-knob and his insect appearance came from the fact that the upper part of the face was concealed by blue goggles set in gold rims quite an inch thick.

The next morning when I went to Lady Montdore's room to say goodbye I found Cedric, in a pale mauve silk dressing gown, sitting on her bed. They were both rubbing cream into their faces out of a large pink pot. It smelt delicious, and certainly belonged to him.

Nancy Mitford, *Love in a Cold Climate*, 1949

He knew that what he was now doing marked a turning point in his life – it was out of line with everything that had preceded it, even out of line with what effect he might hope to produce upon Rosemary. Rosemary saw him always as a model of correctness – his presence walking around this block was an intrusion. But Dick's necessity of behaving as he did was a projection of some submerged reality: he was compelled to walk there, or stand there, his shirtsleeve fitting his wrist and his coatsleeve encasing his shirtsleeve like a sleeve valve, his collar moulded plastically to his neck, his red hair cut exactly, his hand holding his small briefcase like a dandy – just as another man once found it necessary to stand in front of a church in Ferrara, in sackcloth and ashes. Dick was paying some tribute to things unforgotten, unshriven, unexpurgated.

With his miniature leather briefcase in his hand Richard Diver walked from the seventh arrondissement – where he left a note for Maria Wallis signed 'Dicole', the word with which he and Nicole had signed communications in the first days of love – to his shirtmakers, where the clerks made a fuss over him out of proportion to the money he spent. He was ashamed at promising so much to these poor

Englishmen, with his fine manners, his air of having the key to security, ashamed of making a tailor shift an inch of silk on his arm.

F. Scott Fitzgerald, *Tender is the Night*, 1934

The booth behind him contained a handsome young Negro in an expensive fawn suit with exaggerated shoulders. He was lolling back against the wall with one foot up on the bench beside him. He was paring the nails of his left hand with a small silver pocket knife, occasionally glancing in bored fashion towards the animation at the bar. His head rested on the back of the booth just behind Bond and a whiff of expensive hair-straightener came from him. Bond took in the artificial parting traced with a razor across the left side of the scalp, through the almost straight hair which was a tribute to his mother's constant application of the hot comb since childhood. The plain black silk tie and the white shirt were in good taste . . .

Bond suddenly felt the force of what Leiter had told him. They were trespassing. They just weren't wanted . . . 'We'll go to Ma Frazier's, further up the Avenue,' said Leiter. 'Best food in Harlem, or at any rate, it used to be.'

As they went along Bond gazed into the shop windows.

He was struck by the number of barbers' saloons and 'beauticians'. They all advertised various forms of hair-straightener – 'Apex Glossatina, for use with the hot comb', 'Silky Strate. Leaves no redness, no burn' – or nostrums for bleaching the skin. Next in frequency were the haberdashers and clothes shops with fantastic men's snakeskin shoes, shirts with small aeroplanes as a pattern, peg-top trousers with inch-wide stripes, zoot suits . . . 'I'm glad we came up here,' said Bond. 'I'm beginning to get the hang of Mr Big.'

Ian Fleming, *Live and Let Die*, 1954

The corpse of the executed sweater, no matter how I changed its contours as it lay on the back seat of the car, had kept revealing various outlines pertaining to Trapp-Schiller – the grossness and obscene *bonhomie* of his body, and to counteract this taste of coarse corruption I resolved to make myself especially handsome and smart as I pressed home the nipple of my alarm clock before it exploded at the set hour of six a.m. Then, with the stern and romantic care of a gentleman about to fight a duel, I checked the arrangement of my papers, bathed and perfumed my delicate body, shaved my face and chest, selected a silk shirt and clean drawers, pulled on transparent taupe socks, and congratulated myself for having with me in my trunk some very exquisite clothes – a waistcoat with nacreous buttons, for instance, a pale cashmere tie and so on.

Vladimir Nabokov, Lolita, 1959

I observed that he was attired in a white crocheted sweater with two crimson horizontal stripes and with gold safety pins stuck on the tips of each point of the emerging collar of a nylon shirt; in a sky-blue gabardine jacket zipped down the front; and in even tighter blue linen slacks, full at the hips, tapering to the ankle, and falling delicately one half-inch above a pair of pale brown plaited shoes . . .

Then I saw quite a surprising sight: which was a tall spade – very tall – standing in a broken greenhouse, watering plants. Now Spades do garden – it wasn't that – but not ones dressed up like he was, fit to kill: pink slacks, tartan silk outside-hanging shirt, all freshly pressed and laundered.

'What say, man?' I called out to him. 'Do you know Billy Whispers?' . . . as this man came out of the greenhouse, wiping his hands, I saw by the weaving, sliding way he walked towards me that he was a boxer. Round his neck he wore a silver chain, another on

each wrist, and his face had a 'better be careful or I slap you down'
expression.

Colin MacInnes, City of Spades, 1957

Dean was wearing a real Western business suit for his big trip back
to Denver; he'd finished his first fling in New York . . . blue with
pencil stripes, vest and all – eleven dollars on Third Avenue, with a
watch and a watch-chain, and a portable typewriter with which he
was going to start writing in a Denver rooming house as soon as he
got a job there.

Jack Kerouac, On the Road, 1957

We'd had it off on the back seat, see, stripped down a bit for the
job, and when we've done I get out to water the old geranium against
the offside rear wheel (I've been pinting it, see) and generally unjangle
myself, and then I put on my jacket and slip in front into the driver's
seat, not forgetting to give her a last cuddle just to show I done it
all out of love, and not lust, when blow me down if she ain't inciting
me all over again. Well, in for a penny in for a pound, I say, so I've
took out my big white handkerchief and folded it carefully over my
left lapel. I was wearing a navy-blue lightweight suit, in a material
called Tonik, made by Dormeuil, and I didn't want it spoiling. I
don't care whether a bird uses Max Factor Mattfilm or Outdoor
Girl from Woolworth's, if she starts purring it up against your lapel,
it won't look the better for it.

Bill Naughton, Alfie, 1966

1967

In those mod, flower-power days, Fred [Hughes] was conspicuous
– one of the only young people around who insisted on Savile Row
suits. Everyone stared at him because he was so perfectly tailored –
like something out of another era. When he came by that first day,
he was wearing a flared, double-vent dark blue suit, blue shirt, and
light blue bow tie . . . Fred . . . was a cute kid – young – and such a
dandy.

Andy Warhol and Pat Hackett, *POPism: The Warhol '6os*, 1981

All the young aces and dudes out there lollygagging around front of
Zombie's Get-Over Club, wearing their two-tone patent Pyramids
with the five-inch heels that swell out at the bottom to match
the Art Deco plaid bell-bottom baggies they have on with the
three-inch-deep elephant cuffs tapering upward toward the 'spray-
can-fit' in the seat, as it's known, and the peg-top waistband with
self-covered buttons and the silk pattern-on-pattern Walt Frazier
shirt, all of it surmounted by the midi-length leather piece with the
welted waist seam and the Prince Albert pockets and the black
Pimp-mobile hat with the four-inch turn-down brim and six-inch
pop-up crown with the golden chain-belt hatband . . . so that somehow the sons of the slums have become the Brummells and Gentlemen of Leisure, the true fashion plates of 1973, and the Sons of Eli
dress like the working class of 1934 . . . if you tried to put one of
those lumpy mildew mothball lumberjack shirts on them – those
aces . . . they'd vomit.

Tom Wolfe, introduction to René König, *The Restless Image*, 1973

Selecting his brown tie with the artistic squiggles on it he finished
dressing. The flat came complete with a cheval mirror and he studied

his presentation with a critical eye. Not bad, he allowed generously. Terry will never know how much he has done for me.

His hair had grown and he looked like pure suede which was hardly surprising since he'd been having a Mayfair barber treat it at exorbitant cost . . .

No umbrella tonight. No bowler, either. Just his suede hairstyle, brown shirt, brown tie, tweed jacket and cavalry trousers. He thought the orange socks did something for the outfit. Like the Oxfords did, too.

But the hidden glory was his underwear. God, if those sexy birds could only see his mauve jockey shorts and specially dyed emerald green vest!

He felt naked without his umbrella and gloves but Marissa had asked why he thought it necessary to carry his symbol of City gentlemanliness when he was supposed to be relaxing at the club.

Richard Allen, Suedehead, 1971

It was a glorious day; I was sick of being poor so, before I thought better of it, I went into an expensive men's shop on the square and bought a couple of shirts. Then I went down to the Salvation Army and poked around in bins for a while and found a Harris tweed overcoat and a pair of brown wing-tips that fit me, also some cufflinks and a funny old tie that had pictures of men hunting deer on it. When I came out of the store I was happy to find that I still had nearly a hundred dollars.

Once in my room, I spread the clothes on my bed. The cufflinks were beaten up and had someone else's initials on them, but they looked like real gold, glinting in the drowsy autumn sun which poured through the window and soaked in yellow pools on the oak floor – voluptuous, rich, intoxicating.

Donna Tartt, A Secret History, 1992

His friends compared him to Oscar Wilde, largely because of his dress, which was exotic, and his manner of speech, which was exceedingly rapid and flown with wit. His enemies called him the most dangerous man in London.

Where Ivo tended towards damask waistcoats and green carnations, Mark's wardrobe, purchased at Ralph Lauren or Hackett's sales, featured striped poplin shirts with button-down collars and thin silk ties.

Amanda Craig, *A Vicious Circle*, 1996

132.* Brown Shoes. I remember the day I thought I had caught Ivan out. He was wearing a hairy, snot-green tweed suit with black brogues. I pointed at them and said, 'Ivan, the ultimate sin – black shoes with tweed.'

'Oh, you're completely wrong Lorimer, this is very acceptable. I'm glad you noticed it, however. It's a sign of a deeper malaise, something that's been worrying me for years.'

'What's that?'

'It's been difficult, but I've decided that the brown shoe must be condemned. Suede yes, a brown boot – just. But I think the brown shoe is fundamentally below the salt. Something irretrievably *petit bourgeois* about a brown shoe, quintessentially suburban and infra dig. I threw all mine out last week, fourteen pairs, some I've had for decades. Threw them in the dustbin. I can't tell you how relieved I am, the weight off my mind.'

'All brown shoes?'

'Yes. No gentleman should wear a brown shoe, ever. The brown shoe is finished. The brown shoe, Lorimer, has got to go.'

William Boyd, *Armadillo*, 1998

*From Lorimer Black's 'Book of Transfiguration'.

8. 'Dylan was in blue jeans': Youth Style

Fashion does not exist unless it goes down into the streets. The fashion that remains in the salons has no more significance than a costume ball.

Coco Chanel, from Edmonde Charles-Roux,
Chanel and Her World, 1979

If you know the contemporary scene, you could tell them apart at once, just like you could a soldier or sailor, with their separate uniforms.

Colin MacInnes, *Absolute Beginners*, 1959

Since it is in the nature of fashion to progress from what has gone before and to reflect social change, the younger generation has in general differed in dress styles from the older. What was different about the nature of the younger generation after 1945 was the notion of the 'teenager', seeking his or her own identity, and the eventual influence of the 'street' or working-class dress on fashion, a reversal of fashion starting at the 'top' – in other words couture – and filtering down. Before the Second World War, fashion magazines and pattern companies recorded and copied the designs of the couturiers and so the designs eventually hit the ready-to-wear market, or the designs were made at home; and boys went to the same tailors and hairdressers as their fathers. After the war, however, popular culture – music, film and television – related to 'youth' and together the ideas of teenage 'rebel' and 'street style' flourished. By the late 1950s, working-class teenagers had their own styles, which were imitated by middle-

and upper-class teenagers, and by the end of the decade, these street styles were influencing designers. The trend has continued, albeit with a resurgence in couture, which again clearly marks a top strata of fashion that may choose to become more influential. But for many designers, real fashion is a symbiosis between street style influencing catwalk and catwalk feeding the re-interpretation back to the street.

Even if youth and the street did not influence fashion until after the Second World War, the young were none the less conscious of it's power. Writers have noted the way in which 'youngsters' dressed and their attitude towards clothes before the 1950s: Walter Greenwood describes the longing of his young hero to have a new suit like the other lads; the early social-realist novels of Sillitoe and Braine both identify the role of working-class youth in the consumption of fashion and the use of dress as identity; and Angela Carter describes the raw energy in the approach to style of her twin heroines of pre-war south London.

Clothes expressed the beginnings of teenage rebellion in the 1940s. In 1942, when Malcolm X was a young hustler, the larger-than-life zoot suits he wore were the mark of Black and Mexican youth which set them apart from American servicemen and saw violent rioting between the two factions. Likewise zazous, young men about town Albert Camus describes in *The Outsider*, wore braided suits; and in 1944, *Life* magazine reported that teenage girls in America were wearing men's shirts and jeans, a style disliked by parents and teachers, who 'find it shockingly sloppy. This makes the custom exciting . . . and keeps the girls firmly united against all protests.'[1]

The first identifiable group of rebels were Teds or Teddy boys, working-class boys from south London who emerged in 1952 and who, by 1956, had spread throughout the country. Their clothes were a blend of America – the zoot suit – and England – the Savile Row Edwardian look. They wore drape jackets, skin-tight drainpipe jeans tapering to the ankle, luminous socks, brothel creepers, brass rings on their fingers and gamblers' bootlace ties, and often carried a flick knife in their back pockets.[2] They might spend as much as £15 on a new suit every six to nine months; their hair was slicked back into a 'DA' or 'Boston'. They were the new manifestation of the dandy of the street. 'They started everything,' observed Alexander Plunket-Greene, husband of Mary Quant. 'Once they'd made the breakthrough, everyone else could follow and the whole Pop thing went bang.'[3]

Between 1946 and 1951, 15,000 Italian immigrants entered Britain, many of whom worked in the catering trade or opened up coffee bars. They brought with them Italian style, discussed by MacInnes in *Absolute Beginners,* in which he dissects the different youth groups and subcultures in London's Notting Hill and Soho; the hero is one of the modernists, later known as 'mods'. By 1959, there were four million single people aged between thirteen and twenty-five. Their economic power began to dominate certain sections of the market – including clothing – with an estimated annual spending power of £900 million in 1958.[4]

The 'rebel' was at first a primarily male phenomenon. When Mary Quant opened her boutique Bazaar in the King's Road in 1955, she was catering for girls who wanted a look which was about youth. It wasn't until the sixties that the arrival of the miniskirt marked a new spirit of freedom for young women. Mary Quant sold it, Courrèges put it on his catwalk in 1964. 'The sixties' mini was, perhaps, the ultimate surprise focal point. It was: "Wow! Look at me. Isn't life wonderful!" It was young, liberated and exuberant and on the pill. It was called Youthquake. And it looked all girl. It was the beginning of Women's Lib.'[5] Models Jean Shrimpton and Twiggy personified the new spirit. Anti-style, in the tradition of artistic dress, became hip and was sold at the London boutiques Hung on You and Granny Takes a Trip; hippie style, a conglomeration of the second-hand, the antique and the imported from India, took off in London in early 1967. At the same time, Rudi Gernreich and Paco

Rabanne were dressing the fashionable New Yorkers in Pop style.

If 1967 was the 'Summer of Love', protest dress, in the form of 'unisex' jeans and T-shirts, characterized 1968, the year of the student riots. From then on the plethora of styles increased and self-parody began: hippy style became a pale imitation of Hung on You, with cheap imported clothes from India and scraggy Afghan coats teaming up with T-shirts and jeans; working-class style was again as aggressive as the Ted, with skinheads followed by Crombie-coated suedeheads. Glam Rock was a blend of nostalgia – a pastiche of the 1930s and 1940s as sold at Biba – but when teamed up with the sexual ambiguity of rock star David Bowie it became interesting. There was a difference, noted by Tom Wolfe, between 'radical chic' white protest style and the Black dandyism of the streets: 'somehow the sons of the slums have become the Brummells and Gentlemen of Leisure, the true fashion plates of 1973, and the Sons of Eli dress like the working class of 1934 . . .'[6] While the campuses were peopled by 'anything goes', described by Malcolm Bradbury, the subversion of Glam Rock filtered down into punk, a true subculture which plundered the forbidden: S&M, fetishwear, Nazi insignia.

Fashion designers who emerged in the early 1980s looked to this deconstructed language and turned to street style and subculture for inspiration – the androgyny of pop star Boy George and the transvestite Marilyn, the gay language of the leather bar. In the 1980s sportswear and brand-name trainers were worn by Rap bands Public Enemy and Run DMC and their fans, prompting John O'Reilly to predict, 'In ten years' time they won't be talking about pine dressers on the *Antiques Roadshow*. A kid will be on there with a 1969 Adidas tracksuit. People have to understand that the first-ever performance outerwear has a place in our culture. A Reebok Instapump will cost you £440 now. In four years' time £4,000.'[7] But although the 'street' influenced designers, designers were in turn leading the market. Labels became objects of desire, with American Tommy Hilfiger catering to the sportswear-as-style market, and British designers

Owen Gaster and Bella Freud translating the urban ragga style on to their catwalks. 'To my eyes an increasingly frequent chain of events goes like this,' commented anthropologist Ted Polhemus. 'First there is a genuine street-style innovation. This may be featured in a pop music video and street kids in other cities and countries may pick up on the style. Then, finally – at the end rather than the beginning of the chain – a ritzy version of the original idea makes an appearance as part of a top designer's collection. Instead of trickle-down, bubble up. Instead of the bottom end of the market emulating the top end, precisely the reverse.'[8]

When she entered the house she found Harry standing by the slopstone staring into the small mirror suspended there. Around his neck was a collar far too large for him, one of a number given to him by Larry Meath who had discarded them. He had accepted them with beaming gratitude; they were such as he always had dreamed of possessing, for, outside working hours, Larry was always neat about the neck. Even though the collars required altering, a glance at their effect upon him through the glass was sufficient to waken in his heart an abysmal discontentment with his shabbiness. Lacking a new suit would make the wearing of these incongruous. A new suit; a *proper* new suit; one made to special measurement, shaped at the waist, not a reach-me-down that fitted like a sack.

As Sally came into the kitchen he was imagining himself wearing the desired garment. It was made of blue serge; it embraced him, creaseless, precise . . .

The question of a new suit became an obsession. He dreamed of it; wore it so often in fancy that, on waking of a Sunday morning, he was fully convinced that it hung behind the bedroom's curtained-off alcove which served as wardrobe.

It wasn't there. What met his eyes when he opened them was grim reality decorating the bed end, those wretched reach-me-downs bought second-hand from an auction at the Flat Iron Market. Sulkily he would rise . . .

When alone with his mother and father he pestered them unceasingly: 'When am Ah goin' t' have that there new suit?' he mumbled with an expression of sulky petulance.

His mother sighed: 'Ay, lad, what can Ah do? Y'know Sal's on short time, an' y' pa's ne'er sure of a full week's work.'

'Ah know, Ma. But Ah've ne'er had a proper suit yet. An' me nearly eighteen. Ah'm ashamed t'go out of a Sunday,' warmly: 'Luk at Bill Lindsay an' th' others. They can have 'em. Why can't I?'

Mrs Hardcastle glanced at her husband nervously, then said, to Harry, apologetically: 'They get 'um from Good Samaritan, Harry . . . Y'know y' father don't like weekly payments.' She glanced at her husband again. Harry, too, looked at him.

Hardcastle removed his pipe from his mouth, spat into the fire and addressed his newspaper: 'Y'll have t' mek do wi' what y've got, lad. It's tekkin' us all our time t' live. Y'll get one when things buck up.' . . .

Harry's lip quivered: at that rate he'd remain shabby for ever: 'Why can't Ah have one through t' Good Samaritan like th' others?' he mumbled.

'Ah'm shovin' no millstone o' weekly payments round me neck,' replied his father, bluntly: 'What we can't pay for cash down we'll do bout [without].' . . .

He persisted on his own behalf plaguing his father on every suitable occasion. After all, what disgrace was there in availing oneself of the facilities offered by Alderman Grumpole's Good Samaritan Clothing Club? Everybody hereabouts were its patrons, otherwise nobody would have new clothes. The Good Samaritan was a firmly established institution. It angered him to think that only his father's obstinate prejudice against credit dealings stood between him and his desires. Blimey, all this to-do arising out of a legitimate desire to be dressed properly. It made him boil.

His querulous complaints began to wear his father's nerves. The boy seemed absolutely impervious to reason. Weren't they in debt enough without contracting more for such inessential things as new suits? Such a suit as the lad desired would cost three pounds easily. That meant three shillings' interest to be found before Grumpole would issue an order to the outfitter; then would follow twenty week's instalments of three shillings. Three shillings a week, though!

This kind of thing, not being able to provide adequately for one's family, made a man feel an irresponsible fool, humbled him, haunted him to the point of driving him to frantic, foolhardy expedients. Money, money, money. The temptation to go drown worry and misery in drink was, betimes, almost irresistible. Walking abroad he would find himself brooding, muttering to himself, 'Worked every hour God sent, every day o' me life. An' what have Ah t' see for it? Every bloody day, every bloody hour an' worse off'n when Ah was fust wed.'

Harry was unaware that his father's absences from home were contrived. Every time he caught the boy's gaze it said, mutely: 'When am I to have the suit, Father?' He couldn't bear to look. Better to keep out of the lad's way as much as possible. His cause was just; the poor little devil wasn't fit to be seen; he was the only one in the house working full time; and he gave up every penny of his wages. Oh—! Hardcastle felt an urgent desire to be able to take out his brains and plunge them in cold water.

To Harry, his father's stern visage was a perfect mask: had he known he would have been astounded that his father should be afraid of meeting him.

He persisted until one Sunday evening, Hardcastle, in desperation, exclaimed: 'Oh, missis, for God's sake get him that blasted suit. Blimey, sick of it Ah am.'

Victorious, Harry's hungry joy amounted to hysteria. In his excitement the haggard, relaxed expression on his father's face meant nothing to him.

Walter Greenwood, *Love on the Dole*, 1933

What must I have seemed like after Rebecca? I can see myself now, memory spanning the years like a bridge, with straight, bobbed hair and youthful, unpowdered face, dressed in an ill-fitting coat and skirt and a jumper of my own creation, trailing in the wake of Mrs Van Hopper like a shy, uneasy colt. She would precede me in to lunch, her short body ill balanced upon tottering, high heels, her fussy, frilly blouse a compliment to her large bosom and swinging hips, her new hat pierced with a monster quill aslant upon her head, exposing a wide expanse of forehead bare as a schoolboy's knee.

We motored, I remember, leaving London in the morning in a heavy shower of rain, coming to Manderley about five o'clock, in time for tea. I can see myself now, unsuitably dressed as usual, although a bride of seven weeks, in a tan-coloured stockinette frock, a small fur known as a stone marten round my neck, and over all a shapeless mackintosh, far too big for me and dragging to my ankles ... 'I should shed that mackintosh,' he said, glancing down at me, 'it has not rained down here at all, and put your funny little fur straight. Poor lamb, I've bustled you down here like that, and you probably ought to have bought a lot of clothes in London.'

Daphne du Maurier, *Rebecca*, 1938

Next came a group of young fellows, the local 'bloods', with sleek oiled hair, red ties, coats cut very tight at the waist, braided pockets, and square-toed shoes. I guessed they were going to one of the big cinemas in the centre of the town. That was why they had started out so early and were hurrying to the tram stop, laughing and talking at the top of their voices.

Albert Camus, *The Outsider*, 1942

When Shorty let me stand up and see in the mirror, my hair hung down in limp, damp strings. My scalp still flamed, but not as badly; I could bear it. My first view in the mirror blotted out the hurting. I'd seen some pretty conks, but when it's the first time, on your *own* head, the transformation, after the lifetime of kinks, is staggering . . .* On top of my head was this thick, smooth sheen of shining red hair – real red – as straight as any white man's. How ridiculous I was! Stupid enough to stand there simply lost in admiration of my hair now looking 'white', reflected in the mirror in Shorty's room. I vowed that I'd never again be without a conk, and I never was for many years. This was my first really big step towards self-degradation.

The morning after I quit Roseland, I was down at the men's clothing store bright and early. The salesman checked and found that I'd missed only one weekly payment; I had A1 credit. I told him I'd just quit my job, but he said that didn't make any difference; I could miss paying them for a couple of weeks if I had to; he knew I'd get straight.

This time, I studied carefully everything in my size on the racks, And finally I picked out my second zoot. It was a sharkskin grey, with a big, long coat and pants bellowing out at the knees and then tapering down to cuffs so narrow that I had to take my shoes off to get them on and off. With the salesman urging me on, I got another

---

*While participating in the zoot-suit riots in Harlem in 1943 the young hustler Malcolm Little began his political education, which led to his transformation into the Black radical leader Malcolm X. In the Black youth style of the fashion of the day, he had his hair conked, or straightened to make it look less 'Black', and at fifteen, he bought his first zoot suit.

shirt, and a hat, and new shoes – the kind that were just coming into hipster style – dark orange colored, with paper-thin soles and knob-style toes. It all added up to seventy or eighty dollars.

It was such a red-letter day that I even went and got my first barber-shop conk. This time it didn't hurt so much, just as Shorty had predicted.

That night, I timed myself to hit Roseland as the thick of the crowd was coming in. In the thronging lobby, I saw some of the real Roxbury hipsters eyeing my zoot suit, and some fine women were giving me that look. I sauntered up to the men's room for a short drink from that pint in my inside coat pocket.

Malcolm X and Alex Haley, *The Autobiography of Malcom X,* 1965

Arthur washed loudly in the scullery, swilling waves of warm soapy water over his chest and face, blundering his way back to the fire to dry himself. Upstairs, he flung his greasy overalls aside and selected a suit from a line of hangers. Brown paper protected them from dust, and he stood for some minutes in the cold, digging his hands into the pockets and turning back lapels, sampling the good hundred pounds' worth of property hanging from an iron bar. These were his riches, and he told himself that money paid out on clothes was a sensible investment because it made him feel good as well as look good. He took a shirt from another series of hangers near the window and slipped it over his soiled underwear, fastening the buttons and pursing his lips in a whistle that made a shrill split in the room's silence.

A soft drizzling rain fell as he hurried to the bus stop. Clean-shaven and smart, fair hair short on top and weighed down with undue length at the back sent out a whiff of hair cream. From below the overcoat came narrow-bottomed trousers, falling with good creases to the tops of black, shining square-toed shoes.

*

Up in his bedroom he surveyed his row of suits, trousers, sports jackets, shirts, all suspended in colourful drapes and designs, good-quality tailor-mades, a couple of hundred quid's worth, a fabulous wardrobe of which he was proud because it had cost him so much labour. For some reason he selected the finest suit of black and changed into it, fastening the pearl buttons of a white silk shirt and pulling on his trousers. He picked up his wallet then slipped lighter and cigarette case into an outside pocket. The final item of Friday-night ritual was to stand before the downstairs mirror and adjust his tie, comb his thick fair hair neatly back, and search out a clean handkerchief from the dresser drawer. Squared-toed black shoes reflected a pink face when he bent down to see that no speck of dust was on them. Over his jacket he wore his twenty-guinea triumph, a thick three-quarter overcoat of Donegal tweed.

Alan Sillitoe, *Saturday Night and Sunday Morning*, 1954

And then one day things came to a head. In the morning my father announced that he would like to go to Cannes that evening to dance at the casino, and perhaps gamble as well. I remember how pleased Elsa was. In the familiar casino and atmosphere she hoped to resume the role of a *femme fatale*, slightly obscured of late by her sunburn and our semi-isolation. Contrary to my expectation Anne did not oppose our plans; she even seemed quite pleased. As soon as dinner was over I went up to my room to put on an evening frock, the only one I possessed, by the way. It had been chosen by my father, and was made of an exotic material, probably too exotic for a girl of my age, but my father, either from inclination or habit, liked to give me a veneer of sophistication. I found him downstairs, sparkling in a new dinner jacket, and I put my arms round his neck:

'You're the best-looking man I know!'

'Except Cyril,' he answered without conviction. 'And as for you, you're the prettiest girl I know.'

'After Elsa and Anne,' without believing it myself.

'Since they're not down yet, and have the cheek to keep us waiting, come and dance with your rheumaticky old father.'

Once again I felt the thrill that always preceded our evenings out together. He really had nothing of an old father about him. While dancing I inhaled the warmth of his familiar perfume, eau de cologne and tobacco. He danced slowly with half-closed eyes, a happy, irrepressible little smile, like my own, on his lips.

'You must teach me the bebop,' he said, forgetting his talk of rheumatism.

He stopped dancing to welcome Elsa with polite flattery. She came slowly down the stairs in her green dress, a conventional smile on her face, her casino smile. She had made the most of her lifeless hair and scorched skin, but the result was more meretricious than brilliant. Fortunately she seemed unaware of it.

'Are we going?'

'Anne's not here yet,' I remarked.

'Go up and see if she's ready,' said my father. 'It will be midnight before we get to Cannes.'

I ran up the stairs, getting somewhat entangled with my skirt, and knocked at Anne's door. She called to me to come in, but I stopped on the threshold. She was wearing a grey dress, a peculiar grey, almost white, which, when it caught the light, resembled the colour of the sea at dawn. She seemed to me to be the personification of mature charm.

'Oh Anne, what a magnificent dress!' I said.

She smiled into the mirror as one smiles at a person one is about to leave.

'This grey is a success,' she said.

'You are a success!' I answered.

She pinched my ear, her eyes were dark blue, and I saw them light up with a smile.

'You're a dear child, even though you can be tiresome at times.'

She went out in front of me without a glance at my dress. In a way I was relieved, but all the same it was mortifying. I followed her down the stairs and I saw my father coming to meet her. He stopped at the bottom, his foot on the first step, his face raised. Elsa was looking on. I remember the scene perfectly. First of all, in front of me, Anne's golden neck and perfect shoulders, a little lower down my father's fascinated face and extended hand, and, already in the distance, Elsa's silhouette.

Françoise Sagan, *Bonjour Tristesse*, 1954

I went out into the hall and leaned over the banister, just enough to see without being seen. She was still on the stairs, now she reached the landing, and the ragbag colours of her boy's hair, tawny streaks, strands of albino-blond and yellow, caught in the hall light. It was a warm evening, nearly summer, and she wore a slim cool black dress, black sandals, a pearl choker. For all her chic thinness, she had an almost breakfast-cereal air of health, a soap-and-lemon cleanness, a rough pink darkening in the cheeks. Her mouth was large, her nose upturned. A pair of dark glasses blotted out her eyes. It was a face beyond childhood, yet this side of belonging to a woman. I thought her anywhere between sixteen and thirty; as it turned out, she was shy two months of her nineteenth birthday . . .

Truman Capote, *Breakfast at Tiffany's*, 1958

Montana Slim turned to me, pointed at my shoes, and commented, 'You reckon if you put them things in the ground something'll grow up?' – without cracking a smile, of course, and the other boys heard him and laughed. And they were the silliest shoes in America; I bought them along specifically because I didn't want my feet to sweat in the hot road, and except for the rain in Bear Mountain they proved to be the best possible shoes for my journey. So I laughed with them. And the shoes were pretty ragged by now, the bits of coloured leather sticking up like pieces of a fresh pineapple and my toes showing through. Well, we had another shot and laughed.

Jack Kerouac, *On the Road,* 1957

Next, on the first floor, in in fact the best room, but I somehow don't think he'll last there, on account of really critical moments with Mr Omar, is a young coloured kid called Mr Cool (which I need hardly say is not his baptismal name, I don't suppose). Cool is a local product, I mean born and bred on this island of both races, and he wears a beardlet, and listens to the MJQ, and speaks very low, and blinks his big eyes and occasionally lets a sad, fleeting smile cross his kissable lips . . . the kid is always so skint, he's only one suit (a striped Italian black) and no furniture to speak of except for his radiogram . . .

But this particular evening I had to call at a teenage hut inside Soho, in order to contact two of my models, by names Dean Swift and the Misery Kid. Now, about Soho, there's this, that although so much crap's written about the area, of all London quarters, I think it's still one of the most authentic. I mean, Mayfair is just top spivs stepping into the slippers of the former gentry, and Belgravia, like I've said, is all flats in houses built as palaces, and Chelsea – well! Just take a look yourself, next time you're there . . .

This example was called Chez Nobody, and sure enough, sitting far apart from each other at distant tables, were the Dean and the Misery Kid. Though both are friends of mine, and, in a way, even friends of each other, these two don't mix in public, on account of the Dean being a sharp modern jazz creation, and the Kid just a skiffle survival, with horrible leanings to the trad thing . . .

If you know the contemporary scene, you could tell them apart at once, just like you could a soldier or sailor, with their separate uniforms. Take first the Misery Kid and his trad drag. Long, brushless hair, white stiff-starched collar (rather grubby), striped shirt, tie of all one colour (red today, but it could have been royal blue or navy), short jacket but an old one (somebody's riding tweed, most likely), very, very, tight, tight trousers with wide stripe, no sox, short *boots*. Now observe the Dean in the modernist number's version. College-boy smooth crop hair with burned-in parting, neat white Italian rounded-collared shirt, short Roman jacket *very* tailored (two little vents, three buttons), no-turn-up narrow trousers with seventeen-inch bottoms, absolute maximum, pointed-toe shoes, and a white mac lying folded by his side, compared with Misery's sausage-rolled umbrella.

Compare them, and take your pick! I would add that their chicks, if present, would match them up with: a trad boy's girl – long hair, untidy with long fringes, maybe jeans and a big floppy sweater, maybe bright-coloured never floralled, never pretty dress ... smudged-looking's the objective. Modern jazz boy's girl – short hemlines, seamless stockings, pointed-toed high-heeled stiletto shoes, crêpe nylon rattling petticoat, short blazer jacket, hair done up into the elfin style. Face pale – corpse colour with a dash of mauve, plenty of mascara.

Colin MacInnes, *Absolute Beginners*, 1959

The four of us were dressed in the height of fashion, which in those days was a pair of very black tights with the old jelly mould, as we called it, fitting on the crotch underneath the tights, this being to protect and also a sort of a design you could viddy clear enough in a certain light, so that I had one in the shape of a spider. Pete had a rooker (a hand, that is). Georgie had a very fancy one of a flower, and poor old Dim had a very hound-and-horny one of a clown's litso (face, that is), Dim not ever having much of an idea of things and being, beyond all shadow of a doubting Thomas, the dimmest of we four. Then we wore waisty jackets ('pletchoes' we called them) which were a kind of mockery of having real shoulders like that. Then, my brothers, we had these off-white cravats which looked like a whipped-up kartoffel or spud with a sort of a design made on it with a fork. We wore our hair not too long and we had flip horror-show boots for kicking.

'What's it going to be, eh?'

There were three devotchkas sitting at the counter all together, but there were four of us malchicks and it was usually like one for all and all for one. These sharps were dressed in the height of fashion too, with purple and green and orange wigs on their gullivers, each one not costing less than three or four weeks of those sharps' wages, I should reckon, and make-up to match (rainbows round the glazzies, that is, and the rot painted very wide). Then they had long black very straight dresses, and on the groody part of them they had little badges of like silver with different malchicks' names on them – Joe and Mike and suchlike.

Anthony Burgess, *A Clockwork Orange*, 1962

Mark Feld, Peter Sugar and Michael Simmonds were brought up in Stoke Newington. The most important thing in the world to them is their clothes: they have cupboards and shelves bulging with suits and shirts often designed by themselves in bright, strange and violent colours. In their vocabulary they, and the few other contemporaries of whom they approve, are described as 'faces' – the necessary ingredients are youth, a sharp eye for dressing and a general lack of mercy towards the rest of the world . . .

Mark is the most remarkable of the three because he is five years younger than either of the other two and appears to have no visible means of support. His father is a lorry driver and his mother works in Berwick Market: she is joined there by her son on Saturdays when he puts in a full day's work . . . In common with the others his conversation only becomes animated when asked about his clothes. He says, 'I've got ten suits, eight sports jackets, fifteen pairs of slacks, thirty to thirty-five good shirts, about twenty jumpers, three leather jackets, two suede jackets, five or six pairs of shoes and thirty exceptionally good ties.' . . .

'You've got to be different from the other kids,' says Feld. 'I mean, you got to be two steps ahead. The stuff that half the haddocks you see around are wearing I was wearing years ago. A kid in my class came up to me in his new suit, an Italian box it was, he says, "Just look at the length of your jacket," he says. "You're not with it," he says.

"I was wearing that style two years ago," I said. Of course, they don't like that. Not many of them like me much at our school, especially the masters – but they leave me alone now. If it's football or anything – I mean that's not my style at all – they say "Oh never mind about Feld", and I go and sunbathe or something.'

'It's getting harder to be different now,' says Simmonds, the quiet one.

'Yeah,' says Feld. 'Remember three years ago, it was easy then. We used to go round on scooters in Levis and leather jackets. It was a lot easier then.'

But three years ago he would only be twelve.

'That's right,' says Feld.

'Half the tailors you go to just don't want to know,' says Sugar. 'You got to tell them exactly what you want and they say yes, yes, yes, they know, they know what the styles are, all the kids go to them and then they produce a monstrosity with a little box jacket and *vents* and covered buttons and you just can't wear it.'

'You have to leave a small deposit,' says Simmonds. 'And then if you don't like the result, you don't collect. I done that lots of times. I mean you have to.'

Sugar says: 'Bilgorri in Bishopsgate – he's a great tailor. He'll make exactly what you want. It's a real haddocky-looking place he has, but he does what you want. All the faces go to Bilgorri. And John

Stevens. He's very good on trousers. Hardly any place in London makes good trousers. They're all baggy here.'

He tugs at the seat of his own trousers. Barely an eighth of an inch comes away.

'They aren't good on shoulders either,' says Feld. 'They can't make good shoulders like those French shoulders. I bought a jacket back from Paris – I was in Paris with my parents but I didn't like it much – and this jacket was just rubbish over there but it's great here. Great shoulders.'

'We've all had suits from Burton's,' says Sugar. 'We *have*, I admit it. You take a bit of a chance with Burton's but if you can tell them exactly what you want you can get a good suit.'

'C. & A. suits are good too,' says Feld. 'You have to look at them all and try them on but we've all found a suit we like there.'

'You found that sort-of mohair one, didn't you Michael?' said Sugar. 'And I found that tweed one. Just the thing for point-to-points.'

Pause.

'I'm a Conservative,' said Sugar. 'I mean Conservatives are for the rich, really, and everyone wants to be rich, really, don't they.'

'They've been in a long time and they done all right,' said Simmonds.

'Yeah, like he says, they're for the rich, really, so I'm for them,' says Feld.

'Of course, I don't know much about it,' says Sugar.

'The Ban-the-Bomb lot are dead right and everything but I wouldn't march or anything,' says Simmonds.

'It's all exhibitionist isn't it?' says Feld. 'I'm all for that. I mean I'm all for anyone who's exhibitionist. You don't just want to be like everyone else. You got to be different.'

Pause.

'I read a good book the other day,' says Feld. '*The Life of Beau Brummel*. He was just like us really. You know, came up from nothing. Then he met Royalty and got to know all the big blokes and he had

a lot of clothes. He came to nothing in the end through gambling.
I don't gamble.' . . .

'We bought these stick pins from Woolworth's this morning,'
says Sugar. 'Only 3d. each. They are really women's hat pins but you
can't tell can you? We've got pearl ones and gold ones and black
ones and we can ring the changes.'

'You have to watch them, though,' says Feld. 'They work up a
bit if you don't watch them.'

Pause for adjustment of stick pins.

'These shoes cost seven guineas in Pinnays in Bond Street,' says
Feld. 'I think if you pay a bit extra for shoes they last longer.'

Pause.

'We're all a bit exhibitionist,' says Sugar. 'I admit. Some of our
clothes are a bit effeminate but they have to be. I mean you have to
be a bit camp. I mean who cares.'

'You get a lot of jeers and shouts round our way,' says Feld. 'If
you wear something that's a bit different it's "Nancy" and "Look at
that queer."' 'We're not, so who cares,' says Sugar.

'But you get into fights over it all the time, anyway,' says Feld.

'We don't look for them. We're not the type,' says Simmonds.

'Just a bit ago me and Michael were at this dance hall in Hackney,'
says Sugar. 'We twist a lot. We were twisting two years ago and it
used to cause such a lot of trouble that we were told to stop it.
Nowadays everyone twists so we have to have a different twist. I
mean there's the straight twist and the rock twist and the sophisticated
twist, you have to be different. Anyway this lad at Hackney, he'd been
drinking a bit and he grabbed me by the lapels and said, "I hear you've
been looking for me to sort me out." I said I'd never seen him before
and was turning away when he come in with his nut. So I started in
and Michael came in and his mates came in and it was murder. I
wouldn't care if they was my size, but they're always enormous. Mean
that one that hit you, Michael, he must have had a fist THAT size.'

'Yeah,' said Simmonds, remembering.

'I went to the Calypso hall over Croydon way,' says Feld. 'I was wearing a pair of white cotton trousers and a suede jacket. Well, there was a big line of Teds there. You should have heard them when they saw me. Whistling, shouting, laughing. I had to walk all the way past them.'

A short silence for brooding.

'It's because we're different,' says Sugar.

'Anything different they just hit out,' says Feld. 'There's no arguing or settling it with talk, it's just hit out.'

Another pause.

'What I want to do is make money and do just what I like,' says Sugar.

'That's what I want to do. Just what I like. Trouble is I'm lazy. Frankly, mind you, I work hard.'

'John Stevens now,' says Feld. 'You got to hand it to him. All those shops and he's still only twenty-six or something. You got to hand it to him.'

'And that face that does the laundrettes,' says Sugar. 'Only thirty something and he's a millionaire.'

'And blokes like Cliff Richard and Adam Faith,' says Feld. 'I mean, I suppose they're had-its in a way but they've *done* something.'

'And Elvis Presley . . .'

'And Frank Sinatra . . .'

'And Albert Finney . . .'

Pause.

'Remember those winkle-pickers we used to wear from Stan's?' says Feld.

They fall about with laughter.

'Those days it was easy to be different,' says Sugar.

'Harder now,' says Feld.

'Definitely,' says Simmonds.

Peter Barnsley, 'Faces Without Shadows', *Town*, 1962

'Take yer overcoat off Sheil and let yerself go!' Ruby and Lily stop dancing and join the onlookers. The room is thick with the smell of fresh sweat. The music blares on . . . 'See the fella in blue jeans, dancing with the older queen, who's dolled up in a diamond ring . . . Twistin', twistin', twistin' the night away.'

Sheila opens her mouth, swaying desperately. As the music reaches its climax she flings off her coat revealing a gold damask blouse. 'Oh man you oughta see him go . . . Twistin', twistin', twistin' the night away.' It's over and she stands still in the hot circle of women, a laconic grin wide over her face, her richly embroidered Victorian blouse pushed into her old tweed skirt.

'Hey, look at that!'

'Wow, what a blouse!'

'Where did you get that Sheil, off the barrows?'

'Life's so drab you've got to wear something bright ain't you, Sheil?'

'Me mum bought it for me.' Her scrawny arms stick out from the delicately puffed sleeves.

'Don't fib – one of yer boyfriends up the café gave it you.'

'Go and join the ATS in that!'

'Pity they've cleaned up the streets.'

Sheila giggled with coy pleasure, thrusting her chin down into the yellow scarf still wound about her neck.

'Tell you what, Sheila, we'll cut the sleeves off for you, that'll look better!'

With a giant pair of scissors amidst a great deal of cat calls, Ruby did it.

'There you are love, all set for the Jazz Band Ball.'

The blouse had large armholes, and now Sheila's grubby bra was exposed.

'I can see the scruff under your arms, Sheil!' There were howls of laughter.

'Here, Lily, let's give her a low back.' Rube grabbed the scissors and cut a V. The blouse slid sideways revealing a torn vest. The door opened. 'Back to work you women.'

Sheila, still grinning, sat down hugging her arms to her chest till someone threw her a worn cardigan. On the brown lino, amid discarded sweet papers and cigarette ends, the gold sleeves lay gleaming in the raw electric light.

Nell Dunn, *Up the Junction*, 1963

I was supposed to be having the time of my life.

I was supposed to be the envy of thousands of other college girls just like me all over America who wanted nothing more than to be tripping about in those same size-seven patent-leather shoes I bought in Bloomingdale's one lunch hour with a black patent-leather belt and black patent-leather pocketbook to match. And when my picture came out in the magazine the twelve of us were working on – drinking Martinis in a skimpy, imitation silver-lamé bodice stuck on to a big, fat cloud of white tulle, on some Starlight Roof, in the company of several anonymous young men with all-American bone structures hired or loaned for the occasion – everybody would think I must be having a real whirl . . .

Doreen looked terrific. She was wearing a strapless white lace dress zipped up over a snug corset affair that curved her in at the middle and bulged her out again spectacularly above and below, and her skin had a bronzy polish under the pale dusting powder. She smelled strong as a whole perfume store.

I wore a black shantung sheath that cost me forty dollars. It was part of a buying spree I had with some of my scholarship money when I heard I was one of the lucky ones going to New York. This dress was cut so queerly I couldn't wear any sort of a bra under it, but that didn't matter much as I was skinny as a boy and barely rippled, and I liked feeling almost naked on the hot summer nights . . .

I stood quietly in the doorway in my black sheath and my black stole with the fringe, yellower than ever, but expecting less. 'I am an observer,' I told myself, as I watched Doreen being handed into the room by the blond boy to another man, who was also tall, but dark, with slightly longer hair. This man was wearing an immaculate white suit, a pale blue shirt and a yellow satin tie with a bright stickpin.

I couldn't take my eyes off that stickpin.

A great white light seemed to shoot out of it, illuminating the room. Then the light withdrew into itself, leaving a dewdrop on a field of gold.

Sylvia Plath, *The Bell Jar*, 1963

In the morning Benjamin got up earlier than usual. He dressed himself in a pair of khaki pants and an old jacket he had bought in the east at an army surplus store, and went downstairs. Mrs Braddock was in the kitchen. 'You're up early,' she said.

Benjamin walked past her and sat down at the table in front of his grapefruit. 'I'm leaving home,' he said, picking up his spoon . . . 'If you want the cliché . . . I'm going on the road.'

'I see – I see you found it all right,' he said.

She smiled at him and walked into the room, looking at a television set in the corner, then at the bed. She removed the small round hat from the top of her head and set it down on a writing desk against one of the walls.

'Well,' Benjamin said. He nodded but didn't say anything more.

Mrs Robinson walked slowly back to where he was standing. 'Well?' she said, looking up into his face.

Benjamin waited a few moments, then brought one of his hands up to her shoulder. He bent his face down, cleared his throat, and kissed her. Then he lifted his face back up and nodded again. 'Well,' he said again, removing his hand from her shoulder.

Mrs Robinson returned to the writing table and looked down at her hat.

'Benjamin?'

'Yes?'

'I'll get undressed now,' she said, running one of her fingers around the edge of the hat. 'Is that all right?'

'Sure,' Benjamin said. 'Fine. Do you – do you—'

'What?'

'I mean do you want me to just stand here?' he said. 'I don't – I don't know what you want me to do.'

'Why don't you watch,' she said.

'Oh. Sure. Thank you.'

He watched her unbutton the three buttons on the front of her suit, then reach up to unbutton the top button on her blouse. She smiled at him as she moved her hand slowly down the front of her blouse, then leaned for support on the writing table and reached down to remove her shoes.

'Will you bring me a hanger?' she said.

'What?'

She straightened up and frowned at him. 'Benjamin, if you want another drink we'll go down and have one.'

'Oh no,' Benjamin said. 'A hanger. I'll get a hanger.' He hurried to the closet and opened its door. 'A wood one?' he said.

'What?'

'Do you want a wood one?'

'A wood one would be fine,' she said.

'Right,' Benjamin said. He reached into the closet for a wooden hanger and carried it across the room to her.

'Thank you,' she said, taking it.

'You're welcome,' Benjamin said. He walked back to the door. He slid his hands into his pockets and watched her as she removed the jacket of her suit, then the blouse she was wearing and hung them on the hanger.

Suddenly Benjamin began shaking his head. He pulled his hands
up out of his pockets and opened his mouth to say something but
then closed it again.

'Mrs Robin——?'

'What?'

'Nothing.'

She frowned at him.

'Nothing,' Benjamin said. 'Nothing. Do you need another hanger?'

'No,' she said. She looked at him a moment longer, then pushed
her skirt down around her legs, stepped out of it and folded it.
'Would it be easier for you in the dark?' she said, draping the skirt
through the hanger and over the wooden bar.

'No.'

'You're sure?'

'I'm sure. Yes.'

'Hang this up, please?' she said. Benjamin walked across the room
to take the hanger from her and carried it to the closet. When he
had hung it up and turned around she had let a half-slip she was
wearing drop to the floor and was stepping out of it. She slid a girdle
and the stockings fastened to it down around her legs and on to the
floor. 'Will you undo my bra?' she said, turning around.

'Your – your——'

'Will you?'

Benjamin looked at her a moment longer, then suddenly began
shaking his head. He rushed to one of the walls of the room. 'No!'
he said.

'What?'

'Mrs Robinson! Please! I can't!'

'What?'

'I cannot do this!'

Mrs Robinson watched him for a moment, then turned and walked
slowly to the bed. She seated herself and moved back to sit with
her back against the board at the head of the bed. She crossed her

legs in front of her and reached behind her back to unhook the bra.

Charles Webb, *The Graduate*, 1964

1965

At Sam's party Dylan was in blue jeans and high-heeled boots and a sports jacket, and his hair was sort of long. He had deep circles under his eyes, and even when he was standing he was all hunched in. He was around twenty-four then and the kids were all just starting to talk and act and dress and swagger like he did. But not many people except Dylan could ever pull that anti-act off – and if he wasn't in the right mood, he couldn't either. He was already slightly flashy when I met him, definitely not folksy any more – I mean, he was wearing satin polka-dot shirts.

Andy Warhol and Pat Hackett, *POPism: The Warhol '6os*, 1981

She wore a cling sweater in winter-white with a polo neck. The sleeves were pushed carelessly back almost to her elbows. It was tucked into a wine-red skirt of fine tweed, with pleats at each side and pocket flaps. The skirt was held by a broad black leather belt with a double ring, and fell just to the middle of the knee. Her legs, of that same matt tan, were bare. She wore dull gold open sandals with set-back heels, and the touch of coral red on her toenails matched her lips.

Peter O' Donnell, *Modesty Blaise*, 1965

I must have been born with the desire to design clothes – I started so early. My clothes were inherited from a cousin; at the age of five or six I began to resent this and tried to make my own by cutting up the bedspread. I felt they were not me and wanted something sharper.

The look I wanted was clinched for me by another child at dancing class – a tap dancer who wore a basin haircut, forecasting Vidal Sassoon, a black, skinny sweater and a six-inch black pleated skirt over black tights plus white ankle socks. It was the white socks over black, with black patent shoes with ankle straps and a boot button on the top that did it: the surprise focal point. The trick is not any one outrageous item, but in a combination and juxtaposition which is fashionably perverse.

The sixties mini was, perhaps, the ultimate surprise focal point. It was: 'Wow! Look at me. Isn't life wonderful!' It was young, liberated and exuberant and on the pill. It was called Youthquake. And it looked all girl. It was the beginning of Women's Lib.

The nineties mini is the same but different. It says: 'I have made it.'

It's sophisticated and in charge; chairman-of-the-board stuff. It's sexy and very, very female. It looks like Job Done for Women's Lib. And the heyday for grown-up women. And they are only thirty years apart, and yet what a long journey has been made.

And there was no fashion except couture collections intended for individuals of pre-war wealth, shape and deportment. I designed my own clothes. We opened our own shop, Bazaar, above Alexander's. I bought cloth on account at Harrod's, which gave me a year's credit.

The designs were young; clothes to live in. The tunic dresses and skirts were short and worn over tights, which I persuaded the theatrical tights manufacturers to make matching the skinny rib sweaters worn with them. I used a lot of men's suitings – pinstripe and Prince of Wales checks and herringbones, often black and white over mustard yellow skinny rib sweaters. They were short, sharp and wildly successful.

Mary Quant, 'The Meaning of the Mini', *Daily Telegraph*, 1997

1967

Pop fashion really peaked about now – a glance around the gymnasium could tell you that. It was the year of the electric dress – vinyl with a hip-belt batter pack – and there were lopsided hemlines everywhere, silver-quilted minidresses, 'micro-miniskirts' with knee-socks, Paco Rabanne's dresses of plastic squares linked together with little metal rings, lots and lots of Nehru collars, crocheted skirts over tights – to give just the idea of a skirt. There were big hats and high boots and short furs, psychedelic prints, 3-D appliqués, still lots of colored, textured tights and bright-colored patent leather shoes. The next big fashion influence – Nostalgia – wouldn't come till August, when *Bonnie and Clyde* came out, but right now everything mod-mini-madcap that had been building up since '64 was full-blown.

Something extremely interesting was happening in men's fashions, too – they were starting to compete in glamour and marketing with women's fashions, and this signaled big social changes that went beyond fashion into the question of sex roles. Now a lot of the men with fashion awareness who'd been frustrated for the last couple of years telling their girlfriends what to wear could start dressing themselves up instead. It was all so healthy, people finally doing what they really wanted, not having to fake it by having an opposite-sex person around to act out their fantasies for them – now they could get right out there and be their own fantasies.

Andy Warhol and Pat Hackett, *POPism: The Warhol '60s*, 1981

Divided into their tribal units, the hippies heap their belongings on the floor and dance around them. This is how I first saw Passionflower and the rest of her tribe: Arabesque, tall and fair, wearing gauzy harem trousers under her sari and carrying her black baby in a paisley shawl on her back; Willowherb with calf-length skirt from the thrift store, a belted jerkin and feathers stuck in the ends of her two plaits; Tumbleweed in deliberately frayed jeans and fringed leather jacket, his long blond hair held in place by a blue beaded band; Cactusflower with a big black beard that lost its contours in his long hair and the mass of hair on his chest. As they danced, dispensable garments were added to the heap in their midst, Arabesque's trousers, Willowherb's boots, Tumbleweed's jacket, the little black baby rising higher and higher on the pile.

She [Passionflower] nearly always dressed in white, unconventionally, a Mexican shirt as a dress, a Victorian nightgown from the thrift store as a party dress. She never wore a bra and her feet never knew shoes: occasionally sandals or genuine mocassins, and she never took off the four rows of beads.

Toni del Renzio, *The Flower Children*, 1969

Deborah produced wonderful shirts in her shop in Beauchamp Place. They were mostly flower prints and everybody had some. Michael Rainey had some edible-looking, ice-cream-coloured suits in Hung on You – white, pink, pistachio-green and cream. These too were very popular. Moroccan bernouses and yellow babouches, shirts with lace ruffles at neck and cuffs, silks, satins, velvets, gypsy earrings, Indian rings and bracelets and, yes, even bells abounded.

One summer evening Brian Jones was drowned in his swimming pool and some little time afterwards the rest of the Stones gave a memorial concert at the Cockpit in Hyde Park . . .

Eventually, Mick walked on to the stand and came up to the front. He was wearing white, a colour of mourning. It was a Michael Fish short white tunic dress with a very full skirt. He looked sad and he had an open book in his hand, out of which he read a short Shelley poem in honour of Brian. Then the music started, and for two and a half hours twenty thousand people sat and listened. They were as well behaved as any party from the Mother's Union.

Henrietta Moraes, *Henrietta*, 1994

Opening the wardrobe, he selected his gear from its shadowy recesses . . .

Union shirt – collarless and identical with those thousand others worn by his kind throughout the country; army trousers and braces; and boots! The boots were the most important item. Without his boots, he was part of the common herd – like his dad, a working man devoid of identity. Joe was proud of *his* boots. Most of his mates' were new boots bought for a high price in a high-street shop. But not Joe's. His were genuine army-disposal boots: thick-soled, studded, heavy to wear and heavy to feel if slammed against a rib.

Richard Allen, *Skinhead*, 1970

In his pinstripe suit and clean white shirt with his conservative tie clipped in place by a Stratton gold pin, Joe felt quite the city gent. *Funny*, he mused, *how clothes change a guy's outlook.*

He could remember those far-off days when he was ten-foot tall dressed in his bovver boots, union shirt, tight trousers with the loud braces boldy showing. He could touch his hair and recall the pride of a skinhead cut. Recall! His hair was growing now. In another month or two it would be suede . . . in between being a skinhead and being what the Establishment liked to call 'normal' styling. Suede – smooth, élite, expensive.

He smiled to himself as he entered the pub. That was his new image. Suedehead – a smoothie, one of the élite now, and with expensive tastes [and] ambitions.

Richard Allen, *Suedehead*, 1971

Felicity and Merion sit side by side, an anguished Watermouth pair, Felicity in her shirt and long skirt, Merion in incredible thicknesses of garment, including a skin waistcoat and a crocheted long cardigan. Michael Bennard is next to Felicity; he has a large black beard, and wears a frock coat and jeans. Hashmi is next to Merion; he has a fine splayed-out hairdo, and platform shoes . . .

Here he [George Carmody] sits, in his chair, looking beamingly around; as he does so, he shines forth unreality. He is a glimpse from another era; a kind of historical offence. In the era of his hair, his face is perfectly clean-shaven, so shaven that the fuzz of peach hair on his upper features looks gross against the raw epidermis on his cheeks and chin, where the razor has been. The razor has also been round the back of his neck, to give him a close, neat haircut. From some mysterious source, unknown and in any case alien to all other students, he has managed to acquire a university blazer, with a badge, and a university tie; these he wears with a white shirt, and a pair of pressed grey flannels. His shoes are brightly polished; so, as if to match, is his briefcase. He is an item, preserved in some extraordinary historical pickle, from the 1950s or before; he comes out of some strange fold in time. He has always been like this, and at first his style was a credit; wasn't it just a mock style to go with all the other mock styles in the social parody? But this is the third year; he has been out of sight for months, and here he is again, and he has renewed the commitment; the terrible truth seems clear. It is no joke; Carmody wants to be what he says he is.

'You have an advisee called George Carmody.' 'A big fair-haired boy who wears a blazer?' says Miss Callender. 'An unmistakable boy,' says Howard, 'the only student in this university with a trouser press.'

Malcolm Bradbury, *The History Man*, 1975

'Sex were doing something different from everybody else,' says John Lydon, 'and they weren't liked, which was absolutely brilliant. They were totally horrible people. Vivienne was the most awful old bag and that really fascinated me. Vivienne's a killer, a vicious lady. To buy anything in that shop was a real fight. I loved the rubber T-shirt, lock, stock and barrel. I thought it was the most repulsive thing I had ever seen. To wear it as a piece of clothing rather than part of some sexual fetish was hilarious.

'Jordan was always friendly. Genuinely interested. She'd obviously seen us for what we were, which was silly little kids who didn't have a clue. We'd go to the King's Road just to annoy people: it was necessary then. Long hair was everywhere. What was there to do then? There was Soul boys and Roxy Music kind of clothes: all that was very naff, very weedy and not going anywhere. People were very stiff and boring. I was bored with everything.'

Jon Savage, *England's Dreaming*, 1991

The pub was full of kids dressed like me, both from my school and from other schools in the area. Most of the boys, so nondescript during the day, now wore cataracts of velvet and satin, and bright colours; some were in bedspreads and curtains. The little groovers talked esoterically of Syd Barrett. To have an elder brother who lived in London and worked in fashion, music or advertising was an inestimable advantage at school. I had to study the *Melody Maker* and *New Musical Express* to keep up.

But at the front of the place, near the stage, there were about thirty kids in black clothes. And the clothes were full of safety pins. Their hair was uniformly black, and cut short, seriously short, or if long it was spiky and rigid, sticking up and out and sideways, like a handful of needles, rather than hanging down. A hurricane would not have dislodged those styles. The girls were in rubber and leather and wore skin-tight skirts and hole-black stockings, with white face-slap and bright-red lipstick. They snarled and bit people. Accompanying these kids were what appeared to be three extravagant transvestites in dresses, rouge and lipstick, one of whom had a used tampon on a piece of string around her neck. Charlie stirred restlessly as he leaned there. He hugged himself in self-pity as we took in this alien race dressed with an abandonment and originality we'd never imagined possible. I began to understand what London meant and what class of outrage we had to deal with. It certainly put us in proportion.

'Please, Charlie,' Eva implored him. 'Please take off the swastika. I don't care about anything else.'

'In that case I'll keep it.'

'Charlie—'

'I've always hated your fucking nagging.'

'It's not nagging, it's for compassion.'

'Right. I won't be coming back here, Eva. You're such a drag now. It's your age. Is it the menopause that's making you like this?'

Beside Charlie on the floor was a pile of clothes from which he pulled jackets, macs and shirts before throwing them aside as unsuitable. He then applied black eyeliner. He walked out of the flat without looking at either of us. Eva screamed after him, 'Think of those who died in the camps! And don't expect me to be there tonight, you pig! Charlie, you can forget my support for ever.'

'Does he really know what he's doing, Karim?' Some of the kids were as young as twelve; most were about seventeen. They were dressed like Charlie, mostly in black. Some of them had orange- or blue-streaked hair, making them look like cockatoos. They elbowed and fought and gave each other tongue sandwiches, and spat at passers-by and in each other's faces, there in the cold and rain of decaying London, with the indifferent police looking on. As a concession to the New Wave I wore a black shirt, black jeans, white socks and black suede shoes, but I knew that I had uninteresting hair. Not that I was the only one: some older men in 1960s expensive casual clothes, Fiorucci jeans and suede boots, with Cuban heels for Christ's sake, were chasing the band, hoping to sign them.

Hanif Kureishi, *The Buddha of Suburbia*, 1990

Politics, when you were dressing like Lord Byron or a member of some constructivist army, came fairly low down on your list of social responsibilities – more important than religion but far less important than shopping . . . Grey was the colour and alienation was the game. Steve Strange's group Visage had a hit with 'Fade to Grey', while John Foxx's Ultravox, on 'Hiroshima Mon Amour', were 'riding InterCity trains, dressed in European grey'. Grey, as the ghostly non-colour of urban mist, had popped up in Gary Numan's founding vocabulary in reference to the 'friend' of 'Are "Friends" Electric?', who was dressed in a long coat, grey hat, smoking a cigarette, (A fair description of David Bowie during his residence in Berlin, with Iggy Pop as Isherwood to his Auden (on the style index) as well as the eerie hue of half-life, afterlife and indecision.)

Michael Bracewell, *England is Mine*, 1998

FACT

Vestiphobia is the fear of clothes. A fear of wearing flouncy collars, long sleeves, garish ties and bright colours . . . a fear of the whole TREND END in general. Not a fear of being belted swiftly about the head with a pair of heavy cords and a chunky cock-ring belt, but a genuine fear of wearing clothes. Not just being a-feared of red and black lace lingerie or split crotch boxer shorts – I mean scared of clothes! And all those people who you know who don't necessarily 'dress-up' – they're not oblivious to the whys and wherefores of putting on the Ritz . . . clothes actually scare the living daylights out of them.

Fundamentally there are two manifestations of vestiphobia: on the one hand we have VESTIPHOBIACS and on the other VESTIMANIACS. Vestiphobiacs are probably the more pitiful of the two – because they are petrified of actually touching fabric, let alone wearing it; in short they are tortured. They see clothing coming towards them at night – they have visions of scarves wrapping themselves around their necks – shoes kicking them . . . they hear the incessant cackling laugh of the lurex jacket, taunting them to slip it over their shoulders. Ancient Britons were vestiphobiacs; they used to paint themselves blue before going into battle because they thought it was a magic colour that would protect them from harm. But when the Romans defeated them, unsurprisingly they started wearing clothes. Diogenes the Greek philosopher also had an aversion to clothes; he walked around in a barrel because he believed that clothing made people vain. But then Diogenes was always nine pence short of a bob, and he got himself killed for his silly ways.

Vestiphobiacs could be the largest social group in the country (the largest minority – peer group or not – is a m-a-j-o-r-i-t-y) . . . there are just so Goddamn *many* of them. I mean, have you ever had second thoughts after buying a particularly loud Nehru suit (the high-collared suit in the Indian style first popularized by Pierre Cardin in Paris after a trip to India in 1966 and more recently plundered by Scott Crolla), or held back from purchasing a very noisy shirt because you didn't have anything to go 'with-it'? (This in itself is nonsensical, as in the 1960s a white designer polo neck was used to accessorize evening dress – black seersucker dinner jacket with French cuffs, black striped trousers, black silk tie etc. – and broke all conventional rules . . . the white turtle neck pullover and dinner suit was a revolutionary idea that drew international attention – 'Everyone likes a polo, darling.')

It's plain to see that everyone has gone through small sartorial troubles such as these, but those that have these problems are at least coping with clothes (there are elements of the vestiphobiac in all of us), not avoiding them. One particularly common breeding ground for vestiphobiacs is a little place called Cedar Rapids in Iowa, just to the left of Chicago in the big un-fashion conscious US of A. These G U I C K S (both guys and chicks dress identically) seem to assume that anyone not wearing quadrilateral flared jeans, Budweiser sweatshirts, down-home sneakers and blonde nape-length hair is a fetishistic fashion casualty. Clothes in mid-America either signify an allegiance to bad taste . . . or, more commonly, V E S T I P H O B I A.

Fashion has turned on itself more than once in its long, made-to-measure history – inverting ideals and messing things up until they mean nothing at all. The Doctor Marten shoe came into fashion (for the second time) in early 1978, when it became synonymous with sexually emancipated and socially aware young men with drain-pipe jeans, baggy mohair jumpers, short tidy hair and Buzzcocks LPs under their arms. By adopting the D M shoe these pretentious vestiphobiacs were trying to turn a blind eye to fashion, whilst trying not to look too out of date. We can appropriate the dress codes of the proletariat, they cried, without adopting the politics or, the – gulp – class values. In their eyes the D M shoe had bohemian connotations as well as military ones. Sweet boys.

When label-consciousness came back at the turn of the decade, when thin loafers and garish pegs came rambling back into left-field fashion, spreading coloured lights, plastic palm trees, funk and Fiorucci all over this merry land, suddenly label junkies were every-where. And label junkies, as we know, are nothing if not V E S T I-M A N I A C S! These are more easily spotted then vestiphobiacs, because they come out into the open: to flaunt and steal. They can't get enough satin and tat – slacks, cloaks, ponchos, busbys, thermals, jackets, Fair Isles, flannels, bags or jerkins. They dream of wallowing in winceyette, of being coated in yards of the finest beige cashmere – anything and everything to do with clothes and fabrics. Vestimani-acs are scared of appearing out of date, and this magnifies in their minds so that they literally change their clothes every ten minutes

(144 outfits a day). They get confused by the fact that fashion goes backwards as well as forwards and this contributes to their constantly changing wardrobe: the poor things can never be certain that what they're wearing is fashionable. A fashion junkie by any other name, a VESTIMANIAC is scared shitless by clothes.

Oddly enough, it's not the most outrageous and flamboyant clothes that are the bane of both vestiphobiacs and vestimaniacs – it's the classics that present all the problems: the Bass Weejun loafer, Brooks Brothers shirt, Chanel suit and white silk sock forever haunt vestiphobiacs because they can never get rid of them, for the simple reason that they never go out of date; the vestimaniacs never know when the classics are in fashion, so consequently they never know when to wear them.

FICTION

There inevitably comes a point when phobiacs and maniacs can take no more. And when this happens, they either go to meet their tailor (!) or end up in the Miami Vestitution for the Sartorially Anxious. Situated in ample pleasant grounds, just a stone's throw from South Beach under the sweltering Florida sun, this charity-run clinic deals with all manner of sartorially related problems. Ensconced within these big white walls are the remnants of various vestiphobiacs and vestimaniacs. They live at separate ends of the central corridor and although the warders try to keep them apart as much as possible, the maniacs occasionally break out of their padded cells and rampage through the building, tearing the clothes off the backs of the phobiacs, to the phobiac's obvious jubilation – they can't bear wearing those clean white linen suits! This rampaging goes on for an hour or two, then the maniacs get bored with the tunics and give them back – or try to. By this time, the phobiacs are back in their padded cells stretched out naked on the floor, dreaming of the day when they won't have to wear anything at all.

As I said before, there are elements of the vestiphobiac in all of us.

Dylan Jones, 'Vestiphobia – the Fear of Clothes', *iD*, 1985

OK, here it comes . . . the next really monster social trend is the New Seriousness.

The what? I hear you ask. How does it differ from the Old Seriousness? Is there any connection with the Relatively Recent Triviality? All will be revealed, but first let me explain the discovery of this proud new beast.

It was at the ICA that the first inklings came. I was watching the celebrations surrounding the launch of dear Peter York's fab new paperback, which had had – incidentally – quite a zippy little party when it was a hardback last year. The theme of this year's paperback show was to illustrate the social types presented in his tome, *Modern Times* (tuppence-halfpenny from a book boutique near you now), by means of some actual live specimens.

Down the catwalk came Chic Graphiques and Baby Timers and Hard Timers and girls in rubber and boys dressed as girls and indeed the whole panoply of young clubland today. And all these children looked very serious and self-important about their Place in History, which I must say was quite endearing and sweet – like watching one's nephew play the Archangel Gabriel in a nursery-school nativity play.

But the thing about these people was that far from being shining examples of contemporary thought and style, they were actually acting out a show that no one wants to see any more. The whole fancy-dress era is over. A haircut is not enough. Of course, for someone like you, dear reader, it never was. But you must understand that there have been a lot of dedicated followers of fashion in this town who have based their careers on the principle that the *iD* clothes really do make the man. I myself have even said as much.

Lord, how wrong I was. I buttonholed the Great Yorkie after the show and told him that I had seen a new trend in the distance. He was forced to concede that a sea change was upon us, one that threatened his whole career, nay, his very persona. I left him, a forlorn figure in his Crolla Prince-of-Wales suit, weeping into his sponsored Becks bier and surrounded by a horde of outrageously dressed sycophants unable to comfort him.

But there's no room for sentiment in the world of top-flight trending. Ours is a scientific discipline requiring patient research and the accumulation of evidence. Such as . . .

1. The swing-back to modern architecture and design: to wit, the Café Costes, the new Lloyd's building and the Issey Miyake boutique. Nothing could be more calculated to restore the faith of the avant-garde in modernism than the utterly feeble revisionism of magazines like *Interiors* and the apotheosis of the English country house at the National Gallery, Washington DC. Come back Corbusier, all is forgiven.

2. The post-*Witness* fad for the Amish look, where clothing is reduced to pure simplicity and the greatest possible compliment is 'very plain'. This is the perfect style for wearing in the sorts of houses that derive from 1 above.

3. The passionate attack on Sloane culture by Sally Brampton and Tony Parsons in the debut issue of *Elle*. Down with the fripperies of the upper classes! Down with the toadying respect for the values of the country gentry! Good on yer, Sal, you were always a Serious girl – never one to be knowingly frivolous.

4. The return of 'progressive rock'. Yes, pop-pickers, the concept album has returned, courtesy of Kate Bush, and moody boy bands like the Waterboys and the Cult are making heavy records with deep lyrics for pimply adolescents with Camus peeping out of the jacket pocket.

5. The death of fashion. Shurely shome mishtake, you may cry –

there has never ever been more fashion. Can't escape from the stuff. But hold on a mo. Recent research by a Very Big Publishing Company into teenage attitudes revealed that the boppers of today don't want fashion pages. They just want catalogue pictures of all the items of a certain kind that are available in the shops. They'll decide what to wear, thank you very much, not some poseur in the Big Smoke.

These may appear to be trivial phenomena – well, this is a style column, dear – but they have a linking theme of simplicity and rigour. They all want to reduce things to the essence. Which is as serious as popular culture ever gets, and is the visible sign that thought, politics and morality (*particularly* the latter) are also likely to be getting pretty strict as the years go by. That is the new seriousness.

Or to put it in the words of Adolph Loos, written seventy-eight years ago, but still looking tasty today: 'I have made the following discovery and I pass it on to the world: the evolution of culture is synonymous with the removal of ornament from articles of everyday use.' Very plain. Very plain indeed, sir.

Rory Mundane, 'Great Yorkie, the Crash is Coming', *Guardian*, 1985

Mrs Lydiard had arrayed herself for this informal visit in her usual finery. As was proper she had dressed as if for the street, in a navy skirt, a navy and white jacket, and a red wool shawl, the fringed end of which was flung bravely over her left shoulder. By contrast his other visitor was disarmingly pale, untidy even, but perhaps by comparison with Mrs Lydiard's vividly made-up face and pearl ear studs. He had an impression of heaviness, of dullness, though her appearance was nondescript. She wore the usual uniform of jeans and a denim jacket, her feet encased in the grotesquely large shoes. He thought that divested of all this she might be more appealing, but it was impossible to say. Beneath her clumsy clothes she might be any shape at all. The face did not detain him; he was aware of a closed down-turned mouth, undistinguished, rather straggling brown hair. The skin, which was very white, was flawless: that was indecisive; she might be any young person of her kind, without distinguishing characteristics.

Anita Brookner, *A Private View*, 1994

In my closet: white jeans, leather belts, leather bomber jacket, black cowboy boots, a couple of black wool crêpe suits, a dozen white shirts, a black turtleneck, crumpled silk pajamas, a high-class porno movie I've watched hundreds of times starring people who look just like us. I'm pretending to go through stuff until Chloe walks in seconds after I've crouched down inspecting a pair of sandals I bought in Barcelona at a Banana Republic.

'What's the story?' I finally ask. 'Where's my three-snap blazer?'

'About what?' she asks back, tightly.

'Wasn't he a head in a Mr Jenkins ad, baby?'

'I told you he was coming.'

'What do you think that anti-fashion look costs?' I ask. 'Two thousand bucks? Three thousand bucks?'

Bret Easton Ellis, *Glamorama*, 1999

9. 'But the fashion is so hideous': Artistic Dress and Bohemia

Really I must cultivate a pose. It is necessary so often.

Augustus John, from Michael Holroyd, *Augustus John*, 1977

Sorry, my dear, one mustn't be bohemian.

W. H. Auden, from Charles Osborne, *W. H. Auden*, 1982

By the early 1900s, artistic and bohemian dress were recognizable anti-fashion styles. From the days of the Pre-Raphaelite Brotherhood, dress reformers, aesthetes, campaigners for women's suffrage, artists and writers had all campaigned against Fashion, a form of dress imposed by Paris that Wilde called a cycle of ugliness changed twice a year. In turn, these styles affected others: the campaign for artistic and healthy dress influenced the designs of Fortuny and Poiret, and Socialists wore red or black as symbolic protest. Artists/intellectuals took up the oppositional dress which is the subject of this chapter; and as they portrayed it in writing or in art the source material is rich.

It is hard not to overstate the importance of the bohemian dress of the early part of the century (as I will call it): that it was a stance visibly made against the conventions and norms of society and that its legacy in Britain has been the ease with which people express their identity through dress. While the dandy sought to be anonymous and the aesthete aimed for perfection in dress, the bohemian was robustly *there*. Augustus John in a corduroy suit, black slouch hat and gold earrings, and his wives Ida and Dorelia in Pre-Raphaelite-cum-gypsy home-made clothes were as hard to ignore as young women were later while they first wore Doc Martens and boiler-suits.

The Omega Workshop, established by Bloomsbury group members Roger Fry and Vanessa Bell in 1913, used artists to design textiles and produced a range of clothes that dressed Virginia Woolf (she had reservations but gave it her support), Lady Ottoline Morrell and Nina Hamnett. While in *Women in Love* D. H. Lawrence satirized Lady Ottoline, Gudrun and Ursula's bright stockings signified their Arts and Crafts background and the influence of the bright colours of the Ballet Russes or French artist Sonia Delaunay's so-called 'simultaneous' aesthetic, praised in 1914 by Guillaume Apollinaire abandoning 'antiquated fashion in favour of boldly coloured clothing that in shape followed contemporary style'.[1] Sonia Delaunay wore a purple dress with a wide purple and green belt. Under the dress's jacket, she wore a large corsage divided into brightly coloured zones of fabric in which antique rose, yellow-orange, Nattier blue and scarlet appeared on different materials, juxtaposing wool taffeta, tulle, watered silk and *peau de soie*.[2] Her husband Robert Delaunay was resplendent in red coat with blue collar, red socks, yellow and black shoes, black trousers, green jacket, sky-blue vest and tiny red tie.

This style was art as fashion, not artist against fashion, *ergo* against convention, as was usually the case in Britain. When Osbert Sitwell encouraged his sister Edith to dress herself in antique brocade and cultivate her Plantagenet looks, her appearance was a rebellion against what her parents wanted her to be, a 'nice' upper-class English woman. Sitting for her portrait by Roger Fry in 1918, she wore 'a green evening dress, the colour of the leaves of lilies, and my appearance in this, in the full glare of the midsummer light of midday, in Fitzroy Square, together with the appearance of Mr Fry, his bushy, long grey hair floating from under an enormous black sombrero, caused great joy to the children of the district.' 'It was an act of defiance against her upbringing and an act of faith in herself.'[3]

In the 1920s Sonia Delaunay began designing for Heim, her

approach to colour and design part of the Art Deco aesthetic celebrated in the Art Deco exhibition held in Paris in 1925. Elsa Schiaparelli combined art with fashion too in her collaboration with Salvador Dali and Jean Cocteau to produce collections which reflected surrealism, playing with the notion of clothes and the unconscious. 'Dress designing, incidentally, is to me not a profession but an art.'[4] But although art and fashion had become chic, bohemian dress had not, as expressed by writers of the time. In *Cold Comfort Farm*, Stella Gibbons parodies an 'audience had run to beards and magenta shirts and original ways of arranging its neckwear'. Other writers explored alternatives to fashion in dreams of Utopia. In *Clothes*, Eric Gill campaigned for old-style, anti-machine-made dress reform for men and women, arguing for a more natural, beautiful and godly future. Aldous Huxley, however, writes of a bleak *Brave New World*, in which shopping was an ingrained compulsion, caste was colour coded and women dressed in man-made fibres, the clothes covered in zips.

Anti-fashion, as worn by those in the social circles of Bloomsbury, Soho and Fitzrovia, continued through to the 1950s, but it was increasingly a male phenomenon; Soho, for instance, was peopled by artists Lucien Freud, Francis Bacon and Colin MacInnes, who were raffish in their non-fashion corduroy trousers, tieless in woollen jumpers and soft-necked shirts, and wore comfortable sports jackets, breaking the rules of dress of the 'English gentleman'. Ted Hughes wore a 'thrice-dyed black' cord jacket; Kenneth Tynan affected a cape at Oxford; and George Melly dressed in an antiquated waistcoat. Women had not abandoned anti-fashion, however. Poor Margaret in Kingsley Amis's *Lucky Jim*, utterly unaware of the unappetizing nature of her appearance, and hoping that brains counted for more than a ready-made frock as seen in *Vogue*, amusingly exemplifies the fifties' bohemian woman. British art schools suddenly started playing an important role in producing dress designers; Mary Quant was a typical art college product, studying textile design, and socializing and working with artists.

In the 1960s hippie style *à la* King's Road blended the Edith
Sitwell with the Orient; and the trailing frocks of Ottoline Morrell
and puffed sleeves of Virginia Woolf inspired insipid imitation in
campuses and high streets. The ersatz hippies of the mid-seventies
with their long hair, T-shirts and Afghan coats were about narcissism,
not protest; neither marijuana nor LSD, the drugs of the moment,
encouraged radical action. This all changed in 1976 with the arrival
of punk, when the notion of anti-fashion style was reborn, no longer
connected with art: Diana Vreeland lamented that her love of art in
dress was never taken up by fashion: 'But don't you *adore* the look
of white silk slippers with the dark hem of a velvet dress? For months
at *Harpers Bazaar* I went around saying, "Remember Velázquez!"'[5]
Now bohemian style is plundered as part of fashion's retro-neurosis,
with fashion spreads depicting Pre-Raphaelite and Bloomsbury-style
'eccentricity'. The legacy of the style at its greatest, Fortuny's graceful
blend of history and the east, was and is seen in the work of Romeo
Gigli, who launched his own label in 1983. It was not simply his
elongated line and unstructured cut that made him influential: it was
his reinterpretation of a style that had questioned fashion itself.

'Atmosphere is probably a question of touch and go. Even at Queen
Victoria's dinner party – if something had been just a little different
– perhaps if she'd worn a clinging Liberty tea gown instead of
magenta satin—'
  'With an Indian shawl over her shoulders—'
  'Fastened at the bosom with a Cairngorm pin—'
  Bursts of disloyal laughter – you must remember that they are
half-German – greeted these suggestions, and Margaret said pen-
sively: 'How inconceivable it would be if the royal family cared about
art.'

E. M. Forster, *Howards End*, 1910

Femina Daza had put on a loose-fitting silk dress belted at the hip, a necklace of real pearls with six long, uneven loops, and high-heeled satin shoes that she wore only on very solemn occasions, for by now she was too old for such abuses. Her stylish attire did not seem appropriate for a venerable grandmother, but it suited her figure – long-boned and still slender and erect, her resilient hands without a single age spot, her steel-blue hair bobbed on a slant at her cheek. Her clear almond eyes and her inborn haughtiness were all that were left to her from her wedding portrait, but what she had been deprived of by age she more than made up for in character and diligence. She felt very well: the time of iron corsets, bound waists and bustles that exaggerated buttocks were receding into the past. Liberated bodies, breathing freely, showed themselves for what they were. Even at the age of seventy-two.

Gabriel García Márquez, *Love in the Time of Cholera*, 1985

Now that her [Susan's] mean's were adequate she took great pains with her dress, and her clothes, though they cost much more than she could afford, were always beautiful. Her taste was so great, her tact so sure that she was able to make the most of herself. She was determined that if people called her ugly they should be forced in the same breath to confess that she was perfectly gowned. Susie's talent for dress was remarkable, and it was due to her influence that Margaret was arrayed always in the latest mode. The girl's taste inclined to be artistic, and her sense of colour was apt to run away with her discretion. Except for the display of Susie's firmness, she would scarcely have resisted her desire to wear nondescript garments of violent hue. But the older woman expressed herself with decision.

'My dear, you won't draw any the worse for wearing a well-made corset, and to surround your body with bands of grey flannel will certainly not increase your talent.'

'But the fashion is so hideous,' smiled Margaret.

'Fiddlesticks! The fashion is always beautiful. Last year it was beautiful to wear a hat like a pork-pie tipped over your nose: and next year, for all I know, it will be beautiful to wear a bonnet like a sitz-bath at the back of your head. Art has nothing to do with a smart frock, and whether a high-heeled pointed shoe commends itself or not to the painters in the quarter, it is the only thing in which a woman's foot looks really nice.'

W. Somerset Maugham, The Magician, 1908

It has been said that he modelled his appearance on Courbet, but in fact he had no single model in mind, and many transitory moods and influences claimed him. Parental disapproval was always a strong recommendation. One morning about this time [1906] old Edwin John read in a newspaper a description of his son's appearance as being 'not at all that of a Welshman, but rather a Hungarian or a gypsy', and at once sent a letter of reproof which Augustus had no difficulty in treating as Alick Schepeler was always imploring him to treat hers. But the reproof did not go unheeded and, to caricature his father's wishes, he secured a complete Welsh outfit with which to flabbergast Montparnasse.

Michael Holroyd, Augustus John: A Biography, 1977

One day in the springtime of 1912 – a date not long ago in point of time, but infinitely long ago in the point of the changes that Europe has ushered since then – I was lunching at the Savile Club. I had been living for two years in Italy; and there were some faces new to me. There was one that interested me very much; an emaciated face of ivory whiteness, above a long square-cut auburn beard, and below a head of very long sleek dark brown hair. The nose was nothing if not aquiline, and Nature had chiselled it with great delicacy. The eyes, behind a pair of gold-rimmed spectacles, eyes of an inquirer and a cogitator, were large and brown and luminous. The man to whom they belonged must, I judged, though he sat stooping low down over his table, be extremely tall. He wore a jacket of brown velveteen, a soft shirt, and a dark red tie. I greatly wondered who he was. He looked rather like one of the twelve Apostles, and I decided that he resembled especially the doubting one . . . I learned from a friend who came in and joined me at my table that he was one of the Stracheys; Lytton Strachey; a Cambridge man; rather an authority on French literature . . . 'But why,' my friend asked, 'should he dress like that?' Well, we members of the Savile, civil servants, men of letters, clergyman, scientists, doctors and so on, were clad respectably, passably, decently, but no more than that. And 'Hang it all,' I said, 'why *shouldn't* he dress like that? He's the best-dressed man in the room!'

Max Beerbohm, *Lytton Strachey*, 1944

To Vanessa Bell   Asheham, [Rodmell, Sussex]
                                   Sunday [23 April 1916]
Dearest,

I forgot yesterday to ask you what I wanted to ask you – which is, will you out of the overflowing generosity and superabundance of your magnanimous heart (in which I have always believed) design me a sketch for my summer cloak? I bought some grey silk and sent it to Miss Joy, who can't make it for lack of a sketch. What I want is something light and simple – I should think perhaps a kind of kimono. It is the colour of a young elephant, with a slight crinkle. I couldn't get what I wanted, owing to the presence of Amber Reeves, who haunts me. If you could send the sketch straight to Miss Joy, I should bless your shadow.

She has just sent me my blue summer dress, which I like very much – in fact, I think even as an advertisement I should pay the Omega, as I'm always being asked who made my things. It's a superb spring morning, and Lytton and Sanger are in high good temper reading on the terrace. This is far the loveliest country in Europe.

Expecting a letter from you,
I am your faithful
    Singe

To Vanessa Bell   Monday [22 April 1918]

I've been writing about you all morning [in *Night and Day*], and have made you wear a blue dress; you've got to be immensely mysterious and romantic, which of course you are: yes, but it's the combination that's so enthralling; to crack through the paving stone and be enveloped in the mist . . .

Virginia Woolf, *The Question of Things Happening: The Letters of Virginia Woolf*, Vol II 1912–1922, edited by Nigel Nicolson, 1976

1918

There were few women of distinction equal to Virginia's in the room tonight: but all, pretty, or *faded* or plain, wore their own clothes, either more fashionable than elsewhere, without fashion, or smacking of Roger's Omega Workshop, wholesome and home-made. Some of the men were in uniform, but a proportion – equally courageous in their way – had been conscientious objectors and so were able to appear in ordinary clothes – if *ordinary* is not, perhaps, a misnomer for so much shagginess (the suits, many of them, looked as if they had been woven from the manes of Shetland ponies and the fringes of Highland cattle in conjunction), and for such flaming ties as one saw.

Osbert Sitwell, *Laughter in the Next Room*, 1949

John, John, how he's got on,
He owes it, he knows it, to me.
Brass ear-rings I wear and I don't do my hair

And my feet are as bare as can be.
When I walk down the street, the people I meet
All stare at the things I've got on.
When Battersea-Parking, you'll hear folks remarking,
There goes an Augustus John.

from Beatrice Elvery, Lady Glenavy, *Today We Will Only Gossip*, 1964

Augustus found the fashions of the day unpaintable, and his household dressed to suit his painting. Dodo and Edie were skilled dressmakers and evolved the long flowing skirts gathered at the waist, and the loose smock top with the sleeves cut in one. In the drawings and paintings these clothes follow the movement of the figure like timeless, classic draperies. The materials used were those beloved by the artists through the ages; cotton velveteen for the quality of the drapery, and the highlights on the ridge of the fold, the depth of colour in the crease. Shantung was another favourite material; it came in bright clean dyes and the shimmering surfaces described the body beneath.

Some years later when Augustus and Dodo and assorted children were in France, they asked for rooms at the posh Carlton Hotel in Cannes. As they were all dressed in their bright and original clothes, the manager of the hotel took them for gypsies and refused to admit them until Augustus had shown the money bag and found someone to vouch for him . . .

The John clothes did not stop at dresses, but probed deeper to underclothes. The girls suffered bitterly from the cold. For not only were stockings and closed knickers banished, but wool vests or combinations too. I shall never forget the horrible chilliness of draughty linen against the skin. And if that was not enough, there was the new health fad for fresh air. Open windows. We lived with a permanent wind blowing up our legs.

Nicolette Devas, *Two Flamboyant Fathers*, 1966

Dorelia John may have been seen in Babylon or in early Crete, but
before her in this century now women wore those clothes that are
almost Indian and yet entirely European, that are classical and yet
have abstracted something from the gypsies. In fact no one had
developed a more perfect visual expression of the art of living than
Mrs Augustus John, who possesses her rare gifts to this very day.
As a muse, she has been indirectly responsible for much of her
husband's best work; but she is equally creative in her own right.
For the last forty years she has dressed in the same manner: outside
fashion, her clothes and her appearance are never dated. Today Mrs
John wears the uniform of age and seems oblivious to the charm
and impact of her appearance. Yet with her white hair and scarlet
apron over a blue cotton dress, hugging a huge basket of fruit against
her stomach as she brings it in from the orchard, she has the
timelessness, the real fashion of the Bible.

Cecil Beaton, *The Glass of Fashion*, 1954

A COAT

I made my song a coat
Covered with embroideries
Out of old mythologies
From heel to throat;
But the fools caught it,
Wore it in the world's eyes
As though they'd wrought it.
Song, let them take it,
For there's more enterprise
In walking naked

W. B. Yeats, from *Responsibilities*, 1914

Gudrun was the more beautiful and attractive, she had decided again, Ursula was more physical, more womanly. She admired Gudrun's dress more. It was of green poplin, with a loose coat above it, of broad, dark-green and dark-brown stripes. The hat was of a pale, greenish straw, the colour of new hay, and it had a plaited ribbon of black and orange, the stockings were dark green, the shoes black. It was a good get-up, at once fashionable and individual. Ursula, in dark blue, was more ordinary, though she also looked well.

Now she [Hermione Roddice] came along, with her head held up, balancing an enormous flat hat of pale yellow velvet, on which were streaks of ostrich feathers, natural and grey. She drifted forward as if scarcely conscious, her long blanched face lifted up, not to see the world. She was rich. She wore a dress of silky, frail velvet, of pale yellow colour, and she carried a lot of small rose-coloured cyclamens. Her shoes and stockings were of brownish grey, like the feathers on her hat, her hair was heavy, she drifted along with a peculiar fixity of the hips, a strange unwilling motion. She was impressive, in her lovely pale yellow and brownish rose, yet macabre, something repulsive.

She [Minette Darrington] had beautiful eyes, flower-like, fully opened, naked in their looking at him. And on them there seemed to float a curious iridescence, a sort of film of disintegration, and sullenness, like oil on water. She wore no hat in the heated café, her loose, simple jumper was strung on a string round her neck. But it was made of rich yellow crêpe de Chine, that hung heavily and softly from her young throat and her slender wrists. Her appearance was simple and complete, really beautiful, because of her regularity and form, her shiny yellow hair falling curved and level on either side of her head, her straight, small, softened features, provoking in the slight fullness of their curves, her slender neck and the simple, rich-coloured smock hanging on her slender shoulders.

*

It was a quiet and ordinary breakfast, the four men all looking very clean and bathed. Gerald and the Russian were both correct and *comme il faut* in appearance and manner, Birkin was gaunt and sick, and looked a failure in his attempt to be a properly dressed man, like Gerald and Maxim. Halliday wore tweeds and a green flannel shirt and a rag of a tie, which was just right for him.

D. H. Lawrence, *Women in Love*, 1921

1919

Most of the contributors to *Art and Letters* were friends of mine already . . . Percy Wyndham Lewis, who had lately returned to civilian – I nearly wrote civil – life . . . In those days whereof I write, a Norwegian fishing cap made apparently on a pudding-basin model, and I suppose of some kind of cloth (though the material more suggested brawn) – with a short, fat all-round rim, the front of which just afforded shade to his eyes – had long ousted his black sombrero, in the same way that a robust and rather jocose Dutch convexity had replaced the former melancholy and lean Spanish elegance of his appearance.

Osbert Sitwell, *Laughter in the Next Room*, 1949

The sexual meaning of behaviour was only sketchily understood, but the symbolism of clothes was recognized by everyone. To wear suede shoes was to be under suspicion. Anyone who had hair rather than bristle at the back of his neck was thought to be an artist, a foreigner or worse. A friend of mine who was young in the same decade as I says that, when he was introduced to an elderly gentleman as an artist, the gentleman said, 'Oh, I know this young man is an artist. The other day saw him in the street in a brown jacket.'

Quentin Crisp, *The Naked Civil Servant*, 1968

Gene and I went to the wedding and I wore a new coat and skirt, new suede gloves and a small black hat perched on the back of my head. Gene wore his only suit. Unfortunately he had had it dyed green and there was no stuffing in the shoulders; but he looked very tall and narrow and completely unlike anyone else.

Barbara Comyns, *A Touch of Mistletoe*, 1967

Few women yet realize that ornament cannot be done by machinery, and many still cover themselves with the patterns which we associate with nineteenth-century wallpapers. They are terribly at the mercy of shopkeepers who vie with one another in bringing out what they call new 'fashions'. They are addicted to all sorts of illogical cuttings and shapings for which there is neither rhyme or reason, and not even the excuse that it expresses the fancifulness of the manufacturer; for it does no such thing: it expresses nothing but the manufacturers' haste to bring out something 'new'. They have, to a deplorable extent, taken to going to the tailor instead of the dressmaker, and their coats and skirts are now almost as much like blocked tin as are the suits worn by men. The dresses of the majority of women are horribly cheap, and even great ladies, and especially queens, are dressed no better than factory girls.

Eric Gill, *Clothes*, 1931

'I wanted to be like Miss Ashford. She kept the Blue Bird's Cage down in Howling for a month or two last summer. I went in there to have tea once or twice. She was very kind to me. She used to have lovely clothes – that is, I mean, they weren't what you would call lovely, but I used to like them. She had a smock –'

'Embroidered with hollyhocks,' said Flora, resignedly.* 'And I'll bet she wore her hair in shells round her ears and a pendant made of hammered silver with a bit of blue enamel in the middle. And did she try to grow herbs?'

'How did you know?'

'Never mind, I do know. And she talked to you about Brother Wind and Sister Sun and the wind on the heath, didn't she?'

Stella Gibbons, *Cold Comfort Farm*, 1932

Half an hour later it occurred to him to look through the window. The first thing he saw was a green suitcase, with the initials L. C. painted on the lid.† Joy flared up like fire within him. He picked up a stone. The smashed glass tinkled on the floor. A moment later he was inside the room. He opened up the green suitcase; and all at once he was breathing Lenina's perfume, filling his lungs with her essential being. His heart beat wildly; for a moment he was almost faint. Then, bending over the precious box, he touched, he lifted into the light, he examined. The zippers on Lenina's spare pair of viscose velveteen shorts were at first a puzzle, then, solved, a delight. Zip, and then zip, sip, and then zip, he was enchanted. Her green slippers were the most beautiful things he had ever seen. He unfolded a pair of zippi-caminicks, blushed, put them hastily away again; but kissed a perfumed acetate handkerchief and wound a scarf round his neck. Opening a box, he spilt a cloud of scented powder. His hands were floury with the stuff. He wiped them on his chest, on his shoulders, on his bare arms. Delicious perfume! He shut his eyes;

---

*Gibbons is satirizing the artistic dress and pretensions of Elfine, to whom Flora is speaking. 'Embroidered with hollyhocks' describes the decorative style of smocks sold at Liberty's.

†Bernard Marx is in love with Lenina Crowne, who has taken six half-gram tablets of soma to sleep. Unable to keep away, he stands outside the rest house.

he rubbed his cheek against his own powdered arm. Touch of smooth skin against his face, scent in his nostrils of musky dust – her real presence. 'Lenina,' he whispered, 'Lenina!'

There, on a low bed, the sheet flung back, dressed in a pair of pink one-piece zippyjamas, lay Lenina, fast asleep and so beautiful in the midst of her curls, so touchingly childish with her pink toes and her grave sleeping face, so trustful in the helplessness of her limp hands and melted limbs, that the tears came to his eyes.

Aldous Huxley, *Brave New World*, 1932

A day came when this woman found in a dustbin in Bond Street a backless bead frock. No sooner had she seen it than she longed to wear it. As she did not at that time live anywhere in particular, it was difficult to think of a place sufficiently secluded for trying it on. She chose the churchyard in Flitcroft Street and sat among the dead to wait for nightfall. When it was barely dusk her eagerness had overcome her prudence. A crowd collected large enough to attract the attention of the police and she was led away.

The next morning when the magistrate asked her what she had been doing, with a gently mocking laugh at the uncouthness of the question she replied, 'What any woman would be doing at that hour. Changing for dinner.'

Though we never stopped trying, none of us ever achieved such high style as this, but converting one's life into a form of public entertainment turned out to be less difficult than I had imagined.

Quentin Crisp, *The Naked Civil Servant*, 1968

. . . young male poets in corduroy trousers and young female poets with waist-length hair, or at least females who typed the poetry and slept with the poets, it was nearly the same thing . . . One of the poets who was well thought of had acquired a job at Associated News in Fleet Street, in honour of which he had purchased a pair of luxurious pig-skin gloves; he displayed these proudly. There was an air of a resistance movement against the world at this poetry meeting. Poets seemed to understand each other with a secret instinct, almost a kind of prearrangement, and it was plain that the poet with the gloves would never show off these poetic gloves so frankly, or expected to be understood so well in relation to them, at his new job in Fleet Street or anywhere else, as here.

Muriel Spark, *The Girls of Slender Means*, 1963

My appearance, eccentric enough in the rather conventional cast-off clothes of a large uncle plus a few *objets trouvés* like a knitted Victorian waistcoat, made me easier to remember if harder to love. My violent enthusiasm, frequent drunkenness and personal manner of dancing attracted a lot of not entirely kindly amusement. Much later I discovered that Humph had christened me 'Bunny Burn'.

George Melly, *Owning Up*, 1965

Trapnel, in a voice both deep and harsh, requested half a pint of bitter, somehow an unexpectedly temperate choice in the light of his appearance and gruffness of manner. He looked about thirty, tall, dark, with a beard. Beards, rarer in those days than they became later, at that period hinted of submarine duty, rather than the arts, social protest of a subsequent fashion simply for more hair. At the same time, even if the beard, assessed with the clothes and stick he carried, marked him out as an exhibitionist in a reasonably high category, the singularity was more on account of elements within himself than from outward appearance.

Although the spring weather was still decidedly chilly, he was dressed in a pale ochre-coloured tropical suit, almost transparent in texture, on top of which he wore an overcoat, black and belted like Quiggan's Partisan number, but of cloth, for some reason familiarly official in cut. This heavy garment, rather too short for Trapnel's height of well over six feet, was at the same time too full, in view of his spare, almost emaciated body. Its weight emphasized the flimsiness of the tussore trousers below. The greatcoat turned out, much later, to have belonged to Bagshaw during his RAF service, disposed of on terms unspecified, possibly donated, to Trapnel, who had caused it to be dyed black. The pride Trapnel obviously took in the coat was certainly not untainted by an implied, though unjustified, aspiration to ex-officer status.

The walking stick struck a completely different note. Its wood unremarkable, but the knob, ivory, more likely bone, crudely carved in the shape of a skull, was rather like old Skerrett's head at Erridge's funeral. This stick clearly bulked large in Trapnel equipment. It set the tone far more than the RAF greatcoat or tropical suit. For the rest, he was hatless, wore a dark blue sports shirt frayed at the collar, an emerald green tie patterned with naked women, was shod in grey suede brothelcreepers. These last, then relatively new, were destined to survive a long time, indeed until their rubber soles, worn to the thinness of paper, had become all but detached from fibre-less uppers, sounding a kind of dismal applause as they flapped rhythmi-cally against the weary pavement trodden beneath.

The general effect, chiefly caused by the stick, was of the 1890s, the *decadence*; putting things at their least eclectic, a contemptuous rejection of currently popular male modes in grey flannel demob suits with pork-pie hats, bowler-crowned British Warms, hooded duffels, or even those varied outfits like Quiggin's, to be seen here and there, that suggested recent service in the *maquis*. All such were rejected. One could not help speculating whether an eyeglass would not be produced – Trapnel was reported to have sported one for a brief period, until broken in a pub brawl – insomuch that the figure he recalled, familiar from some advertisement advocating a brand of chocolates or cigarettes, similarly equipped with beard and cane, wore an eyeglass on a broad ribbon, though additionally rigged out in full evening dress, an order round his neck, opera cloak over his shoulder. In Trapnel's case, the final effect had that touch of surrealism which redeems from complete absurdity, though such redemption was a near thing, only narrowly achieved.

Perhaps this description, factually accurate – as so often when facts are accurately reported – is at the same time morally unfair. 'Facts' – as Trapnel himself, talking about writing, was later to point out – are after all only on the surface, inevitably selective, prejudiced by subjective presentation. What is below, hidden, much more likely to be important, is easily omitted. The effect Trapnel made might indeed be a little absurd; it was not for that reason unimpressive. In spite of much that was all but ludicrous, a kind of inner dignity still somehow clung to him.

Anthony Powell, *Books Do Furnish a Room*, 1971

An irregular knocking on the door at the far end of the room was at once followed by the bursting-open of this door and the entry of a tall man wearing a lemon-yellow sports coat, all three buttons of which were fastened, and displaying a large beard which came down further on one side than on the other, half-hiding a vine-patterned tie. Dixon guessed with surging exultation that this must be the pacifist painter Bertrand whose arrival with his girl had been heralded, with typical clangour, by Welch every few minutes since teatime. It was an arrival which must surely prove an irritant sooner or later, but for the moment it served as the best possible counter-irritant to the disastrous madrigals. Even as Dixon thought this, the senior Welches left their posts and went to greet their son, followed more slowly by the others who, perhaps finding the chance of a break not completely unwelcome, broke into conversation as they moved. Dixon delightedly lit a cigarette, finding himself alone: the amateur violinist had got hold of Margaret; Goldsmith and the local composer were talking to Carol, Goldsmith's wife, who'd refused, with enviable firmness, to do more than sit and listen to the singing from an armchair near the fireplace; Johns was doing something technical at the piano.

'Oh, I see all right, James. I see perfectly.' This time her voice was flat. She wore a sort of arty get-up of multicoloured shirt, skirt with fringed hem and pocket, low-heeled shoes, and wooden beads . . . She went on like this while Dixon looked her in the eyes. His panic mounted in sincerity and volume. Her body moved jerkily about; her head bobbed from side to side on its rather long neck, shaking the wooden beads about on the multicoloured shirt. He found himself thinking that the whole arty get-up seemed oddly at variance with the way she was acting. People who wore clothes of that sort oughtn't to mind things of this sort, certainly not as much as Margaret clearly minded this thing. It was surely wrong to dress, and to behave most of the time, in a way that was so unprim when you were really so proper all of the time.

Kingsley Amis, *Lucky Jim*, 1954

By this time I had become a complete hippy. I dressed in Afghan robes and clothes from Hung on You, or crushed-velvet trousers and shirts with stars on them from Granny Takes a Trip. I got boots from Granny made in most fetching William Morris prints, chrysanthemum and honeysuckle. They laced up to the knee, and, depending on how stoned I was, took at least ten minutes to put on. The Chelsea Cobbler sold a more elegant zip-up suede boot and I acquired a true Marvel comic pair in bright red and green, covered in gold stars, from Mr Freedom. I spent quite a lot of time shopping, going into the antiques market to buy old forties summer dresses, lace petticoats and embroidered shawls. The weather seemed to be

summer always and there were varieties of acid about called Purple
and Sunshine Yellow.

Henrietta Moraes, Henrietta, 1994

Frederica stands on a small platform at one end of a large studio,
lit from above. She is dressed in a short black woollen dress and a
knitted jacket in black, as long as the dress. Her hair is loose and
long: her sharp face looks out from between curtains. The students
sit in chairs with swinging notepad arms, the men in dark jeans, the
women in shirts and smocks mostly in dark, fruity colours, all slightly
acid. They have pale lips and eyes made up like sinister dolls, with
long lashes and a bruised look. They are professional waifs.

At the other end of the studio ... the model, Jude Mason ... is
partly dressed: below his spare haunches he is naked: he sits on the
edge of the platform, his knees drawn up amongst his long grey veil
of hair, his balls poised on the dust between his dirty feet. He wears
a velvet jacket in a faded speedwell blue, a skirted jacket, from the
turn of the seventeenth and eighteenth centuries in style, with filthy
lace cuffs and a kind of jabot or cravat. Under this jacket and beneath
the cravat, he is unclothed, his body lean like dark metal.

A. S. Byatt, Babel Tower, 1996

My father was more frivolous when my mother wasn't around. I
put on one of my favourite records, Dylan's 'Positively Fourth
Street', to get me in the mood for the evening.

It took me several months to get ready: I changed my entire outfit
three times. At seven o'clock I came downstairs in what I knew
were the right clothes for Eva's evening. I wore turquoise flared
trousers, a blue and white flower-patterned see-through shirt, blue
suede boots with Cuban heels, and a scarlet Indian waistcoat with

gold stitching around the edges. I'd pulled on a headband to control my shoulder-length frizzy hair. I'd washed my face in Old Spice.

Dad waited at the door for me, his hands in his pockets. He wore a black polo-neck sweater, a black imitation-leather jacket and grey Marks and Spencer cords. When he saw me he suddenly looked agitated.

Hanif Kureishi, *Buddha of Suburbia*, 1990

10. 'Did you get the brassière, darling?': Shopping

'I want something striking,' she said. 'I don't want any old thing, you know. I want something different from what anybody else has.'

W. Somerset Maugham, *Of Human Bondage*, 1915

I believed later that a form of personality disorder overtook her when she shopped, which made her entirely unable to distinguish reality from advertising copy. Fashion is her soul's *métier*, I thought. What I know now is that fashion was all there was for her. Its amnesia suited her down to the ground.

Linda Grant, *The Cast Iron Shore*, 1996

The process of purchasing fashionable clothes and accessories has always been part of fantasy. In a new suit of clothes, you can imagine you look like anyone you wish; gazing through shop windows, as Jean Rhys describes, one can dream. Today the runway shows and massive advertising campaigns provide the fantasy. The key to realization is the act of purchase. One form of purchase was the customized service offered by London department stores at the turn of the century described by W. Somerset Maugham in *Of Human Bondage*; another the fashion show, like the one described by Lucile staged at her Hanover Square salon. Those who could afford it bought their clothes in Paris or from a dressmaker in London; Violet Gordon Woodehouse, Virginia Woolf and Edith Sitwell all had dressmakers to make their clothes, as the fashionable was invariably not what they were looking for. Woolf's squeamishness over shopping in Leicester Square and her frustration over not being able to get to her dressmaker during the General Strike casts a light on her priorities; the statements of the Jewishness of the shopkeepers by Woolf and Rhys reveal an anti-Semitism that created a resentment towards the system of fashion. Huxley's vision of a throwaway, shopaholic future in *Brave New World* is surely a comment on his own times, in which the new was feverishly awaited, 'I simply must get one like it' a mantra for the future.

For those who preferred dressmakers, there were many different kinds. Proust describes most of the Paris couturiers as mere dressmakers, bar a few who were *haute* couturiers – artists in fabric. In London in the 1930s there were top dressmakers such as Bunny Roger – 'There was very little that if you were queer you could do, especially a strange-looking queer – '[1] and couturiers such as Norman Hartnell and Hardy Amies who both dressed royalty. But there were dressmakers to suit almost every budget, to whom one went for a custom-made garment, taking along a few pictures of the latest *modes* from a fashion magazine which could be copied, as described by Molly Keane in *Good Behaviour*, The difference between anticipation and reality is also described by Rosamund Lehmann.

In the 1920s and 1930s factory-produced ready-mades made fashion more accessible and 'wholesale couture' or 'middle-class fashions' were produced by manufacturers and retailed in small shops or department stores.[2]

In the mid-fifties, with the growing power of youth's currency, boutiques began to spring up: Mary Quant's Bazaar in Chelsea, Biba in Kensington, John Michael in the King's Road, His Clothes in Carnaby Street, Tiger Morse in New York. Shopping became part of the fashion experience; single changing rooms, loud music, stars mixing with ordinary youngsters, moving along from shop to shop as part of the parade – just as it had been in London and Paris in the pre-department store enclosures. Street markets – Camden and Portobello – offered antique and second-hand clothes for those who

wanted to look just like the Beatles on the cover of *Sgt. Pepper*,
likewise in the seventies and eighties, second-hand clothes shops
were the haunts of those whose sought to make a personal and
radical stance against mainstream fashion. In the 'designer eighties',
when credit cards allowed unheard-of accessibility, shopping in
specially designed boutiques – Katharine Hamnett, Joseph, Vivienne
Westwood, Paul Smith – was an affirmation of arrival, therapy for
the stressed yuppie working to earn enough to pay for the emblems
of his or her success. Retail therapy, as it became known, was as
much a reality then as it had been in the late 1940s, when Dior's
New Look soothed women aching to recover from the sartorial
hardship of the Second World War.

Now across the 'First' World shopping has become part of popular
culture, it is not only the British who are a nation of shopkeepers. In
this culture, US-style shopping malls, once part of the glamour of the
big city – alongside the Bon Marché, Harvey Nichols and Harrod's,
Bergdorf Goodman and Macy's, chic dressmakers' salons and designer
boutiques – have become cities in themselves, leisure-centre metropoli
with brand names – Nike, Adidas, The Gap – providing 'youth' with
a global uniform that eschews individuality. Shops provide identity
and fantasy, and shopping is part of a leisure industry.

'Tell me, do you think women's fashions for motoring pretty?'

'No,' replied Elstir, 'but that will come in time. You see, there are
very few good dressmaking houses at present, one or two only,
Callot – although they go in rather too freely for lace – Doucet,
Cheruit, Paquin sometimes. The others are all ghastly.'

'So there's a vast difference between a Callot dress and one from
any ordinary shop?' I asked Albertine.

'Why, an enormous difference, my little man! Oh, sorry! Only,
alas! what you get for three hundred francs in an ordinary shop will

cost two thousand there. But there can be no comparison; they look the same only to people who know nothing at all about it.'

Marcel Proust, *Remembrance of Things Past: Within a Budding Grove*, 1919

In the salon where she [Madame de Greffulhe] stood moulded by this marvellous sheath of metal, bordered with sable, there reigned an awe as if in a fairy's chamber. The saleswoman inclined her head, ravished, the *première* passed an artist's hand over the seams of the stuff, and through the bull's-eye window of the door one could see the eager, indiscreet faces of the staff, and could hear their flattering exclamations: 'What a miracle!' or else: 'There is splendour for you!' The Countess, haughty and morose amidst this concert of praise, lifted her head and pointed her nose in every direction. When I came in, I bowed to her and said she had reason to be satisfied, for her dress was very beautiful. Then, lifting her head, so that her ill humour should fall from as high as possible, she said to me:

'I thought that you only knew how to dress midinettes and hussies, but I did not know that you were capable of making a dress for a great lady.'

I answered her, that her robe had in precise fact been made by those midinettes, and that the great ladies of Belgium could always trust themselves to the taste of the midinettes of Paris, and they would only gain thereby. And I left the place absolutely scandalized to find, in a woman of her age and her opulence, such lack of tact, joined with such perfidy and conceit. My words were repeated by my staff. In Russia, they would have deserved the knout, in Italy, castor oil, in France, they made everyone laugh. When she came to me again, to order more dresses, her revengeful saleswoman named such enormous prices that she was not rich enough to pay them.

Paul Poiret, *My First Fifty Years*, translated by
Stephen Haden Guest, 1931

Her dressmaker was now Venturette in Beauchamp Place. Venturette, whose real name was Hélène, was a charming Frenchwoman whom Violet had taken up to help design her evening dresses. 'They were very picturesque, subtle and original,' according to Rupert's daughter, Elizabeth, best known as the cookery writer Elizabeth David, 'especially when Aunt V. was dressed up with her extraordinary jewellery, necklaces, bracelets, earrings, all dangling and clanking – but Hélène told me that sewing the dresses was a terrible task, and Aunt V. was so capricious that suddenly she would decide she'd like to have the linings of all the flounces changed from white to red or something of that kind, and nothing would do but that she must have the dress ready for dinner the following evening. Hélène told me that she had sometimes to sit up all night sewing in order to finish a dress for Aunt V. who was not by any means always grateful or pleased.'

Jessica Douglas-Home, *Violet*, 1996

Ethel began to order her wedding dress which cost a good bit. She chose a rich satin with a humped pattern of gold on the pure white and it had a long train edged with Airum lilies. Her veil was of pure lace with a crown of orange blossum. Her bouquett she ordered to be of white dog daisies St Joseph lilies and orange blossums tied up with pale blue satin ribbon.

You will indeed be a charming spectacle my darling gasped Bernard as they left the shop. Then they drove to the tailor where Bernard ordered an elligant black suit with coat tails lined with crimson satin and a pale lavender tie and an opera hat of the same hue and he intended to wear violets in his buttonholes also his best white spats diamond studs and a few extras of costly air. They both ordered a lot of new clothes besides and Bernard gave Ethel a very huge tara made of rubies and diamonds also two rich braclets and Ethel gave him a brand new trunk of shiny green leather.

Daisy Ashford, *The Young Visiters or Mr Salteena's Plan*, 1919

Femina Daza, always resistant to the demands of fashion, brought back six trunks of clothing from different periods, for the great labels did not convince her. She had been in the Tuileries in the middle of winter for the launching of the collection by Worth, the indisputable tyrant of *haute couture*, and the only thing she got was a case of bronchitis that kept her in bed for five days. Laferrière seemed less pretentious and voracious to her, but her wise decision was to buy her fill of what she liked best in the second-hand shops, although her husband swore in dismay that it was corpses' clothing. In the same way she brought back quantities of Italian shoes without brand names, which she preferred to the renowned and famous shoes by Ferry, and she brought back a parasol from Dupuy, as red as the fires of hell, which gave our alarmed social chroniclers much to write about. She brought only one hat from Madame Reboux, but on the other hand she filled a trunk with sprigs of artificial cherries, stalks of all the felt flowers she could find, branches of ostrich plumes, crests of peacocks, tailfeathers of Asiatic roosters, entire pheasants, hummingbirds and a countless variety of exotic birds preserved in mid-flight, mid-call, mid-agony; everything that had been used in the last twenty years to change the appearance of hats. She brought back a collection of fans from countries all over the world, each one appropriate to a different occasion.

Gabriel García Márquez, *Love in the Time of Cholera*, 1985

In those days one paid a visit to one's dressmaker and was received into the uncompromising atmosphere of a shop, with hard chairs, a few unbecoming mirrors and a door, which opened on to a little fitting room. Nobody had thought of developing the social side of choosing clothes, of serving tea and imitating the setting of a drawing room. Trying on, or selecting clothes, was a thing of as much secrecy as fitting a wooden leg might be expected to be.

In many of the then fashionable dressmakers' establishments the models were displayed on horrid lay figures – dreadful affairs of saw-dust and wax faces, calculated to inspire a positive revolt against what-ever dress they happened to be attired in. Then, greatly daring, some resourceful soul conceived the idea in Paris of having living models.

But there was no parade, oh! dear no! Nothing so frivolous. Remember, they were fighting prejudice. A good woman had to look good, or her virtue was not to be believed in. There must be nothing which might shock the susceptibilities of the *grandes dames* who visited the salons, nothing which might suggest that the poor little mannequin had a personality of her own, that she was capable of any more emotion than the sawdust dummy, which she replaced. She must not show the glow of youthful flesh, or the curves of young ankles. So to prevent it they encased her in a garment of rigid black satin, reaching from chin to feet, which were shod in unappetizing laced boots. Even the most nervous mamma could safely take her son with her to the dressmaker's when temptation appeared in such unalluring guise, that is to say, if it could be called temptation at all, for as a guarantee of the respectability of the establishment the director could be relied upon to choose only the plainest of girls to show off his creations.

I shall never forget being taken to see the models at a famous house in Paris and the positive shock I felt when I saw lovely evening dresses in pale shades of rose and blue being worn by girls whose arms and necks, in dingy black satin, emerged from the low-cut *décolletés*. I decided that nothing on earth would induce me to show such atrocities.

Slowly the idea of a mannequin parade, which would be as entertaining to watch as a play, took shape in my mind. I would have glorious, goddess-like girls, who would walk to and fro dressed in my models, displaying them to the best advantage to an admiring audience of women. After I had visualized it all, the rest seemed possible. I set about looking for pretty girls, not so easy in those days as it would be now. At the beginning of this century there were outstanding beauties, but the majority of girls, and certainly of working girls, were not one quarter as good-looking as they are today. You might go out into the street then and see not more than four pretty women in a whole morning, whereas now at least one in every ten will have a piquant, pleasing face, and one in every thirty or forty will be really lovely. The general standard in women's looks has improved enormously, which I think supplies one reason why a very beautiful woman does not arouse as much attention today as in those days when beautiful women were few and far between.

It was some time before I succeeded in finding my mannequins, six of them, who would be able to do justice to my dresses . . . Oh! the coaching and the anxious thought I gave them. The hair and the hands were soon set right by sending them to my own hairdresser's. That cheered me up, for slowly I saw my chrysalides' wings beginning to appear. Then I set about teaching them to walk as I imagined young goddesses would walk. (The characteristic, languorous, insolent glide of the mannequins of today was a later development; I hate it and would never have allowed my girls to adopt it.) I used to make them walk up and down the showroom with books on their heads until they had acquired a perfect poise of head and shoulders. When my six had achieved the art of walking beautifully the battle was won. Feminine psychology did the rest. Is there a woman in the world who will not respond in her own personality to the influence of lovely clothes?

At last the great day of my first parade – the first real mannequin parade ever held – arrived.

The showroom was crowded. Princess Alice, the dearest, most human of all my royal patrons, sat near the front. I think she knew I was nervous, for she gave my hand an affectionate little squeeze, and told me how she was looking forward to seeing the models. Ellen Terry was there, kind and thoughtful, helping late arrivals to find their places; Lily Langtry, so beautiful that she made everyone turn to look at her, as she came in with much more of a regal entry than the several royal ladies who were present . . . It would be easier in fact, to say that society was present *en masse*, at least feminine society, for as yet no man had even thought of visiting such an entertainment.

There was never such a triumph for me as that wonderful afternoon! For hours afterwards my head rang with the applause and the showers of congratulations which these women, the highest and the greatest in the country, lavished on me. Orders flowed in by the dozen, so that the saleswomen could hardly cope with them. My star had risen: I knew that from that moment my career as a dressmaker would be smiled upon by fortune.

'Lucile', Lady Duff Gordon, *Discretions and Indiscretions*, 1932

To Vanessa Bell   Monday [22 April 1918]

. . . but I can't describe to you what an agony this afternoon was to me. You know the horror of buying clothes, especially for one forced as I am to keep my underclothes pinned together by brooches. However things have come to a pass; so I flung myself into a shop in Holborn. I should certainly always paint shops with lots of looking glasses and boxes bursting with white frills, and all the young ladies powdered and painted, and their hair scraped tight back, and one enormous Jewess in black satin issuing solemnly from a wardrobe. The impropriety seemed to me beyond anything we know. So it went on: I tried shop after shop; and then in a perfectly random way went and bought a wine-coloured black striped coat or dress for £6.10! in Leicester Sqre. Good Heavens! What a world we live in! The pressure of solid matter never seems sufficient to keep one altogether straight.

Virginia Woolf, *The Question of Things Happening: The Letters of Virginia Woolf*, Vol II 1912–1922, edited by Nigel Nicolson, 1976

So at Lady Shelton's house we met quite a few people who seemed to be English. I mean some of the girls in London seem to be Ladies which seems to be the opposite of a Lord. And some who are not Ladies are honorable. But quite a few are not ladies or honorable either, but are just like us, so all you have to call them is 'Miss'. So Lady Shelton was really delighted to have we Americans come to her house. I mean she took Dorothy and I into the back parlor and tried to sell us some bead headbands she seems to make by sewing quite a few beads on a piece of ribbon to tie around your head in the evening. So I asked her how much they were and she said five pounds. So I asked her how much it was in money and it seems it is twenty-five dollars. I mean I am going to have quite a hard time with Dorothy in London because she should not say what she said about an English lady. I mean she should not say that she really thought that Lady Shelton's headbands were quite useful because any girl who would pay twenty-five dollars for one of them would need to have her head bandaged.

Anita Loos, *Gentlemen Prefer Blondes:*
The Illuminating Diary of a Professional Lady, 1926

6 May 1926

The shops are open but empty. Over it all is some odd pale unnatural atmosphere – great activity but no normal life. I think we shall become more independent & stoical as the days go on. And I am involved in dress buying with Todd [editor of *Vogue*]; I tremble & shiver all over at the appalling magnitude of the task I have undertaken – to go to a dressmaker recommended by Todd, even, she suggested, but here my blood ran cold, with Todd. Perhaps this excites me more feverishly than the Strike.

Virginia Woolf, *Diaries: Volume III 1925–1930*,
edited by Anne Olivier Bell, 1980

'Good morning,' said Clarissa in her charming voice. 'Gloves,' she said with her exquisite friendliness and putting her bag on the counter began, very slowly, to undo the buttons. 'White gloves,' she said. 'Above the elbow,' and she looked straight into the shop woman's face – but this was not the girl she remembered? She looked quite old. 'These really don't fit,' said Clarissa. The shop girl looked at them. 'Madame wears bracelets?' Clarissa spread out her fingers. 'Perhaps it's my rings.' And the girl took the grey gloves with her to the end of the counter.

Yes, thought Clarissa, it's the girl I remember, she's twenty years older . . . There was only the other customer, sitting sideways at the counter, her elbow poised, her bare hand drooping, vacant; like a figure on a Japanese fan, thought Clarissa, too vacant perhaps, yet some men would adore her. The lady shook her head sadly. Again the gloves were too large. She turned round the glass. 'Above the wrist,' she reproached the grey-headed woman; who looked and agreed.

They waited; a clock ticked; Bond Street hummed, dulled, distant; the woman went away holding gloves. 'Above the wrist,' said the lady, mournfully, raising her voice. And she would have to order chairs, ices, flowers, and cloakroom tickets, thought Clarissa. The people she didn't want would come; the others wouldn't. She would stand by the door. They sold stockings – silk stockings. A lady is known by her gloves and her shoes, old Uncle William used to say. And through the hanging silk stockings quivering silver she looked at the lady, sloping shouldered, her hand drooping, her bag slipping, her eyes vacantly on the floor. It would be intolerable if dowdy women came to her party! Would one have liked Keats if he had worn red socks? Oh, at last – she drew into the counter and it flashed into her mind:

'Do you remember before the war you had gloves with pearl buttons?'

'French gloves, madame?'

'Yes, they were French,' said Clarissa. The other lady rose very sadly and took her bag, and looked at the gloves on the counter. But they were all too large – always too large at the wrist.

'With pearl buttons,' said the shop girl, who looked ever so much older. She split the lengths of tissue paper apart on the counter. With pearl buttons, thought Clarissa, perfectly simple – how French!

Virginia Woolf, *Mrs Dalloway in Bond Street*, 1923

Living and its cost depend on the habits of a people, and in England these 'habits' include the possession of a private income of so much a year and the possibility of getting money easily and spending it lavishly.

It is this state of affairs that has led to 'shopping', which is as untranslatable as 'Season' and 'society'. Possibly it is the lack of trivial amusements which is responsible for shopping. Making purchases, or rather foraging, can be done in one's own neighbourhood, and the English housewife still likes to go to the local shops with her market-bag, a duty which, strange to say, is not usually relegated to the servant. But to go 'shopping' one must go to town. In London there is no westward movement, as there is in Berlin, and the trip to town constitutes the first prerequisite of shopping. With her head, her heart, and her handbag full of a thousand and one trifles, the good lady makes her way to town. Very often the adventure which started with such myriads of ideas merely ends in her changing her novels at the Times Book Club in Wigmore Street. The blessed institution of the allowance saves her from any wild extravagance. As a girl she had her £100 a year from her father, and managed her own budget. Her father's allowance is now increased by her husband's contribution, and the latter, relieved of all further responsibility in the matter, stabilizes this item in his budget.

Thus shopping becomes a means of killing time, a sort of

occupation which can be practised as an art, an occupation affection-
ately cherished. It may take weeks to decide on some important
purchase, with endless discussions with a friend, who after a trying
morning at Harrod's is treated to lunch. Even the wife's income is
not spent according to the theory of marginal profit. Exorbitant
sums will be spent on a good article, the value of which, in her eyes,
rises in proportion to the price paid. From the standpoint of the
economist such a woman pays far too much for every article she
buys, and lives beyond her means, but each individual article will be
good. She prefers to limit herself to a small wardrobe of choice
garments, and gladly forgoes the variety she might get by the purchase
of cheaper goods. But a spoilsport in the shape of the policeman
has interfered with the art of shopping; he orders the housewife's
car from one parking place to another, and from one street corner
to the next. He is responsible for the fact that shopping is beginning
to lose its charm, which consisted in loafing and sauntering from
one shop to another.

Karl Silex, *John Bull at Home*, 1933

Ten days before the wedding Paul moved into rooms at the Ritz,
and Margot devoted herself seriously to shopping. Five or six times
a day messengers appeared at his suite bringing little by-products of
her activity – now a platinum cigarette case, now a dressing gown,
now a tiepin or a pair of links – while Paul, with unaccustomed
prodigality, bought two new ties, three pairs of shoes, an umbrella
and a set of Proust.

Evelyn Waugh, *Decline and Fall*, 1928

Mrs Harty wore a stuffed satin heart hung on a corset lace. It swung,
full of pins, between her breasts. I felt some connection between it
and the sacred heart of Jesus flaming away in its holy picture, the

constant small light burning below. Mrs Harty plucked pins out of hers and lurched about on her club foot, standing back to survey her work, or pouncing forward to remedy a fault. While the light shrank from her windows she swooped on me and round me with her scissors, and mumbled at me as she changed pins from her heart to her lips, and then to the seams of my dress; at last she staggered away . . . I could feel her dissatisfaction, and through it my bulk loomed to me – a battleship through fog. 'The wholly all about it is,' she said, 'there's not enough of it in it.'

I could not imagine the wedge-shaped gaps to be filled, and the strains that the pink chiffon would not take. I knew better than to look into the narrow slit of mirror. 'Do you know what we'll do – how would it work, I wonder, if we used our gold to drape our troubles?'

I demurred – then I agreed. Panels of gold lace swept from my hips to the ground, chiffon clouded my bosom.

'And a big rose in gold and pink – imagine – on one shoulder.' The rose was not there. She sketched it in the air, and pinned the air down my left bosom. I moistened my lips and nodded in agreement. In the wintry light, between the fox, the badger and the sacred heart of Jesus, I began to feel a storybook little-princess character taking me over – possessing me.

'Now. Look at yourself.' She turned me about like a child or a dummy to face my reflection. I spun willingly round on my Louis heels. I closed my eyes, I spread my hand like a fan across my chest. I decided how I should smile – I smiled. I opened my eyes, I pulled in my stomach, and I leaned a little forwards to my reflection. Gold lace fell in points and godets to the floor. Flesh and chiffon were indistinguishable in the sweetheart neckline. I caught my breath, and for a moment I was standing alone with the beautiful doll that was me.

Mrs Harty broke the silence. She too was looking enchantedly from me to my reflection. 'Well, Miss Aroon,' I could feel her searching for the absolute word, 'wouldn't you make a massive statue?'

Molly Keane, *Good Behaviour*, 1981

About clothes, it's awful. Everything makes you want pretty clothes like hell. People laugh at girls who are badly dressed. Jaw, jaw, jaw . . . 'Beautifully dressed woman . . .' As if it isn't enough that you want to be beautiful, that you want to have pretty clothes, that you want it like hell. As if that isn't enough. But no, its jaw, jaw and sneer all the time. And the shop windows sneering and smiling in your face. And then you look at the skirt of your costume, all crumpled at the back. And your hideous underclothes. You look at your hideous underclothes and you think, 'All right, I'll do anything for good clothes. Anything – anything for clothes.'

A dress and a hat and shoes and underclothes.

I got a taxi and told the driver to go to Cohen's in Shaftesbury Avenue.

There were two Miss Cohens and they really were sisters because their noses were the same and their eyes – opaque and shining – and their insolence that was only a mask. I knew the shop; I had been there with Laurie during rehearsals.

I said, 'Can I try on the dark blue dress and coat in the window, please?' and the thin one advanced smiling. Her red lips smiled and her heavy lids drooped over her small, shiny eyes.

This is a beginning. Out of this warm room that smells of fur I'll go to all the lovely places I've ever dreamt of. This is the beginning.

The fat Miss Cohen went into the back room. I held my arms up and the thin one put on the dress as if I were a doll. The skirt was long and tight so that when I moved in it I saw the shape of my thighs.

'It's perfect,' she said. 'You could walk right out in it just as it is.'

I said, 'Yes, I like this. I'll keep it on.' But my face in the glass looked small and frightened.

It was four o'clock when I left the flat. There was a black velvet dress in a shop window, with the skirt slit up so that you could see the light stocking. A girl could look lovely in that, like a doll or a flower. Another dress, with fur round the neck, reminded me of the one that Laurie had worn. Her neck coming out of the fur was a pale-gold colour, very slim and strong looking.

The clothes of most of the women who passed were like caricatures of the clothes in the shop windows, but when they stopped to look you saw that their eyes were fixed on the future. 'If I could buy this, then of course I'd be quite different.' Keep hope alive and you can do anything, and that's the way the world goes round, that's the way they keep the world rolling. So much hope for each person. And damned cleverly done too.

Jean Rhys, *Voyage in the Dark*, 1929

Blanche soon realized that, dressed as she was, she was unlikely to find work as a mannequin even if she did possess the perfect figure. She saw her reflection superimposed on the plate-glass windows so that she almost became part of the window display. There was the hump-backed coat and the heavy brown leather gloves that smelt of Bovril. In despair she wrote to Mr Hobbs demanding five guineas for a new overcoat: 'I look so different to the other girls in my worn old country coat. It is a child's one really. I'll never get work dressed as I am,' she wrote and, to her surprise, a registered letter arrived a few days later containing a five-pound note. The letter said she was to study hard and return the money as soon as possible because it was only a loan. Minnie Dawes offered to help her choose the coat, but she preferred to shop on her own even if the thought of opening great glass doors and being accosted by a haughty shop assistant was a little frightening. After two afternoons spent in window shopping and a considerable amount of thought in bed at night, she chose a navy velour wrap-over coat with a grey fur collar and from her small store of money bought a pair of suede gloves.

Barbara Comyns, *A Touch of Mistletoe*, 1967

Mrs Smiling's second interest was her collection of brassieres, and her search for a perfect one. She was reputed to have the largest and finest collection of these garments in the world. It was hoped that on her death it would be left to the nation.

She was an authority on the cut, fit, colour, construction and proper functioning of brassieres; and her friends had learned that her interest, even in moments of extreme emotional or physical distress, could be aroused and her composure restored by the hasty utterance of the phrase:

'I saw a brassiere today, Mary, that would have interested you . . .'

'Did you get the brassiere, darling?'

A shadow fell upon Mrs Smiling's face.

'No. It was no use to me. It was just a variation on the "Venus" design made by Waber Brothers in 1938: it had three elastic sections in front, instead of two, as I hoped, and I have it already in my collection. I saw it from the car as I drove past, you know; I was misled by the way it was folded as it hung in the window. The third section was folded back, so that it looked as though there were only two.'

'And that would have made it more rare?'

'But naturally, Flora. Two-section brassieres are *extremely* rare. I intended to buy it – but, of course, it was useless.'

Stella Gibbons, *Cold Comfort Farm*, 1932

In the nurseries, the Elementary Class Consciousness lesson was over, the voices were adapting future demand to future industrial supply. 'I do love flying,' they whispered, 'I do love flying, I do love having new clothes, I do love . . .' . . .

'One of these days,' said Fanny, with dismal emphasis, 'you'll get into trouble.'

'Conscientious objection on an enormous scale. Anything not to consume. Back to nature.'

'I do love flying, I do love flying.'

'Back to culture. Yes, actually to culture. You can't consume much if you sit still and read books.'

'Do I look all right?' Lenina asked. Her jacket was made of bottle-green acetate cloth with green viscose fur at the cuffs and collar.

'Eight hundred Simple Lifers were mowed down by machine-guns at Golders Green.'

'Ending is better than mending, ending is better than mending.'

Green corduroy shorts and white viscose-woollen stockings turned down below the knee.

'Then came the famous British Museum Massacre. Two thousand culture fans gassed with dichlorethyl sulphide.'

A green-and-white jockey cap shaded Lenina's eyes; her shoes were bright green and highly polished.

'In the end,' said Mustapha Mond, 'the Controllers realized that force was no good. The slower but infinitely surer methods of ectogenesis, neo-Pavlovian conditioning, and hypnopaedia . . .'

And round her waist she wore a silver-mounted green Morocco-surrogate cartridge belt, bulging (for Lenina was not a freemartin) with the regulation supply of contraceptives.

'The discoveries of Pfitsner and Kawaguchi were at last made use of. An intensive propaganda against viviparous reproduction . . .'

'Perfect!' cried Fanny enthusiastically. She could never resist Lenina's charm for long. 'And what a perfectly sweet Malthusian belt!'

'Accompanied by a campaign against the Past; by the closing of museums, the blowing up of historical monuments (luckily most of them had already been destroyed during the Nine Years' War); by the suppression of all books published before AF 150.'

'I simply must get one like it,' said Fanny.

'There were some things called the pyramids, for example.'

'My old black-patent bandolier . . .'

'And a man called Shakespeare. You've never heard of them, of course.'

'It's an absolute disgrace – that bandolier of mine.'

'Such things are the advantages of a really scientific education.'

'The more stitches the less riches; the more stitches, the less . . .'

'The introduction of Our Ford's first T-model . . .'

'I've had it nearly three months.'

'Chosen as the opening date of the new era.'

'Ending is better than mending; ending is better . . .'

'There was a thing, as I've said before, called Christianity.'

'Ending is better than mending.'

'The ethics and philosophy of under-consumption . . .'

'I love new clothes, I love new clothes, I love . . .'

Aldous Huxley, *Brave New World*, 1932

By the morning I had made my plans. Sooner or later I should have to go to B. for more money, but it seemed hardly decent to do so yet, and in the meantime I must exist in some hole-and-corner way. Past experience set me against pawning my best suit. I would leave all my things at the station cloakroom, except my second-best suit, which I could exchange for some cheap clothes and perhaps a pound. If I was going to live for a month on thirty shillings I must ·

have bad clothes – indeed, the worse the better. Whether thirty shillings could be made to last a month I had no idea, not knowing London as I knew Paris. Perhaps I could beg, or sell bootlaces, and I remembered articles I had read in the Sunday papers about beggars who have two thousand pounds sewn into their trousers. It was, at any rate, notoriously impossible to starve in London, so there was nothing to be anxious about.

To sell my clothes I went down into Lambeth, where the people are poor and there are a lot of rag shops. At the first shop I tried the proprietor was polite but unhelpful; at the second he was rude; at the third he was stone deaf, or pretended to be so. The fourth shopman was a large, blond young man, very pink all over, like a slice of ham. He looked at the clothes I was wearing and felt them disparagingly between thumb and finger.

'Poor stuff,' he said, 'very poor stuff, that is.' (It was quite a good suit.) 'What yer want for 'em?'

I explained that I wanted some older clothes and as much money as he could spare. He thought for a moment, then collected some dirty-looking rags and threw them on the counter. 'What about the money?' I said, hoping for a pound. He pursed his lips, then produced a *shilling* and laid it beside the clothes. I did not argue – I was going to argue, but as I opened my mouth he reached out as though to take up the shilling again; I saw that I was helpless. He let me change in a small room behind the shop.

The clothes were a coat, once dark brown, a pair of black dungaree trousers, a scarf and a cloth cap; I had kept my own shirt, socks and boots, and I had a comb and razor in my pocket. It gives one a very strange feeling to be wearing such clothes. I had worn bad enough things before, but nothing at all like these; they were not merely dirty and shapeless, they had – how is one to express it? – a gracelessness, a patina of antique filth, quite different from mere shabbiness. They were the sort of clothes you see on a bootlace seller, or a tramp. An hour later, in Lambeth, I saw a hang-dog man, obviously a tramp, coming towards me, and when I looked again, it was myself, reflected in a shop window. The dirt was plastering my face already. Dirt is a great respecter of persons; it lets you alone when you are well dressed, but as soon as your collar is gone it flies towards you from all directions.

I stayed in the streets till late at night, keeping on the move all the time. Dressed as I was, I was half afraid that the police might arrest me as a vagabond, and I dared not speak to anyone, imagining that they must notice a disparity between my accent and my clothes. (Later I discovered that this never happened.) My new clothes had put me instantly into a new world. Everyone's demeanour seemed to have changed abruptly. I helped a hawker pick up a barrow that he had upset. 'Thanks, mate,' he said with a grin. No one had called me mate before in my life – it was the clothes that had done it. For the first time I noticed, too, how the attitude of women varies with a man's clothes. When a badly dressed man passes them they shudder away from him with a quite frank movement of disgust, as though he were a dead cat. Clothes are powerful things. Dressed in a tramp's clothes it is very difficult, at any rate for the first day, not to feel that you are genuinely degraded.

George Orwell, *Down and Out in Paris and London*, 1933

Effie shook out her purchases in her room, laid the dresses out over the couch, piled the dainty lingerie, price tags still modestly fluttered from shoulder ribbons, on the window seat. In a daze she wandered through Fifth Avenue shops, ordering this and that, never asking the price, though certainly the long-dormant charge account, once gracefully sponsored by Belle Glaezner, could not bear such demand without investigation sooner or later. This new wardrobe was one she had treasured in the back of her mind, something she had planned half-asleep through the long lonely nights. It had nothing to do with her present needs or tastes, it was definitely a wardrobe for the Effie of long ago, a re-costuming of the glamorous scenes of her honeymoon. Let other women of her years prepare for age; here was one who was building for her youth. Useless to bring common sense to bear when she saw the blue-flowered hat in Saks, useless for the saleswoman to hint that it was a little too on the bridesmaid side, for this was the hat Effie should have worn to Caroline Meigs's garden party so that Andy could have looked at no one else. Remembering the plain dark blue taffeta she had worn running away to Connecticut with Andy on her wedding night, she corrected herself now by buying a rose-colored print, and here too on the black couch were the elaborately strapped French slippers Andy had wanted for her but which she would not have. Here were the ridiculously fragile underthings Andy was always suggesting for her, the chiffon stockings, all the feminine extravagances she had laughed at him for admiring. Ordering two insanely expensive chemises from a Madison Avenue shop, Effie was brought to a pause by the suspicious interrogation in the salesgirl's eyes. You can't pay for these, said the look, and for whom do you buy these bridal treasures? – surely not for your old poor person, modest finances betrayed by ready-made coat, counter hat, bargain gloves, pawnshop antique silver necklace, basement pocketbook. Effie drew up her shoulder haughtily at this inquisition, flung out Mrs Anthony Glaezner's name as the charge's name, and then she thought, Why it's true, she's right, I can't pay for these things. I will have to explain to Belle soon, and for that matter when and where will I wear them and for whom?

Dawn Powell, Turn, Magic Wheel, 1936

Years before, when he was about sixteen, he had been a door-to-door stocking salesman in England. But the ad through which he had got that job had simply stated: 'Door-to-door salesman needed. No salary. Commission only.' Instruction in selling technique had been limited to the one injunction, 'Get your foot in the door and keep it there. Don't be talked out of a sale.'

'In this grea-a-a-at country we have a little know-how. Little old England sure has a long ways to catch up,' Esmond exulted in his American politician's voice. 'Come with me tomorrow and I'll show you how it's done. You'll simply be fascinated by it. Wait till you hear all the new expressions I've learned. Perhaps, after you've learned the routine, they'll give you a job, too.'

The selling territory assigned to Esmond was in a middle-class residential district of Washington not far from where we were living. Esmond opened up the cardboard briefcase and explained the workings of the elaborate kit – for the use of which he had been induced to leave a five-dollar deposit with the Silkform Company. 'The first day, we don't do any actual selling at all. We do a thing called softening up the territory,' he explained. 'That's done with the magnificent free gifts, and they only cost one-half cent each, so I'm afraid they are not terribly magnificent.' I came across some pencilled sheets in the kit, notes in Esmond's peculiar and almost illegible handwriting: 'all made different by creator', 'fasten support', 'big toe sightseeing – hard time', 'careful house-keeper', 'woven exclusively, discriminating American woman', 'economy size package' . . .

'What's all this?' I asked.

'Oh, you'll see. Part of the tried and true Silkform method.'

Jessica Mitford, *Hons and Rebels*, 1960

While other girls' mothers read *Woman's Own* and *Good Housekeeping* and ran up their own frocks, mine was totally impractical (we were always the first to have shop products; later she would live almost exclusively on fish fingers). She made a close fortnightly study of *Vogue* but the costumes depicted in it rarely appeared outside the Home Counties, however much she inspected the list of stockists.

She would wander through the Bon March and George Henry Lee on Church Street with her nose turned up. Even in Cripps she could never find what she had seen in magazines. She wanted to be a Kensington wife, a society beauty, ideas so absurdly far above her station that once a year she would go to one, board a train and with my father travel down to London, he to attend the April fur auctions, my mother to swan about the West End and Knightsbridge pretending she did that sort of thing every day. She never sat in a London taxi with an air of excited expectancy, but always one of languid indifference.

This expedition, in the spring of 1938, was particularly significant. My mother and father were not to know it but the auction of that year was to be one of the last great sales before the war. More important, I myself was to be outfitted by my mother's own hand, my new dress allowance spent.

'From the moment she enters the room the head waiter is her slave and flagging violin takes new heart,' I read in *Vogue*, on the train, while the countryside flashed past unremarked. Once we had pulled out of Crewe, that was what down south meant to me, endless fields, a blank space until one reached London. 'Exquisite in every detail, she chooses for her perfume the Yardley lavender to which fashionable women instinctively turn for daytime and formal wear. The winsome beauty of this lovable fragrance gives that air of refinement and charm which adds so much to the enjoyment of every occasion. 2/6d to two guineas.'

This was all I ever read. I wanted nothing more in life than for a head waiter to be my slave and to revive the spirits of a stringed instrument . . .

She believed in beginning at the beginning, which commenced with a visit to a discreet little shop off the Edgware Road to purchase a foundation garment. The whole of my trunk was encased in patented elastic tricot. 'It will massage away the young lady's unwanted flesh, tone the muscles and wake up the circulation, madam,' the saleslady told my mother. 'Of course the fit is not perfect, but we can make one up to her individual vital statistics.' Which were 32-35-34, the result of too many sweets on the way home from school. 'The young lady will find it restrains without constriction.' Despite my fawn socks and the suspenders which flapped against my bare legs, I saw in the mirror the figure of my dreams.

We took the bus to Mayfair. 'Divest your mind of the cobweb of old ideas. Turn a fresh eye on the fashion front,' my mother advised me. She was not reading from *Vogue*. I believed later that a form of personality disorder overtook her when she shopped, which made her entirely unable to distinguish reality from advertising copy. Fashion is her soul's *métier*, I thought. What I know now is that fashion was all there was for her. Its amnesia suited her down to the ground. She had to have the new to obliterate the past. 'I don't remember,' she would say later. 'I only lived for today. I really don't remember.'

What *I* recall of the wardrobe we bought that day was a Digby Morton suit: a coral pink tweed jacket banded with lamb in the same earth-brown shade as the skirt beneath. It was clean-cut and young, my mother said, and it cost a fortune. Suits were everywhere that season. There was a hat, too, like a pixie's which someone had maliciously snipped off halfway up the crown. To complete the outfit we bought shoes with butterfly bows tied around the ankle. They were not Patou, my mother said, but a good imitation. We spent for ever looking at tweeds. Whatever I liked my mother vetoed. 'Oh, Sybil, you'll be dismayed to see how soon the fitting-room chic disappears if the material is not good, and this' – she rubbed it between her fingers – 'is not.' Tweed bagged in the seat. I pined for a black crêpe Maggy Rouf afternoon dress, jokingly buttoned with porcelain vegetables, but my mother was horrified, not by the black crêpe, which was universally considered wildly unsuitable for a woman under thirty, but because a dress was a matter of drop-dead seriousness.

I remember, too, a Weil lipstick – a gold case with a scarlet coolie cap. Rejected, too flashy. I was bought instead two pairs of Mirrasilk stockings packed in a cardboard golden casket and finally what my mother called 'a synopsis of your boudoir' – a crocodile vanity case, filled with jars and bottles with chromium-plated tops. It cost an enormous amount, eight guineas, and I kept it long after my boudoir consisted of little more than a succession of plywood closets in some Mid-Western . . .

Linda Grant, The Cast Iron Shore, 1996

To Diana Mosley   20 rue Bonaparte, VI
                                          19 February 1947

To cheer myself up I went and ordered a suit at Dior. The skirt has sort of stays at which one tugs until giddiness intervenes – the basque of the coat stuck out with whalebone . . . Terribly pretty. I shall have the coat copied in white linen so that I can wear it the whole summer except in the really boiling (!!) weather . . .

Nancy Mitford, Love From Nancy: The Letters of Nancy Mitford,
edited by Charlotte Mosley, 1993

What next? I proceeded to the business centre of Parkington and devoted the whole afternoon . . . to buying beautiful things for Lo. Goodness, what crazy purchases were prompted by the poignant predilection Humbert had in those days for check weaves, bright cottons, frills, puffed-out short sleeves, soft pleats, snug-fitting bodices and generously full skirts. Oh Lolita, you are my girl, as Vee was Poe's and Bea Dante's, and what little girl would not like to whirl in a circular skirt and scanties? Did I not have something special in mind? coaxing voices asked me. Swimming suits? We have them in all shades. Dream pink, frosted aqua, glans mauve, tulip red, oolala black. What about playsuits? Slips? No slips. Lo and I loathed slips . . .

Another, much older woman, in a white dress, with a pancake make-up, seemed to be oddly impressed by my knowledge of junior fashions; perhaps I had a midget for a mistress; so, when shown a skirt with two 'cute' pockets in front, I intentionally put a naïve male question and was rewarded with a smiling demonstration of the way the zipper worked in the back of the skirt. I had next great fun with all kinds of shorts and briefs – phantom little Lolitas dancing, falling, daisying all over the counter. We rounded up the deal with some prim cotton pyjamas in popular butcher-boy style. Humbert the popular butcher.

Vladimir Nabokov, *Lolita*, 1959

'Excuse my familiar asking: but where can I get a shirt like that?'
   'Like this?'
   'Yes? It's hep. Jumble style, but hep.'
   He reached out a long, long hand and fingered it.
   'In Jermyn Street,' I said with some self-satisfaction, but asperity.
   'Number?'
   I told him.
   'Thanks so very much,' said Johnny Macdonald Fortune. 'And now I must be on my way to Maida Vale.'

Colin MacInnes, *City of Spades*, 1957

'Shall we go up the Pay-as-You-Wear shop and choose a couple of frocks?'
   'I thought you were skint.'
   'Pay as you wear, berk! You only have to put down about fifteen bob deposit.'

'And then you pay the rest off weekly?'

'Yer meant to but you don't bother. Sylvie got a fabulous two-piece up there; one pound down and she wasn't going to pay no more. When they sent her this letter she rings up and says, "I'm Miss Macarthy's mother. I'm afraid they've taken her away to Banstead mental home." But they sent her a red note saying they was putting the matter to the solicitors, so she's rung up again and said, "It's so sad, Miss Macarthy's passed away, so please don't send no more letters."'

Nell Dunn, *Up the Junction*, 1963

The necktie is suffering a sea change. At last the little fellow is filling out. The summer when everyone wrapped a skimpy herbaceous border round his neck is over, and boutiques like Hem and Fringe in Pimlico and Dandy, opposite the tail end of Baker St, and grand old Turnbull and Asser, Jermyn St, are selling rich and splendid ties, five or six inches wide at 2 or 3 gns. I only hope they are heralding a new era of splendour for the tie. Rich fabrics with sprawling damask designs would be a welcome change from dainty Tana lawn. Beale and Inman still make their very pretty fine woven silk ties, and both Turnbull and Asser and Hermès have cashmere square-ended ties in a dozen good colours, 50s. to 70s. Pauline Fordham at Palisades has white satin ties, handprinted in gold, orange and purple, 2 gns. John Jesse designed the navy and white op art tie and shirt . . . Shirts are still a real problem. Turnbull and Asser have the best materials and the best makers. Philip Stevens . . . is your man if you want a little fantasy. He has made many of the prettiest shirts around; lace and ruffles festoon his attic shop. There are lots of nice shirts in voile and batiste at John Michael. The only shirt I saw otherwise was the lovely herringbone number, . . . £4 5s., at the Trend shop, Simpson.

Christopher Gibbs, 'Shopping Guide', *Men in Vogue* (London), 1965

Every visiting star seemed to come to Biba [in 1966]. Mia Farrow, who had just married Frank Sinatra, came in with Samantha Eggar. Sarah helped them choose dresses, bags, shoes and underwear. The next day she received a huge bouquet of flowers from Mrs Sinatra and later we received a letter from Frank Sinatra's secretary asking us to send all the colours of the cheesehole hat, which had amused him very much. The hat was felt cut with giant holes like an Emmental cheese.

John Lennon's new painter girlfriend Yoko had come to the shop to borrow a dress which Rosie helped her choose to use in her exhibition that night. Later, as we were watching the TV news, Yoko came on and cut up our smock into little pieces in front of a million viewers. Next day, Rosie was wondering if she still had a job.

When Barbra Streisand came in she was pregnant. The girls offered her a private room to change in but she refused, and joined the mob in the dressing room. She bought lots of smocks. Princess Anne came in with her lady-in-waiting. She had a smashing figure. No one dared approach her. Fiona von Thyssen was a regular when she visited London. Mick Jagger and Marianne Faithfull would come in, Marianne in a transparent blouse that shocked even our lot.

Barbara Hulanicki, *From A to Biba*, 1983

1966

Tiger Morse opened her tiny new boutique called Teeny Weeny on upper Madison Avenue at the end of August. Her policy there was man-made materials only – vinyl, Mylar, sequins. There were mirror bricks all over the walls. Wherever I saw fragmented mirrors like that around a place, I'd take the hint that there was amphetamine not too far away – every A-head's apartment always had broken mirrors, smoky, chipped, fractured, whatever – just like the Factory did. And Tiger did take a lot of amphetamine. She always boasted, 'I am living proof that speed does *not* kill.'

A little bit later Tiger got the backing of some big company to design a line of pajamas and nightgowns for them, and to launch that, she gave a big party at the Henry Hudson Baths on West 57th Street that was sort of a fashion show 'happening' around the pool, with models walking out on to the diving board, sometimes diving in, sometimes just turning around and walking back. As I said, it was Tiger who made happenings pop, turning them from something artistic into big parties. She'd stand around in her silver jeans and huge sunglasses, having a ball herself. People got so drunk they jumped into the pool with all their clothes on and then later tried to dive to the bottom for things like wallets that had fallen out of their pockets.

I'd done a few movie sequences with Tiger at her old boutique, Kaleidoscope, on East 58th Street, above Reuben's Restaurant, where she had about six seamstresses sewing for her and hundreds of jars of beads and sequins all around. Before that she'd sold her clothes out of a house on 63rd Street near Madison. In those days she did very expensive, chic, silk-and-satin brocade-and-lamé-type – a little froufrou sometimes – the kind of outfits that would have a hand-stitched lining that was more elaborate than the dress itself. Then Tiger went off to England, and after she came back she went plastic and started to make dresses out of shower curtains. Eventually she took over the Cheetah boutique on Broadway, right outside the club – it stayed open as late as Cheetah did, and people would just pop in and buy new disco clothes on their way in to dance.

Andy Warhol and Pat Hackett, *POPism: The Warhol '60s*, 1981

She has met an actor called Leon, twenty-seven years old, who wears yak coats and does small parts at the Traverse and on television, on the train up to London one Friday. Now, every so often, she takes a weekend in London, and spends it at his flat, having first been careful to ensure that proper arrangements have been made about the children. She calls these her shopping trips, for she shops too: she makes avaricious love to Leon over the weekend, and then moves on to Biba, coming back home on the mid-morning train on Monday with a brighter look on her face and several dresses, each in their elegant, dark-brown plastic bags.

Malcolm Bradbury, *The History Man*, 1975

'What a great suit,' I thought as I fondled the vivid yellow fabric. Flared lapels, two-tone side vents and crimson piping down the back of the jacket! Unbelievable. You'd have to have balls to get inside that with a straight face. And serious money. Look at the name. Gear like this couldn't come in under a grand. I mean, this was top-flight Kevin Graceland. Memphis style. I grasped the label. £100. A mistake, surely? 'No, no,' said the hovering salesman, 'a special price. Nearly new. Only worn once. Gentleman brought it in yesterday. Just a tiny, tiny stain on the cuff. Would you like to try it on?'

'Er, no thanks . . .'

There was a brief moment of shock as I shuffled uneasily in front of the mirror. Could I hear laughter somewhere? Hold on though, I didn't look *that* bad. OK, it was a little large ('an easy cut', I was informed) but it did lend me certain qualities . . . But there was something more. I looked indispensable somehow. As if I could make a difference. As if someone was paying me impossible sums to do something no one else could do. It was great. It was all over. Swaying in the sweet smell of polished wood and light bulbs I asked if they'd take two cheques. They would ('just this one time'). Did I want to keep it on? It was now or never. And with a freshly lit cigarette clenched between my teeth I breezed out on to the streets of Soho.

Jake Michie, *Suit*, 1991

When I told my friends I was looking for the Ideal Christmas party frock, they responded with cries of envy and a torrent of advice. 'Go to Joseph, Harvey Nichols, Gianni Versace, Ally Capellino, French Connection, Emporio Armani,' they exclaimed, inadvertently revealing their own private fantasies. My friend Andrea, with whom I have shopped tirelessly in London, Florence and Istanbul in the last couple of years, promptly offered to take the day off work and come with me to avoid mistakes.

Two gay friends tried to send me to Top Shop at Oxford Circus, which I remember as a subterranean cavern where I could never find the size or colour I wanted; when I went in search of a 10 or a 12 or exactly the same dress in blue, I always seemed to come back and find that other customers had left dusty footprints on my discarded clothes in the communal changing room. 'I'd buy all my clothes there if I was a girl,' one of my gay friends said, 'and I'd look really fab.'

I pointed out that as neither he nor I fall into the category of girls, this was not exactly helpful. I once read a survey which claimed that women lose interest in clothes at the age of thirty-five and I simply couldn't believe it. It hasn't happened to me. Who are these women who migrate unresistingly from Warehouse to Marks and Spencer as middle age appears on the horizon?

Perhaps they're just married. I've always bought more interesting outfits when I live alone. In fact the last time I split up with someone I gave away virtually all my clothes soon after, unable to believe I'd acquired such a dreary wardrobe. I also grew my hair and bought shoes with much higher heels – one of the few things I have in common with the Princess of Wales, who leapt into her stilettos the day after her separation from Prince Charles was announced.

A boyfriend once asked me to help him choose a suit in Paris and I had a terrific afternoon, rifling through racks of Yves Saint Laurent without having to pay the bill, but it would never have crossed my mind to do the same thing in reverse. Most straight men, in my experience, have only a vague impression of what women are wearing. I once tested this proposition by asking the man I was living with what he thought of a brand new Ally Capellino suit. 'I've always liked that,' he said in a slightly hurt tone. 'I don't know why you don't wear it more often.'

John Berger wrote famously in 'Men look at women' *Ways of Seeing*. Women watch themselves being looked at.' It's a seductively simple proposition but also complete rubbish, casting women as voyeurs of their own disempowerment. Anyone who works in the fashion industry will tell you that women buy clothes to impress other women, but it is also the case that, at a deeper level, what we wear is a powerful way of making statements about ourselves. In that sense, it's not directly to do with other people at all, but a clue to the inner self.

When I was in an unhappy phase of my life and buying horrible clothes, I wasn't trying not to attract men so much as expressing my anxiety about the whole notion of sexuality. These days, when I try on a foxy black dress, I buy it without a second thought – unless you count an anxious vision of my next credit card statement – because I feel comfortable in it. Shopping has become a pleasure again, a welcome return to frivolity, which is why the kind of shopping I love most is looking for party dresses.

All the boring, everyday considerations – will it wash, does it have to be dry-cleaned, will I get sick of it in six months? – go out of the window. Very few women I know would go as far as dressing in Vivienne Westwood – I was taken aback when a couple of friends, knowing my occasionally reckless taste in clothes, warned me off this season's bustle skirts – but the absence of any one strong line this season, although it has caused consternation among fashion editors, gives the women in the street unprecedented freedom.

Unfortunately, the moment I see something I like, I want to know if it's available in black. At a literary dinner in London a couple of months ago I realized what a bad habit this is, the range of colours worn by both male and female guests so dark and sombre that the pre-dinner drinks party resembled a wake. I was furious with myself for not wearing red, thinking of the slinky 1930s evening dress I'd looked at and returned to the wardrobe, but I've been wearing black so long it's become second nature.

It's a habit I'm trying to break. It may not seem a bold step but I've put the process into reverse, trying on dresses in black to see if I like the shape, then going back to the rail to see what other colours they come in. Brown and midnight blue are beginning to creep into my wardrobe and while the phrase 'little black dress' still echoes seductively in my ear the moment I walk into a clothes shop, I'm doing my best to resist it.

Joan Smith: 'Frock till you drop', *Guardian*, 1994

THE TWELVE COMMANDMENTS FOR WOMEN

1. Since most women do not know themselves they should try to do so.
2. A woman who buys an expensive dress and changes it, often with disastrous result, is extravagant and foolish.
3. Most women (and men) are colour-blind. They should ask for suggestions.
4. Remember – twenty per cent of women have inferiority complexes. Seventy per cent have illusions.
5. Ninety per cent are afraid of being conspicuous and of what people will say. So they buy a grey suit. They should dare to be different.
6. Women should listen and ask for competent criticism and advice.
7. They should choose their clothes alone or in the company of a man.

8. They should never shop with another woman, who sometimes consciously and often unconsciously is apt to be jealous.
9. They should buy little, and only of the best or the cheapest.
10. Never fit the dress to the body, but train the body to fit the dress.
11. A woman should buy mostly in one place where she is known and respected and not rush around trying every new fad.
12. And she should pay her bills.

Elsa Schiaparelli, *Shocking Life*, 1954

Notes

Introduction

1. Anne Hollander, *Seeing Through Clothes*, New York 1975, pp. 418–9.
2. Oscar Wilde, 'Dress', Lecture 1884.
3. Mark Anderson, *Kafka's Clothes: Ornament and Aestheticism in the Hapsburg Fin de Siècle*, Oxford 1992, pp. 3 and 33.
4. Thoman Mann, *The Magic Mountain*, 1924.
5. Virginia Woolf, *Orlando*, London 1928.
6. Virginia Woolf, *Diaries: Volume III 1925–1930*, edited by Anne Olivier Bell, London, 1980, 4 July 1926.
7. Elsa Schiaparelli, *Shocking Life*, London 1954, p. 72.
8. Colette, *My Apprenticeships; and, Music Hall Highlights*, 1957.
9. Marcel Proust, *Remembrance of Things Past: Within a Budding Grove*, London 1981, p. 783; Diana Festa-McCormick, 'Proustian Optics of Clothes: Mirrors, Masks, Mores', *Stanford French and Italian Studies 29*, Saratoga: Anima Libri, 1984, pp. 4–5. From Valerie Steele *Paris Fashion*, pp. 210–11, Oxford 1988.
10. John Harvey, *Men in Black*, London 1995, p. 230.
11. Malcolm McLaren, 'Hype-Allergic', *Details*, July 1992, p. 54.
12. *Harpers & Queen*, March 1998, pp. 124–5.
13. Virginia Woolf, op. cit. 14 May 1925.

Chapter One

1. Elizabeth Wilson, *Adorned in Dreams*, London 1985, pp. 11–12.
2. Camille Paglia, 'No Law in the Arena: A Pagan Theory of Sexuality' from *Vamps and Tramps*, New York 1994, p. 19.

3. 'Lucile', Lady Duff Gordon, *Discretions and Indiscretions*, London 1932, p. 78.

4. Elizabeth Wilson, op. cit., p. 13.

5. Ibid., p. 125, quoting Simone de Beauvoir, *The Second Sex*, London 1953, p. 509.

6. Ibid.

7. Germaine Greer, *The Female Eunuch*, London 1970, p. 34.

Chapter Two

1. Marcel Proust, *Remembrance of Things Past: The Captive*, p. 527, translation by C. K. Scott Moncrieff and Frederick A. Blossom, New York 1922–97, quoted by V. Steele in *Paris Fashion*, Oxford 1988, p. 211. (See also Diana Festa-McCormick, 'Proustian Optics of Clothes: Mirrors, Masks, Mores', *Stanford French and Italian Studies 29*, Saratoga: Anima Libri, 1984, pp. 93–103.)

2. Georgina Howell, *In Vogue: Six Decades of Fashion*, London 1975, p. 4.

3. Lady Duff Gordon, *Discretions and Indiscretions*, London 1932, p. 258.

4. Aldous Huxley, *Antic Hay*, London, 1923.

5. Doris Langley Moore, *Pandora's Letter Box, Being a Discourse on Fashionable Life*, London 1929, pp. 93–4.

6. Terence Greenidge, *Degenerate Oxford*, London, 1930, p. 107.

7. Taylor Croft, *The Cloven Hoof*, London 1932, p. 62.

8. Hugo Vickers, *Cecil Beaton*, London 1985, p. 41.

9. Andy Warhol and Pat Hackett, *POPism: The Warhol '60s*, London 1981, pp. 293–4.

10. Alkarim Jivani, *It's Not Unusual: A History of Lesbian and Gay Britain in the Twentieth Century*, London 1997, pp. 159–60.

11. Richard Martin, 'The Gay Factor in Fashion', *Esquire Gentleman*, spring 1993, p. 137.

Chapter Three

1. Valerie Steele, *Paris Fashion*, Oxford 1988.
2. Adolf Loos, *Ornament and Crime*, Vienna, 1908.
3. Elizabeth Wilson, *Adorned in Dreams*, London 1985, p. 40.
4. Valerie Steele, op. cit., p. 120.
5. Ibid.
6. Ibid.
7. Ibid., p. 122, quoting Cecil Beaton, *The Glass of Fashion*, London 1954.
8. Elizabeth Wilson, op. cit., p. 43.
9. Ibid., p. 89, quoting *Vogue*, February 1953.
10. Colin McDowell, *The Dictionary of Twentieth-Century Fashion*, London 1984, p. 295.

Chapter Four

1. Elsa Schiaparelli, *Shocking Life*, London 1954, p. 69.

Chapter Five

1. *The Canterbury Tales*, from F. N. Robinson, *The Complete Works of Geoffrey Chaucer*, Boston 1961; and the *Oxford English Dictionary*, Oxford 1933.
2. Sigmund Freud, *Basic Writings*, London 1938. Quoted by Lawrence Langer, *The Importance of Wearing Clothes*, London 1959, p. 81.
3. Valerie Steele, ibid., pp. 33–4.
4. Dr Richard Krafft-Ebing, *Psychopathia Sexualis with Especial Reference to the Antipathic Sexual Instinct: A Medico-Forensic Study*, 1886. Quoted by Valerie Steele, op. cit., p. 31.

Chapter Six

1. J. C. Flugel, *The Psychology of Clothes*, London 1930, pp. 111–2.
2. The Duke of Windsor, *A Family Album*, London 1960, p. 45.

3. Ibid., p. 115.

4. Diana de Marly, *Fashion For Men*, London 1985, p. 119.

5. Aileen Ribeiro, *Dress and Morality*, London 1986, p. 158.

6. Ibid., p. 158.

7. Nik Cohn, *Today There Are No Gentlemen*, London 1971, pp. 22–3.

8. Hugo Vickers, *Cecil Beaton*, London 1985, p. 531.

9. Judith Watt, 'By Design', *For Him Magazine*, 1989, p. 143.

10. Malcolm McLaren, 'Hyper-Allergic', *Details*, July 1992.

Chapter Seven

1. James Laver, *Dandies*, London 1968, p. 21.

2. Valerie Steele, *Paris Fashion*, Oxford 1988, pp. 87–8.

3. Ellen Moers, *The Dandy*, London 1960, p. 304.

4. Quoted by Mark Anderson, *Kafka's Clothes, Ornament and Aestheticism in the Hapsburg Fin de Siècle*, Oxford 1992, p. 180.

5. Mark Anderson, op. cit., p. 51.

6. Ibid., pp. 219–20.

7. Caroline Evans and Minna Thornton, 'Chanel: The New Woman as Dandy', *Women and Fashion*, London 1989, pp. 123–4.

8. Edna Woolman Chase, *Always in Vogue*, London 1954, p. 95.

9. Quoted by Charles Spencer in the *London Magazine*, October 1967, p. 71, from Howard Greer, *Designing Male*, New York 1949.

10. In an interview with the author, 1988.

Chapter Eight

1. Quoted by Aileen Ribeiro, *Dress and Morality*, London 1986, p. 164, from *Life* (New York), 11 December 1944.

2. Nik Cohn, *Today There Are No Gentlemen*, London 1971, p. 29.

3. Ibid., p. 35, quoting Alexander Plunket-Greene.

4. Catherine McDermott, *Streetstyle*, London 1987, p. 14.

5. Mary Quant, 'The Meaning of the Mini', *Daily Telegraph*, 18 October 1997.

6. Tom Wolfe, introduction to René Konig, *The Restless Image*, London 1973, p. 23.

7. John O'Reilly, 'All That is Solid Melts into Air Jordans', *Guardian*, 23 October 1998.

8. Ted Polhemus, *Streetstyle: From Sidewalk to Catwalk*, London 1994, p. 10.

Chapter Nine

1. Quoted by Whitney Chadwick, *Living Simultaneously*, 1993, from Michael Bracewell, 'Dressing for the Gallery', *Tate Magazine*, No. 16, winter 1998, p. 38.

2. Valerie Steele, *Paris Fashion*, Oxford 1988, p. 230.

3. Victoria Glendinning, *Edith Sitwell: A Unicorn Among Lions*, London 1981, p. 53.

4. Elsa Schiaparelli, *Shocking Life*, London 1954, p. 46.

5. Diana Vreeland, *D. V.*, New York 1984, p. 105.

Chapter Ten

1. Bunny Roger in an interview with the author, 1988

2. Elizabeth Wilson, *Adorned in Dreams*, London 1985, p. 79

Permissions

Every effort has been made to contact copyright holders. The publishers are willing to correct any omissions in future editions of the book.

Beaton and Rupert Crew Limited; SIMONE DE BEAUVOIR: *The Second Sex*, Jonathan Cape, 1953, reprinted by permission of Random House UK; MAX BEERBOHM: *Lytton Strachey*, The Rede Lecture, 1943, Cambridge University Press; ARNOLD BENNETT: *The Journals of Arnold Bennett, 1921–1928*, edited by Newman Flower, Cassell and Company, 1933, reproduced by permission of Cassell and Co.; E. F. BENSON: *Lucia in London*, London, 1927; *Mapp and Lucia*, London 1935; reproduced by permission of A. P. Watt Ltd on behalf of The Executors of the Estate of K. S. P. McDowall; CELIA BERTIN: *Paris à la Mode*, 1956, Victor Gollancz, London, copyright by Librairie Hachette 1956, reproduced by permission The Orion Publishing Group Ltd; J. E. BLANCHE: *Portraits of a Lifetime*, 1937; ALAIN DE BOTTON: *How Proust Can Change Your Life*, copyright © Alain de Botton 1997, reprinted by permission of Macmillan Publishers; ELIZABETH BOWEN: *The Little Girls*, Jonathan Cape, 1964, copyright © Elizabeth Bowen 1964, reproduced by permission of Curtis Brown Ltd; WILLIAM BOYD: *Armadillo*, Hamish Hamilton, 1998, copyright © William Boyd 1998; MICHAEL BRACEWELL: *The Crypto-Amnesia Club*, Serpent's Tail, 1988, copyright © Michael Bracewell 1988, reproduced by permission of Serpent's Tail; *England is Mine*, 1997, copyright © Michael Bracewell 1997, reprinted by permission of HarperCollins Publishers Ltd; MALCOLM BRADBURY: *The History Man*, Hutchinson, 1975, copyright © Malcolm Bradbury 1975, reproduced by permission of Random House UK; JOHN BRAINE: *Room at the Top*, Methuen, 1957, copyright by John Braine 1957; *Life at the Top*, Eyre and Spottiswood, 1962, copyright © John Braine 1962, reprinted by permission of David Higham Associates; VERA BRITTAIN: *Letters from A Lost Generation*, edited by Alan Bishop and Mark Bostridge, Virago Press, Little Brown and Company, 1998, copyright © Alan Bishop and Mark Bostridge 1998; ANITA BROOKNER: *A Private View*, copyright © Anita Brookner 1974, reproduced by permission of Random House UK; JULIE BURCHILL: *Diana*, copyright © Julie Burchill 1998, reproduced by permission of The Orion Publishing Group; 'Material Boys', *Guardian*, 3 October 1998, reproduced by permission the Guardian and Observer Newspapers Ltd; ANTHONY BURGESS: *A Clockwork Orange*, William

India, Edward Arnold, 1924, Penguin Books, 1936; copyright © The Provost and Scholars of King's College, Cambridge and the Society of Authors as the literary representatives of the E. M. Forster Estate; JOHN GALSWORTHY: *Swan Song*, 1928, by permission of The Society of Authors as the literary representative of the Estate of John Galsworthy; STELLA GIBBONS: *Cold Comfort Farm*, Penguin Books, 1932, copyright by Stella Gibbons 1932, reproduced with permission of Curtis Brown Ltd; CHRISTOPHER GIBBS: 'Shopping Guide', *Men in Vogue*, November 1965, copyright © *Men in Vogue*, The Condé Nast Publications Ltd; ERIC GILL: *Clothes*, Jonathan Cape, 1931; BEATRICE ELVERY, LADY GLENAVY: *Today We Will Only Gossip*, Constable, 1964; ELINOR GLYN: *The Vicissitudes of Evangeline*, George Duckworth and Sons, 1905; LADY DUFF GORDON, 'LUCILE': *Discretions and Indiscretions*, Jarrolds, 1932; LINDA GRANT: *The Cast Iron Shore*, copyright © Linda Grant 1996, reproduced by permission of Granta Books; 'Cut and Thrust', *Guardian*, 5 February 1996, reproduced by permission of Guardian and Observer Newspapers Ltd; MONICA GRANT: *The Ragga & the Royal*, copyright © Monica Grant 1994; WALTER GREENWOOD: *Love on the Dole*, Jonathan Cape, 1933, reproduced by permission of Random House UK; GERMAINE GREER: *The Female Eunuch*, copyright © Germaine Greer 1970, reprinted by permission of Gillon Aitken Associates Ltd; GUARDIAN: 'Pass Notes: Isabella Blow,' 23 February 1998, reproduced by permission of Guardian and Observer Newspapers Ltd; RADCLYFFE HALL: *The Well of Loneliness*, Jonathan Cape, 1928, reproduced by permission of Random House UK; SUSANNA HERBERT: 'When I see fashion now, I suffer', *Daily Telegraph*, 15 January 1998, reproduced by permission of Telegraph Newspapers; JAMES LEO HERLIHY: *Midnight Cowboy*, Jonathan Cape, 1966, copyright © James Leo Herlihy 1965, reproduced by permission of Jeffrey Bailey; PHILIP HOARE: *Serious Pleasures: A Life of Stephen Tennant*, copyright © Philip Hoare 1990, reprinted by permission of Gillon Aitken Associates Ltd; ALAN HOLLINGHURST: *The Folding Star*, Chatto and Windus, 1994, copyright © Alan Hollinghurst 1994, reprinted by permission of Gillon Aitken Associates Ltd; MICHAEL HOLROYD: *Augustus John, A Biography*, 1974, reproduced

Faber and Faber; D. H. LAWRENCE: 'The Thimble', first published in
Seven Arts, March 1917, and in *The Mortal Coil and Other Stories*, Penguin
Books, 1971, reproduced by permission of Laurence Pollinger Ltd and the
Estate of Frieda Lawrence Ravagli; *Women in Love*, 1921, reproduced by
permission of Laurence Pollinger Ltd and the Estate of Frieda Lawrence
Ravagli; ROSAMUND LEHMANN: *Invitation to the Waltz*, 1932, reproduced
by permission of the Society of Authors as the literary representative of
the Estate of Rosamund Lehmann; WYNDHAM LEWIS: *The Apes of
God*, London, 1930, copyright by Wyndham Lewis 1930, reproduced by
permission of the Peters, Fraser and Dunlop Group Ltd; ANITA LOOS,
Gentlemen Prefer Blondes, 1925, copyright by Anita Loos 1925, renewed by
Anita Loos 1952, assigned to the Anita Loos Trusts 1984, reproduced by
permission of the Anita Loos Trusts; COLIN MACINNES: *City of Spades*,
1957, copyright by the Colin MacInnes Estate 1957; *Absolute Beginners*, first
published by MacGibbon and Kee, 1959, copyright © the Colin MacInnes
Estate 1959; COMPTON MACKENZIE: *Extraordinary Women: Themes and
Variations*, Martin Secker & Warburg, 1928, reproduced by permission of
the Society of Authors as the literary representative of the Estate of
Compton Mackenzie, COLIN MCDOWELL: *Dressed to Kill, Sex, Power and
Clothes*, Hutchinson, 1992, reproduced by permission of Random House
UK; 'Depravity Bites', *Guardian*, 9 August 1997; JAY MCINERNEY: *Model
Behaviour*, Bloomsbury, 1998, copyright © Jay McInerney 1998; MALCOLM
MCLAREN: 'Hype-Allergic', *Details*, July 1992, reproduced by kind per-
mission of the author; THOMAS MANN: *The Magic Mountain*, 1924, published
as *Der Zauberberg*, copyright by S. Fischer Verlag 1924, this translation
copyright by Martin Secker & Warburg 1928; *Death in Venice*, Alfred A.
Knopf, Inc., 1925, translated by Kenneth Burke, 1925, reproduced by
permission of Random House UK; GABRIEL GARCÍA MÁRQUEZ: *Love
in the Time of Cholera*, 1985, Penguin Books, 1989, copyright © Gabriel
García Márquez 1985, 1988, reproduced by permission of Random House
UK; RICHARD MARTIN: 'The Gay Factor in Fashion', *Esquire Gentleman*,
spring 1993, reproduced by kind permission of the author; W. SOMERSET
MAUGHAM: *The Magician*, William Heinemann, 1908, reproduced by per-

Index of Authors